Especially Chosen
To Be
Broken For Purpose

*Overcoming Brokenness
Growing Into
Wholeness And Purpose*

Rev. Dr. Jasmine Rosetta Gordon

XULON PRESS

Xulon Press
2301 Lucien Way #415
Maitland, FL 32751
407.339.4217
www.xulonpress.com

Paperback ISBN-13: 978-1-6305-0913-2

Ebook ISBN-13: 978-1-6305-0914-9

Invite Rev. Dr. Jasmine R. Gordon for preaching,
teaching, speaking, conference keynote, book study,
book signing, and workshops.

For information contact:
DRJASMINE RGORDON MINISTRY
P. O. BOX 361421
Decatur, GA 30036
United States

https://drgordonministries.org

Broken for Purpose
This is the theme of the book

"*It was good for me to be afflicted so that I might learn your decrees (commands)*" (Psalm 119:71).

"*He heals the broken hearted and binds up their wounds*" (Psalm 147:3).

"*Because of the Lord's great love we are not consumed, for his compassions never fail. They are new every morning; great is your faithfulness*" (Lamentations 3:22-23).

"*Fight the good fight of faith. Take hold of the eternal life to which you were called when you made your good confession in the presence of many witnesses*" (1 Timothy 6:12).

Dedication

With profound delight this book is lovingly dedicated to a circle of very special individuals whom I deeply appreciate for being there for me, believing in me, supporting me, reminding me, pushing me, challenging me and encouraging me always.

Daughter Marcia you had been my biggest supporter and constant cheer leader. I could always "see you at the finish line" with your favorite colors pom pom cheering me on. Thank you, Marcia, for holding me accountable. You never failed to always call me and ask, "Mom, when are you going to finish the book? Just do it mom, you know you can do it. You need to stop working so hard and use the time to write your book." Daughter, you care so much about others and you have a big heart.

Son **Nigel** this book is dedicated to you. You are an excellent father and husband. I admire how you love the Lord. Thanks for your consistent encouragement over the years telling me to write. You were the one who encouraged and convinced me to accept my first college professorship assignment when you were a teenager. You believe in me, respect me, and look up to me.

Thank you, it means a lot to me. Son, you are a purpose driven businessman and you care about the welfare of others and God will see about yours.

Mr. Desmond Muir you were relentless for many years reminding and encouraging me to write my book. You were faithful in calling me very often to ask about the book. Your encouragement caused me to self-reflect and believe in myself that I could do it. Thank you!

Sister Rosetta, for years you were always there to call me up and encourage me to take time out to write my book. You always said to me that you want to see me on the Oprah Winfrey's show with my book. Thanks for your encouragement.

Dedication goes to my granddaughters MichelleLee and Stacy, grandsons Michael, Josiah, Christopher, and Alexander, great granddaughter Arionna and great grandson Noah. Dedication to my siblings, sisters Hyacinth, Verona, Rosetta, Violet, and my late sister Paulette, brothers Desmond, Delroy, Averton, and Dwight. To my many nieces, nephews and cousins this is also for you. *I dedicate this book to all of you and may you be inspired*.

Remember, you can and should birth the seed which God has planted inside of your heart. Whatever your dreams are go after them even when no one else believes in you or supports you. People will try to distract you and will even speak ill of you. *Remember, your dream is like a seed which will not die. It may become dormant but it will not go away. It is just waiting to be planted in the ground. All that a seed needs to grow and be fruitful are waiting for it in the ground. Your seed is waiting on you to be activated so go ahead and activate your seed and watch it grow*.

My late Mother and Father: With a heart full of gratitude I pay a very special tribute to Mama and Papa. Surely, I owe so much to them. Our parents were intentional in raising us well, for they were persistent in giving my siblings and me a quality life filled with invaluable life lessons on values, morals, self-worth, compassion, work ethics, kindness and the importance of education. My precious parents did not have college degrees or school diplomas, yet, they were excellent teachers who taught us so much. They sent us to school without fail and they instilled in us how valuable it is to have a good education. They taught us as we were growing up what it meant to love others, to be compassionate and kind hearted. These values they taught us are more valuable than material things that will come and go. My parents lived out these values by their examples. Rest In Peace Mama and Papa. We will continue to teach our children and grandchildren about them and our precious memories of them will live on in our hearts and minds as we continue to practice what we were taught.

To all my students whom I taught over the years: At the university, college, high school, middle school and elementary school levels, to each of you I say the blessings, honor and pleasure of teaching you were mine. Thanks for allowing me to touch your lives and make a difference. Remember to pursue excellence always!

The Christian Community: This book is dedicated to the global Christian community of believers to whom I have ministered as a Bible Teacher, Chaplain, Preacher,

Counselor, Mentor, Workshop Facilitator, Conference Presenter and any other capacity in which I served you.

Finally, with great delight **I dedicate this book to my childhood home church**, Fort William Church of God Holiness now (Fort William Assembles of Holiness) which is in Fort William, Westmoreland, Jamaica. I received my very solid Christian foundation from my early childhood at my home church where I was very active in ministry from childhood. I praise God that I still get the opportunity to preach at my childhood church whenever I visit home, Jamaica.

Table of Contents

PART FOUR: THE TUNNEL - HEALING

PART FIVE: DELIVERANCE & RESTORATION

Table of Contents

Preface

Seek ye first the kingdom of God and His righteousness and all other things will be added unto you **(Matthew 6:33)**

I know the plans I have for, you says the Lord. Plans to prosper you and not to harm you. Plans to give you hope for the future **(Jeremiah 11:29).**

It was early in January 2012, during one of my morning devotions, as I reflected, contemplated and agonized over the experiences that caused my heart to be broken and torn into pieces that the Holy Spirit ministered to my soul and spoke to me very clearly. The Holy Spirit said, *"**Broken hearts can be made whole again**."* Those words caught my attention and as I thought about those words the Holy Spirit kept on speaking to me saying, *"**A broken heart was first whole**."* I was fully constrained to listen and as I listened the Holy Spirit continued to minister to me saying, *"**Sometimes hearts are broken to teach a valuable spiritual lesson or some lessons**."* I am fully persuaded that God always has a **purpose** in whatever He does.

The thoughts ministered to me by the Holy Spirit gripped my attention and my soul deeply as I sobbed and poured out my broken heart to God. As the Spirit continued to minister to me, in my heart I was experiencing a deep pain that opened up like a spring that burst forth and gushed out from the depth of my soul and began to flow in tears nonstop from my torn heart. *This was six going on seven years of pent up broken heartedness 2005-2012*. It is not my intention in this book to share those specific experiences that caused my heart to be broken. The purpose of this book is to share my deep heart pain and my journey in overcoming my own broken hearted experiences with the hope that you will be encouraged on your journey towards healing. My emotional experience that morning was like a "*broken dam a reservoir*" that could not hold back the controlled and now very restless waters any longer.

The secret pain deep in my shattered heart caused my tears to flow uncontrollably just like the release of escaped water from a broken dam. That morning I wept before God and talked to Him about what was hurting my heart so deeply. Over those six to seven years I prayed, fasted, studied the Bible and cried to God but this particular day was very different. It felt like God was saying to me, "*I have tried you long enough and this is now a turning point. I especially chose you and took you through those experiences of heart break for my divine purpose.*" I understood God to be saying to me that my brokenness has served its purpose and He is ready to take me through another phase of preparedness in readiness to operate fully in His divine purpose.

The word *love* kept ringing in my spirit and the Word of God tells us very clearly what love is. "**Whoever claims to *love God* yet hates a brother or sister is a liar. For whoever does not love their brother and sister, whom they have seen, cannot love God, whom they have not seen**" (1 John 4:20). As I thought about love as the Bible explains it, I kept wondering, how can we as children of God say that we love God and yet, within the body of Christ, inflict severe hurt on others who are our church brothers and sisters and at the same time behave as if it is business as usual?

Generally speaking, I have observed that even within the body of Christ, the church, people are being hurt to the extent that some of them ended up leaving their church for another church. Additionally, there are others who leave the church all together and never to return for they turn away from God. These people have been badly hurt, heartbroken, wounded, feeling helpless, hopeless, neglected and needing soul healing. Many people are so badly hurt within the church that they do not stay silent. Instead, some tell of their mistreatment by people in the church to anyone and everyone who will listen. I thought of this group of people and prayed to God on their behalf feeling very sorry that they suffered such pain. Church hurt is very real and it can certainly be devastating to a person. I thank God for the strong and solid foundation in Christ that I received from my childhood for as painful as my experiences were my faith kept me holding on to hope for my hope is in Christ Jesus.

I am thankful to God that I studied the Bible and stored away the Word of God deep in my heart for at that moment the Holy Spirit reminded me of when Jesus asked His disciples a profound self reflective question. "***Then Jesus turned to the Twelve and asked, 'Are you also going to leave?' Simon Peter answered him, 'Lord, to whom shall we go? You have the words of eternal life***" (John 6:67-68). Although my heart was crushed deeply I knew that there was no turning away from God or leaving for another church without being led by the Holy Spirit. That day I lingered in God's presence while the Holy Spirit kept ministering to me and working on my shattered heart.

My spiritual eyes began to open widely and I began to see more clearly in the realm of the Spirit. Ideas kept rising up and swimming through my thoughts revealing the conditions of a **broken and wounded heart** and the journey that it will take in overcoming and growing into wellness and wholeness. Later on by the help of the Holy Spirit, I realized that God was also inspiring me to journal my experiences that would minister to me as I wrote. Journaling became part of my healing process and I soon realized that my healing journey experiences could also be shared in ministering to anyone seeking healing from a broken, wounded and hurting heart.

In the months that followed it became clearer to me that God was also inspiring me with a specific ministry focus "***Soul Care Healing.***" Time went on and from my painful experiences emerged insights for ministry pur-poses and ***Christian Literature about soul healing and soul care***. The Holy Spirit gave me the name of the book that I should write and it was very clear to me and quite overpowering to the extent that I "Google" to search for the title. I wanted to see if there were any books on the market with that identical title and there was none. I was further overwhelmed with excitement and was deeply amazed at God's strong presence with me and the clarity with which He speaks to me! I spent much time thinking about the concept of soul care healing and soon after I began to minister to people about "**Soul Care Healing.**" This concept was something new to me as well as to those to whom I ministered. This was an "eye opening" experience that required of me deep reflective thinking. Whenever I ministered to people about soul care healing the reactions were always the same. "**Wow, soul care healing! This makes sense. Interesting! I never heard of this before**!"

Over time the Holy Spirit began to share with me by imparting in my spirit the many areas in one's life in which one can be heartbroken that could lead to intense heart pain and how this book that I will write will be a source of "**ministry tool for healing.**" Years before I actually started writing the Holy Spirit confirmed to me that this book when written will minister to the hearts of many people far and wide.

This book is all inclusive and it will be guiding humanity across religious convictions, cultures, ethnicity, demographic regions, male and female, wide ranges of age groups, the rich, and the poor. This book will be useful for group counseling sessions, marriage counseling, and anyone striving towards soul healing, health and wholeness of heart. Also, Clergy, Laity, Chaplains, and Bible Teachers will all find this book useful as a supplementary resource and for Bible study. I recommend this book as a text supplement for any College Christian Education and Counseling programs.

I am recommending this book for personal use as a resource for devotional purposes and spiritual growth development. It may also be used as a supplemental resource for your small group discussions. Some other suggestions for the use of this book as a substantive read will include "**book study**" for females, males, couples, youth groups, family devotions among others. Use this book as a teaching series by deeply studying the content chapters and Scriptures. You may consider this book as a manual for bringing healing to the wounded, broken and hurting heart. Without doubt this book will also gently lead you to understanding the power of forgiveness, repentance, reconciliation, and transformation.

Since my teen years I had been engaged in ministry on many levels, however, from the experiences of my broken heart, my ministry, "*Soul Care Healing Women's Fellowship*" was born first in my heart in early 2012 and was officially launched on Saturday, February 9, 2013, in my home. This ministry focuses mainly on the inner healing of the hurting heart and soul. Our first annual one day conference was on April 23, 2016. The ministry has now grown to include *GORDON MINISTRY INSTITUTE*; *Soul Care Healing Prayer Ministry*; *Soul Care Healing Global Mission*; *Gordon Chaplaincy Ministry* among other ministry activities. God's divine purpose for me has been revealed and it is clearer to me than ever before.

God's divine purpose for my broken heart was for the birthing of this ministry "*Soul Care Healing*" and my close relationship with the Holy Spirit has been my constant support in the process. A profound sense of the possibilities of this ministry swept over my soul. This reality constrained me to take a thoughtful assessment on how to care for my soul and make sure it is in right standing with God. Truly, my heart got happy and I was overjoyed. My ministry strongly took on a new dimension and meaning.

During the span of time 2005-2011, I had some suspision of what was happening but it was too unreal to believe. Early in the year 2011 God uncovered and exposed to me what was happening and this was emotionally devastating. This is exactly what the Apostle Paul spoke about when he said that this was not a "flesh and blood" fight but a fight with and against the powers that are in very high places. "*For we wrestle not against flesh and blood, but against principalities, against powers, against the rulers of the darkness of this world, against spiritual wickedness in high places*" (Ephesians 6:12).

The year 2011, the seventh year in my brokenness journey, was a significant turning point for God shifted the dynamics and revealed to me the "plot" and needless to say that this revelation was crushing although it confirmed what I had observed and suspected for a long time. "*Because the Lord revealed their plot to me, I knew it, for at that time he showed me what they were doing*" (Jeremiah 11:18). This revelation and confirmation gave me holy boldness and led me to take some extraordinary and meaningful actions in moving forward in my God given ordained purpose.

Those actions I took in fall 2011, further provoked the "oppressor" (someone who uses power unjustly to prevent and deny people or keep people under control). I knew that if I abide in God's will, and remain faithful in the face of opposition that God Himself through His divine grace and mercy would give supernatural ability for me to operate in my purpose.

The year 2012 was a new beginning for during this particular year God outlined my strategies and His plan and direction for me moving forward. It was during this year that I first began sharing and bringing to light my wounded and broken heart experiences. To share with others the pain of my heart was very hard and intimidating so I began to open up to only two persons I considered close and trusting. I suffered alone for years for I did not want to be labeled as one who caused trouble in the church. I trusted God to take care of the situation in His own way and in His own time. Yet, there were times when I felt crushed in my spirit, lonely, humiliated, embarrassed, ignored, and with no sense of truly belonging. This should never happen to a child of God but I reminded myself that some situations are allowed by God.

The year 2011 through 2017 was another seven year period that was extremely difficult for me. My bold and God driven move in 2011 provoked "the oppressor" and things were done that caused the pain in my heart to grow worse instead of better. This leader behaved towards me in ways that were unjust and burdensome. Yet, I did not leave the church although I had been treated in ways that did not demonstrate God's love. It was on Christmas Sunday of 2017 that the pastor did something in church that resulted in a significant and very difficult turning point for me. On that day of which I speak it became very clear to me that it would be the last Sunday that I would attend that particular church. I did not make the decision to walk away and leave that church I was led away by the spirit. As a result of this very painful experience on Christmas Sunday 2017, I was sick for the following three to four weeks.

The year 2018 marks another eight year period which was another new beginning. The New Year started and for me there was no pull on my heart or in my spirit to return to that church. The Holy Spirit made clear to me by revelation "*I had to set you free for you would have stayed right there and My purpose within you would be unfulfilled or aborted. This very painful experience had to be permitted as My way to lose you and let you go for you could not give birth in this environment to the now mature seed growing on the inside in the womb of your heart.*" I then realized and accepted the fact that I had to move on from that church. Today I still cannot find words to explain how extremely difficult and emotionally painful that was for me to do in spite of the years of heartbreak. It is not easy to let go and move on after spending approximately twenty seven years at one church.

During the years of 2018 and 2019 I visited a few churches but was not in a hurry to join any particular church quite yet. I intentionally sought God in prayer for His direction for a church home for I wanted to be sure about my decision. To be transparent I also felt somewhat vulnerable in joining another church too quickly and while my heart was hurting and feeling very sad to leave. I also wanted to be persuaded of being led by God to the church that I would join. Believe it or not there are jealous people within the church and some of these people fail to understand that not everyone is focused on some positions and appointments or what they themselves are focused on but rather some people such as myself are more focused on a higher calling in Christ Jesus Himself and God's divine purpose for their own lives.

The thought of starting all over again in a new church was not easy. However, the Holy Spirit encouraged me saying that sometimes we have to start all over again in order to grow in our wholeness and God's divine purpose for our lives. I learned that starting over in order to develop into the person God calls us to be is a good thing. Consider that God is shifting and moving you to a new and different environment where you will experience peace of heart and mind and will be able to operate in your purpose. When God takes you out of that place to a new place He will add years to restore the lost time. I now know that although things were rough at that former church God in His own divine way was preparing me for His divine favor.

Sunday February 3, 2019, is a date that I will never forget. I visited a particular church and during the service the Holy Spirit spoke to me and I wrote immediately in my journal, "*I am pregnant in the final trimester, I am about to give birth, I am giving birth*." Interestingly enough this had no relation to the pastor's sermon. That same Sunday evening I attended a revival service at another church and during the sermon the preacher said, "***You are pregnant already***." This I also documented in my journal. I looked at what I had written that morning and was truly amazed at how God confirmed what the Holy Spirit had said to me that morning. Throughout that month of February, the Holy Spirit worked with me in my heart bringing to my remembrance and helping me to understand the meaning of the seed that was planted in my heart in January 2012. Seven years later in March 2019, the Holy Spirit constrained me and I "***gave birth***." I had no other choice but to give "birth" to this purpose seed by embarking on writing this book.

March is the month in which I should have been making my final preparations for my annual conference in April, however, the Holy Spirit directed me to use the time to write the book instead of planning for the conference. The thought of forgoing the conference was not easy for me to do but after much praying and seeking God He assured me that was what I needed to do. Once I yielded my spirit to do as God instructed I was liberated. God said that I needed to give birth and I have. Once I started writing this book I was filled with excitement and it actually gushed out of the belly of my spirit like an enormous water fall. Here again God used my major heartbroken experiences and my healing journey to birth and create this manual (book of instructions) and guide (order or directions) of healing that will encourage and support you in your own quest for healing, wholeness and purpose.

Have an enjoyable and transforming reading experience. I promise that you will never be the same while reading or after reading this healing manual and I encourage you to share your experience with this book and encourage others to read it as well.

I especially want to express a heart full of gratitude to everyone who has supported me by purchasing this book. I know this book will bless and inspire you on your brokenness to wholeness journey as well as in your God given purpose as you seek to discover the purpose for which your heart was broken.

The Framework

Jesus said to them, 'Surely you will quote this proverb to me: 'Physician, heal yourself!' And you will tell me, 'Do here in your hometown what we have heard that you did in Capernaum (Luke 4:23).

Your encounter with this book is a divinely directed life transforming experience for you. From the pulpit to the pews and the larger communities, the people of God and humanity in general are hurting emotionally, psychologically, spiritually, personally, professionally and otherwise. Although people are hurting, for many reasons they choose to cover their heart pain and hurt instead of dealing with those painful experiences. This divinely inspired and directed book will provide a framework for your inner healing from heart pain.

My personal experiences of heartbreak have equipped me with the tools that I will use to guide you gently, intentionally, lovingly, compassionately and strategically by taking you through my healing journey and show you how I overcame my years of broken heart experiences. I will share with you my continuous journey into heart wholeness and growth in Christ. You could consider this book a "***healing manual***" for it provides spiritual and practical insights that one can follow to a desired outcome of inner heart healing. This brokenness journey is a struggle but let me assure you that God will sustain you all the way through to your breakthrough for He is your constant companion and strongest defense. I have prayed for you numerous times and will continue to do so and I know you will never be the same while reading and after reading this book.

I have systematically outlined and arranged this book into six distinct and organized parts as the framework and you are encouraged to read accordingly for it will serve you very well.

Part One: Preparation:

Chapter one introduces you to a unique **survival kit** that contains meticulously selected tools. For a successful healing journey you will need to use all the tools that are provided in the survival kit. Some examples of the tools are personal choice, prayer, faith, the Word of God and several more.

Chapter two reveals to you how I made myself very transparent and vulnerable in sharing deeper about my wounded and shattered heart and the deep emotional pain I experienced. I also shared candidly and sincerely how I was able to remain in the "secret place of the Most High God" during this very difficult time.

Chapters three and four present a picture of the unknown journey that is ahead of you and the courage that it will require of you to embark on this unknown journey of your healing.

Part Two: God's Great Work:

This part of the book gently introduces you and gives you an insight into the great work that God is doing on the inside of your heart during your time of brokenness. This section will deepen your understanding to the fact that God has permitted these experiences for you in order for you to fully grasp the measures He is taking to prepare you for your great purpose ahead.

Although you hurt and suffer, take comfort that this is just for a season so you should rejoice in God anyway for this too shall pass. Please know that God will preserve you through it all for you carry the purpose seed He has planted in your heart. Your heartbreak results in great pain and emotional suffering but in the end this brokenness of heart will result in your divine healing, transformation, and the joyous discovery of your gifts and divine purpose.

Part Three: The Tunnel Purging:

Part three introduces you to the first of two tunnels, *Purging*. In this section of the book I will guide you gently through the purging and cleansing that one must under-take in order to experience "*soul care healing*." There are some things that I discussed which I call impurities that we must purge ourselves from including denial, anger, bitterness, hatred, discouragement and so much more. These are the realities I discovered and some of which

I experienced as I had to navigate my way through the mending and healing of my shattered heart. For anyone to experience inner healing these impurities **MUST** be purged from the heart.

Part Four: The Tunnel Healing:

Part four introduces you to the second of the two tunnels, *Healing*. In this section of the book I teach about what I call the "*Power Stations*." Once you have travelled through the "Purging" tunnel and have cleansed your heart and soul of the impurities you are now ready for healing to take place. The power stations along this tunnel include obedience, forgiveness, love, humility, grace, mercy and much more. Every station in this tunnel plays a unique and significant role in your complete inner healing and transforming journey.

Part Five: Deliverance and Restoration:

In part five, I prayerfully and carefully selected biblical examples of persons including Jesus who experienced brokenness of heart and soul and how they overcame and were restored to wholeness of heart. When we submit to God and His will we will experience deliverance and restoration from those things that hinder us and we will be well positioned to fulfill God's purpose for us. In this part of the book I explain what submission is and what it means to submit to God in order for us to experience deliverance. When we submit ourselves to God we give Him full control and freedom to work in and through us like the "*Potter and the Clay.*" You will learn that although God has given us the power of personal choice He desires that we choose to have Him work freely with us to fulfill His purpose.

Part Six: Gratitude and Praise:

Part six is the last section of the book and it is quite reflective. In this part of the book I shared my personal deep thoughts and insights of emerging from death to newness of life. I meticulously explained that there are scars left by my wounded heart experiences and that these scars will serve to remind me of where God has brought me from and how far I have come in overcoming my brokenness and growing into my divine purpose. In this section I also warned that the fight does not end but instead it continues and it intensifies so we must be on the alert and keep fighting at a different level of preparedness. I ended this section by offering Christ and salvation to anyone who is not saved.

This book is written with passion and purpose: It is my desire, passion and purpose to make an impact in the Christian community and beyond by the writing of this book which is an anointed work of ministry in itself. I say this with the blessed assurance for the Holy Spirit ministered this truth to me before and during writing. If you are heartbroken this book will minister to you deeply in many ways. With the presence of the Holy Spirit you will not be able to contain the inspiration experienced for you will be constrained by the Holy Spirit to witness to others and share the blessings you received from reading this book. In addition, there may be those who are on their healing journey but may need some extra support which this book will provide.

God has planned and fashioned this anointed work of ministry, this book, to assist people globally as they journey through their inner hurt and healing process. We all do have the same basic needs for the wholeness of our emotional, psychological and social well being.

Journaling is strongly recommended as you read this book for it is good to write your thoughts down for reflection and track your healing and growth. I charge you to read prayerfully and with an open heart and mind in allowing God through the power and presence of the Holy Spirit to speak to you as you read. Take time to meditate, pray and reflect as you read and open your heart to God's divine healing of your heart and soul and enjoy your special journey.

The ultimate goal of this book is to aid in your "**Soul Care Healing**" journey and to enhance and promote your spiritual and personal growth development. This book is also good for anyone who may have never experienced heartbreak for by reading this book they will be armed with necessary tools to assist and minister to someone whom they may know to be heartbroken. Additionally, this book will help to prepare someone on how to deal with situations should they become broken in heart for any particular reason. You will find that I offer heartwarming insights and powerful Scripture messages that will be priceless tools on your journey. My purpose is to inspire, motivate, empower and guide you as you develop into a more dynamic you. Be healed so that you can be an inspiration in the healing of others.

Introduction

The LORD is close to the broken hearted (Psalm 34:18)

I am the LORD, I change not. So you, the descendants of Jacob, are not destroyed (Malachi 3:6).

My sacrifice, O God, is a broken spirit; a broken and contrite heart you, God, will not despise (Psalm 51:17).

I am introducing this book as a divinely inspired and divinely directed resource that will facilitate your healing from heartbreak in your life experiences. Trust the Master's plan which is God's divine plan and purpose for your brokenness and inner healing journey towards wholeness and purpose. When you are healed you become healthy; when you are whole there is balance and harmony among all of your systems including physical, behavioral, cognitive, emotional, and spiritual for you are cured in your heart, soul and body. Divine healing yields harmony among the systems as God originally intended for them to be.

JUST BROKEN!

No one is immune to experiencing a broken heart. Moreover, a broken heart does not have to be forever for in due time one could experience **Overcoming** the broken heart and **Growing** into wholeness and purpose. I was perfect and whole before I became scarred and imperfect. God created me in His own image and in His own likeness as whole and for a purpose. "***So God created mankind in his own image, in the image of God he created them; male and female he created them***" (Genesis 1:27). When God made man and placed him in the Garden of Eden he was perfect and without sin. Man was **whole** and complete. Man was whole in heart, soul, and body. "***I praise You because I am fearfully and wonderfully made; Your works are wonderful, I know that full well***" (Psalm 139:14).

In the story of the "*Fall*" sin crept into man's heart and man became "*broken*" in heart and soul. Sin corrupted man's heart and that is a broken condition for as a result man became separated from his creator, God. The origin of brokenness of spirit, soul and body can be traced back to the Garden of Eden with Adam and Eve and their disobedience to God.

Status in life cannot protect and shield anyone from heartbreak and one can be broken in any area of one's life. The human condition is the common denominator for in every culture, race, social status, religion, and educational achievement we are all the same with the same basic need. Someone may even experience multiple areas of brokenness at the same time or over a period of time. Some of the areas of the human condition that are vulnerable to brokenness could include but are not limited to the following:

- Broken- heart
- Broken- spirit
- Broken- mind
- Broken- dreams
- Broken- promises
- Broken- will
- Broken- desire
- Broken- home
- Broken- relationships
- Broken- marriage, separation or divorce
- Broken- families
- Broken- friendships
- Broken- serious health issues
- Broken- finances
- Broken- parent and child relationships
- Broken- church relationships and fellowships
- Broken- mental illness
- Broken- the death of a spouse
- Broken- the death of a parent
- Broken- the death of a child
- Broken- your child is born with special needs
- Broken- old age and failing health
- Broken- old age and abandonment by family
- Broken- miscarriage or abortion
- Broken- the death of a sibling (brother or sister)
- Broken- sibling rivalry, quarrels, abandonment
- Broken- the promotion you did not receive

- Broken- domestic violence and abuse
- Broken- verbal and physical abuse
- Broken- mental illness
- Broken- your fiancé broke off the engagement
- Broken- Pastor's concern for members
- Broken- ongoing conflict with in-laws
- Just broken! The list continues.

Have you ever been heartbroken in any area of your life such as spiritual, personal, professional, social or otherwise? Are you broken right now? Have you identified or know the cause of your broken heart? Do you desire to be healed and to begin growing in your wholeness and purpose? Are you healed from your brokenness? Are you in the process of being healed from your brokenness? Do you know of anyone who is broken hearted? I want you to know that healing can emerge from your broken pieces and places. Miracles can come from your broken pieces and places. Yes, God can cause a spring of fresh healing waters to flow from the deserted place of your broken heart and soul and prepare you for your ordained purpose.

The children of Israel could have the answers to these questions. They had an experience as they journeyed from Egypt through Marah. *On their journey from Egypt, the Children of Israel got to Marah where they were very thirsty because they had no water in three days. There at Marah they found that there was no water except for one spring and the water was bitter. They complained to Moses who cried to God on their behalf. God showed Moses a piece of wood and gave him instructions to throw the wood in the water. Moses did as God instructed him and the water became fit to drink. Before leaving Marah, God gave the Israelites specific instructions of his expectations, commands and decrees that if they follow God promised them healing. After they left Marah, the Children of Israel traveled on to the oasis of Elim. When they got to Elim, they found that there were twelve springs of fresh, clear water and seventy palm trees that awaited them. They camped there near the water and rested under the trees for a few days before continuing their journey* (Exodus 15:22-27). Did you know that God can make your bitter water sweet? Oh yes, God will do just that for you if you ask Him and allow Him.

Child of the Most High God, I assure you that if you remain faithful to God and rely on His unchanging Word, He will bring you out of your brokenness situation to a refreshing experience as He did for the children of Israel. God can bring you from your place of "***bitter water to sweet water***" and into a good place, a place of plenty, a place of wholeness, a place of divine purpose, a place where you can set up camp and linger for a good while like the Children of Israel.

The testimony you share of overcoming brokenness of heart can and should be from your own brokenness experience in that you tell about how God brought you out victoriously. If you have the desire to be whole do not lose hope! God says, "***Come unto me all he who labor and are heavy laden and I will give you rest, take my yoke upon you and learn of me for my yoke is easy and my burden is light***" (Matthew 11:28). God wants to deliver and restore you to wholeness in order for you to operate in your purpose.

ESPECIALLY CHOSEN To Be BROKEN For PURPOSE: Overcoming Brokenness Growing Into Wholeness And Purpose! As I reflected on the subject of inner healing, the longer I thought about it and immersed myself in the possibilities the Holy Spirit revealed to me that I am broken now but the assurances of healing are great. Hearing this was quite inspiring to me! The words ***overcoming and growing*** are very profound and have deep interpretations and self applications! They suggest to some of us and remind some of us of our brokenness state and the efforts we must make to overcome and be healed. Growing in wholeness and purpose brings into focus the fact that I am broken but God intends for me to be healed. God is perfect and He created perfect humans in Adam and Eve. Everything God made He said it was good! When God looked at everything He made He was pleased (Genesis 1:31). David says, "***I will praise You, for I am fearfully and wonderfully made, Your works are wonderful, I know that full well***" (Psalm 139:14).

Adam and Eve were whole for they were pure and without sin. They both lived in paradise in the *Garden of Eden*. They enjoyed a marvelous relationship with God their maker. Each day they anticipated God's visit to the garden to fellowship with them and it was a time of great fellowship between them and their Maker. When the serpent deceived Adam and Eve in the Garden of Eden by getting them to do what God had instructed them not to do, they no longer looked forward to God's visit to the Garden to spend time in fellowship with them. Instead, they were ashamed and intentionally hid themselves when they knew that it was time for God to visit. So likewise, when we are experiencing heartbreak we in some ways hide ourselves physically by staying away from friends, family members and even church. We also try to hide our emotions by behaving in ways to cover our inner hurt by pretending that all is well and we are okay.

After Adam and Eve ate the fruit this was the beginning of their brokenness and they were never the same thereafter. Everything changed for them from that moment and they realized that their disobedience was the cause of their separation from God. I imagine that grief and regret gripped their hurting souls with no end in sight that they could see. God in His compassion and loving mercy devised a plan to restore Adam and Eve. God covered them with animal skin while at the same time God had some consequences for their willful disobedience.

Likewise, when we become broken in heart things are never the same. Our thinking, mood, behavior, and attitudes change during our time of brokenness. We are either broken or whole. In our case, it took the plan of redemption through Jesus' dying on the cross to make provision for our restoration so that we can be whole again which is God's way of covering us. God's plan of redemption does much more than covering our sins for it removes our sins and cleanses us in our hearts from all unrighteousness.

We cannot begin to **grow into wholeness and fulfill our purpose** until we begin to **overcome** our brokenness. Overcoming begins first with an aware-ness and acknowledgment of our broken condition. In our brokenness we labor through our heart pain and the struggles for a breakthrough. Can you forgive yourself and accept God's forgiveness? When we do reach that place of repentance and forgiveness where we repent of our wrong and we forgive others of their wrong towards us it is a place of rest. What a relief! At this "place of rest" we find rest to our souls which brings peace and we will begin the process of healing which will move us towards wholeness and purpose.

As we are overcoming our brokenness, the fur-ther removed we are from our brokenness is the more growth experiences we have in growing into our whole-ness. Brokenness brings *grief and pain* but wholeness brings *joy and peace*. As you read this divinely inspired book, I know that the Holy Spirit will minister to your soul and you will be led to identify the root cause of your brokenness so that you can begin your healing process. The Holy Spirit will aid you; sustain you; and guide you in the purging of your heart and soul. The Holy Spirit is your divine and constant helper who will facilitate your healing.

I am on a mission to minister to wounded and hurting hearts and one of my tools that I am using is this divinely inspired book. No medical physician can prescribe med-ication for the healing of a broken heart. A counselor, psychiatrist, therapist, and life coach may all try to point you in the direction of things that you can do for mental and physical health. However, it is only the living Word of God through the power of the Holy Spirit that can heal and restore your broken heart. It is only the Word of God that reaches man's heart and nothing else. You must feed your soul by absorbing the Word of God as you read and study prayerfully.

> *For the Word of God is quick, and powerful, and sharper than any two-edged sword, piercing even to the dividing asunder of soul and spirit, and of the joints and marrow, and is a discerner of the thoughts and intents of the heart* (Hebrews 4:12).

Part One
Preparation

Entrance To The Unknown

"A voice of one calling in the wilderness, 'Prepare the way for the Lord, make straight paths for him" (Mark 1:3).

As you enter this unknown journey which leads towards your healing, you have no idea what hurdles you will face along the way or what the outcome of your journey will be. In the natural you get ready by putting things in order. You design a plan and the groundwork for what is to be your expected journey and its outcome. Likewise you must prepare for this spiritual cleansing and healing journey.

Consider journaling your thoughts during and after each read which can be quite therapeutic. Be intentional and consistent to journal and record your insights into Scripture as well as your progress on your own healing journey.

Enter into His gates with thanksgiving and into His courts with praise, be thankful unto Him and bless His name, for the Lord is good and His mercies

everlasting, and His truth endures to all generations (Psalm 100:4-5).

If for any reason you feel intimidated you are not alone for this is what most people experience when they are faced with the challenges of having to do something new especially if this could be a big life changing decision. It takes much courage to enter the unknown not knowing what to expect and what the outcome will be. Likewise, this healing journey you are embarking on is unknown to you for you have never trod this way before and you do not know what is awaiting you around the corner.

CHAPTER 1

Your Survival Kit:
READY! SET! GO!

"So you also must be ready, because the Son of Man will come at an hour when you do not expect him" (Matthew 24:44).

This know also, that in the last days perilous times shall come. For men shall be lovers of their own selves, covetous, boasters, proud, blasphemers, disobedient to parents, unthankful, unholy; Without natural affection, trucebreakers, false accusers, incontinent, fierce, despisers of those that are good (2 Timothy 3:1).

B e forewarned, there is a rough road and a difficult journey ahead of you. This chapter lays the foundation for a successful journey from brokenness to wholeness and purpose. This chapter is to introduce you to your "**survival kit**" which undoubtedly is needed for every step of your journey to sustain you. If you choose to travel without this survival kit you are knowingly exposing yourself to danger and all kinds of attacks on every side from the enemy. You must without fail embrace every essential item in your **survival kit** and use each one to your advantage.

It is not optional that you have this kit and for a successful journey you are strongly advised to be sure to use it. In your survival kit you **MUST** have the following essential items or tools: [1] personal choice, [2] prayer, [3] the Word of God, [4] faith, [5] Trust [6] humility, [7] time, [8] the Whole Armor of God, [9] hope [10] patience [11] songs of praise and [12] endurance. These will be your spiritual nutrients that will sustain you along the way on your difficult journey and there can be no substitute for nothing else can take their places.

PERSONAL CHOICE

> *If you forsake the Lord and serve foreign gods, he will turn and bring disaster on you and make an end of you, after he has been good to you. But the people said to Joshua, 'No! We will serve the Lord* (Joshua 24:20-21).

> Joshua said, "*But as for me and my household, we will serve the Lord*" (Joshua 24:15).

PERSONAL CHOICE: In the Scripture above Joshua made his personal choice that he would serve God and not foreign gods. As you embark on this journey, it is important that you know your **God given rights to choose**! The greatest right you have is that of personal choice. You have the right to make personal choices and it is a God given blessing. From the beginning of time, man had been given the power to choose for himself. In our daily lives we have to make choices some of which affect us personally while others include and affect other people. We choose which college to attend; where to live; the friends we keep; the clothes we wear on any given day and the kind of car we want to drive. You will read about the account of the personal choice that Adam and Eve made in Genesis chapter three. When God made Adam and Eve and placed them in the Garden of Eden He gave them clear and specific instructions concerning personal choice.

God told them that they could eat from all the trees in the garden but not from the tree in the center of the garden. This was a big choice God gave them. The power to make wise choices is something that you should be very careful in exercising. God says,

> **This day I call the heavens and the earth as witnesses against you that I have set before you life and death, blessings and curses. Now choose life, so that you and your children may live** (Deuteronomy 30:19).

Although God gives us the free will to make personal choices, He advises us on how we should choose. If we make unwise choices there are consequences, for God will punish those who do not make Him their first choice above everyone and everything else.

PRAYER

Bless them that curse you, and pray for them which despitefully use you (Luke 6:28).

Here my cry, O God; listen to my prayer. From the ends of the earth I call to you, I call as my heart grows faint; lead me to the rock that is higher than I. For you have been my refuge, a strong tower against the foe (Psalm 61:1-3).

Simon, Simon, listen! Satan has demanded to sift all of you like wheat, but I have prayed for you that your own faith may not fail; and you, when once you have turned back, strengthen your brothers (Luke 22:31).

PRAYER: Prayer is our lifeline to God and it is the avenue through which we talk with God. Whenever we pray it is in Jesus' name that we pray for we go to God through Jesus. The Bible teaches that no one gets to God but through Jesus His Son. "*Jesus said unto him, I am the way, the truth, and the life: no man cometh unto the Father, but by me*" (John 14:6).

When you pray you should remind God of His Word and promises to you. "*Put Me in remembrance; Let us contend together; State your case, that you may be acquitted*" (Isaiah 43:26). In prayer we acknowledge our

4

dependency on God our heavenly Father. "***Then you will call on me and come and pray to me, and I will listen to you***" (Jeremiah 29:12). Jesus prayed to His Father God on our behalf. "***My prayer is not that you take them out of the world but that you protect them from the evil one***" (John 17:15). We are encouraged to pray if and when we are in trouble. "***Is anyone among you in trouble? Let them pray. Is anyone happy? Let them sing songs of praise***" (James 5:13). Prayer invokes God's presence in getting close to us. We must extend our faith in God when we pray. First, we must approach God in faith for it is counterproductive if we pray in doubt. Prayer is an intimate relationship with God and it should be built on trust. In our prayer we demonstrate that we love God deeply and value our relationship with Him. "***Therefore I tell you, whatever you ask for in prayer, believe that you have received it, and it will be yours***" (Mark 11:24).

Child of God, this is wise instruction concerning what our attitude towards prayer should be. "***Rejoice always, pray continually, give thanks in all circumstances; for this is God's will for you in Christ Jesus***" (1 Thessalonians 5:16-18). When you pray you acknowledge your insufficiency and your dependence on God. Jesus is our perfect example, for when He fed the multitude, He first took the loaves, lifted them up to God and prayed, then, He broke them and gave to His disciples who then gave to the people. Sometimes we have to spend time in prayer and fasting.

If my people, who are called by my name, will humble themselves and pray and seek my face and turn from their wicked ways, then I will hear from

heaven, and I will forgive their sin and will heal their land (2 Chronicles 7:14).

We should always pray our way through every situation. In prayer we receive peace of mind knowing with full assurance that God will supply all of our need according to His riches in glory. The Bible teaches us that our personal prayers should be our private time in communication with God. This is an intimate time with God when we are free to open our hearts and reveal to God all those things that are of concern to us. God our Heavenly Father will always supply our needs according to His riches in glory. "**But when you pray, go into your room, close the door and pray to your Father, who is unseen. Then your Father, who sees what is done in secret, will reward you**" (Matthew 6:6).

THE HOLY WORD

> **The word of God is quick, and powerful, and sharper than any two edged sword, piercing even to the dividing asunder of soul and spirit, and of the joints and marrow, and is a discerner of the thoughts and intents of the heart** (Hebrews 4:12). **Thy Word have I hid in mine heart, that I might not sin against thee** (Psalm 119:11).

THE HOLY WORD: On this journey you must have the Word of God and it is not optional for nothing else can take the place of God's Holy Word. We must know the Word of God for it is the most powerful weapon that we will need to defeat the enemy. Jesus Himself used the Word when He was tempted by Satan who upon hearing the Word fled from Jesus. The Word of God is your life giving and life sustaining source.

> *In the beginning was the Word, and the Word was with God, and the Word was God* (John 1:1).

> *Take the helmet of salvation and the sword of the Spirit, which is the word of God* (Ephesians 6:17).

> *Jesus answered, It is written: 'Man shall not live on bread alone, but on every word that comes from the mouth of God* (Matthew 4:4).

> *Blessed rather are those who hear the word of God and obey it* (Luke 11:28).

As you travel along this healing journey you will need the Word of God as your comforter; for your deliverance; the guide of your path; it will give you assurance; and in it is your protection. The Word of God is food for the soul and we must spend time reading and studying it in order for our souls to live and thrive spiritually. Everything that you need is found in the Word of God. True peace of heart and mind is found in the Word of God. You will hear God speak to you through His Holy Word.

FAITH

> **Now faith is the substance of things hoped for, the evidence of things not seen** (Hebrews 11:1).

FAITH: In (Greek faith is (*pestis*); in Latin faith is (*fides*) meaning "trust" and "belief"). Jesus is our perfect example of having trust, belief, and obedience in God the Father. It is by our faith in God that we are saved by His grace and received salvation. "**For it is by grace you have been saved, through faith and this is not from yourselves, it is the gift of God**" (Ephesians 2:8). Faith is to believe even without having any concrete evidence of the outcome. Faith is holding on to the Word of God which will not fail. For your journey from **brokenness to wholeness** you must have faith, unwavering faith in God. Since faith produces work your faith will be evident in your actions. "**What good is it, my brothers and sisters, if someone claims to have faith but has no deeds? Can such faith save them**?" (James 2:14).

Faith is one of the most important items that must be in your survival kit and it is not optional. "**And without faith it is impossible to please God, because anyone who comes to him must believe that he exists and that he rewards those who earnestly seek him**" (Hebrews 11:6). Not only is it hard to please God it is impossible to please Him without faith. Your journey with God is a walk of faith, for you must trust God completely with all your heart that He knows what is best for you. Our faith should be grounded in the Word of God. "**So then faith comes**

8

by hearing, and hearing by the word of God" (Romans 10:17). God Himself is the source of our faith.

> **Looking unto Jesus, the author and finisher of our faith, who for the joy that was set before Him endured the cross, despising the shame, and has sat down at the right hand of the throne of God** (Hebrews 12:2).

Lack of faith is to doubt God which is fear and this comes with a great price. Our example is the Children of Israel who due to their lack of faith ended up in the wilderness for forty years where most of them died, all those who were twenty years old and older who were counted in the census and who had grumbled against God (Numbers 14:29). They did not believe that with God's help they could defeat the Canaanites and so the Children of Israel complained to Moses that he had brought them from Egypt there in the desert to die. They even wished that they had died in Egypt and they wanted to choose a leader who would take them back to Egypt (Numbers 14:2-4).

This rebellious and doubting behavior of the Children of Israel was enough for God. At that point God had a conversation with Moses and Aaron saying, "**How long will this wicked community grumble against me? I have heard the complaints of these grumbling Israelites**" (Numbers 14:26). Due to their lack of faith in God He decided that they would not be allowed to enter the Promised Land of Canaan.

As surely as I live, declares the Lord, I will do to you the very thing I heard you say: In this wilderness your bodies will fall, every one of you twenty years old or more who was counted in the census and who has grumbled against me. Not one of you will enter the land I swore with uplifted hand to make your home, except Caleb son of Jephunneh and Joshua son of Nun (Numbers 14:28-30).

Lack of faith in God will keep you spellbound and prevent you from taking action. Since you must act it requires that you exercise your strongest faith in God for the outcome that you desire is according to the measure of your faith. I assure you that in God there is no defeat for His hands are strong and mighty enough to deliver you from any and all circumstances that you will and must face on this journey.

TRUST

Trust in the Lord with all of your heart and lean not on your own understanding; in all your ways (acknowledge) submit to him, and he will (direct) make your paths straight. Do not be wise in your own eyes; fear the LORD and shun evil. This will bring health to our body and nourishment to your bones (Proverbs 3:5-8).

*"**Trust in the Lord, and do good; dwell in the
land and enjoy safe pasture**"* (Psalm 37:3).

TRUST: In (Latin trust is (***fiducia***) meaning "firmness"). This firmness is having confidence in something or someone and this is the confidence that we are called upon to have in God. "***But I trust in you, Lord; I say, 'You are my God.***" Trust and faith are intertwined which means that you cannot have one without the other. The Greek word for faith is (***pistis***) and the Latin word for faith is (***fides***) meaning trust and belief. God calls on us to trust Him with ALL of our hearts. To trust God with all of our hearts means that we should not lean on our own understanding. God alone knows everything and not us. Our understanding is limited and when we lean on our own understanding we trust our own knowledge. To trust in the Lord means much more than believing in Him. Trusting God is an abiding confidence in who He is and what He can and will do. When we trust God He promises to lead and direct our paths. While we trust God we should stay away from evil. "***That is why I am suffering as I am. Yet this is no cause for shame, because I know whom I have believed, and am convinced that he is able to guard what I have entrusted to him until that day***" (2 Timothy 1:12).

Trusting God comes with a special blessing and doing what God requires means that one is obedient and will be specially blessed. It is extremely important that we trust God and do good for our joy and safety depend on our wise choice. "***Trust in the Lord, and do good; dwell in the land and enjoy safe pasture***" (Psalm 37:3). "***But***

blessed is the one who trusts in the Lord, whose confidence is in him" (Jeremiah 17:7). One who trusts in the Lord is likened to a tree that is planted by the water that sends out its roots by the stream, and does not fear when heat comes; for its leaves remain green, and is not anxious or worry in the year of drought for it does not cease to bear fruit (Jeremiah 17:8).

Trusting God and giving Him full control of your circumstances means that you are aware that nothing can happen to you without Him knowing. When you trust God to this extent it gives you extra strength, courage, and peace as you face the difficulties and pain of your broken heart. Knowing that God will never leave or forsake you gives you holy boldness. When we trust God the experience is like healing to our flesh and refreshment to our bones. Trusting God brings healing to our souls and refreshes our spirit thus giving us the strength to cope and make wise decisions as we deal with the pain in our broken hearts.

Jesus is our perfect example of what it means to trust God completely. When Jesus was on earth they saw Him trusting His Father God completely on many occasions including during to his death on the cross. Victory over our circumstances is promised to us when we trust God wholeheartedly.

> ***When I am afraid, I put my trust in you. In God, whose word I praise, in God I trust and am not afraid. What can mere mortals do to me?*** (Psalm 56:3-4).

"Fear of man will prove to be a snare, but whoever trusts in the LORD is kept safe" (proverbs 29:25).

But when you ask, you must believe and not doubt, because the one who doubts is like a wave of the sea, blown and tossed by the wind (James 1:6).

HUMILITY

He was oppressed and He was afflicted, Yet He did not open His mouth; Like a lamb that is led to slaughter, And like a sheep that is silent before its shearers, So He did not open His mouth (Isaiah 53:7).

HUMILITY: Jesus is our perfect example of humility and God takes great delight when we humble ourselves. *"For those who exalt themselves will be humbled, and those who humble themselves will be exalted"* (Matthew 23:12).

What does it mean to be humble? The state of being humble has its origin in the Latin word humilis, meaning "low." Humility is the quality of being humble and it means putting the needs of another person before your own, and thinking of others before yourself. Humility also means not drawing attention to yourself and it could also mean acknowledging that you are not always right. If you are humble you are also teachable, gentle, and you exercise self control.

God requires that you be humble. Child of God, as you continue on this journey from **brokenness to wholeness**, be sure to maintain humility of heart for God will not be able to walk closely with you if you have a prideful heart. God cares for the humble but He looks at the proud from a far distance (Psalm 138:6).

TIME

> **But do not forget this one thing, dear friends; With the Lord a day is like a thousand years, and a thousand years are like a day** (2 Peter 3:8).

> **Teach us to number our days, that we may gain a heart of wisdom**" (Psalm 90:12).

> **My times are in your hands; deliver me from the hands of my enemies, from those who pursue me** (Psalm 31:15).

> **Do not boast about tomorrow, for you do not know what a day may bring** (Proverbs 27:1).

TIME: God alone is in full control of time and time is not promised to anyone. Wasted time will delay your journey and healing! Therefore, we should use our time wisely knowing that the present is all that we have. "**There is a time for everything, and a season for every activity under the heavens**" (Ecclesiastes 3:1). On this brokenness to wholeness journey we should endeavor to smoothly move from one station to the next. We should not spend undue time at any given station so be careful not to waste your time. "***Making the most of every opportunity, because the days are evil***" (Ephesians 5:16). Time is limited and quite valuable, as a result, for the most part of our daily lives we try to manage our time so that we get the most out of our day.

In God's plan He creates opportunities for us to do that which needs to be done. He gives night and day, cold and heat, summer, fall, winter, spring and so on. God our Heavenly Father creates the perfect conditions for our successful journey. "***As long as the earth endures, seedtime and harvest, cold and heat, summer and winter, day and night will never cease***" (Genesis 8:22).

Time waits on no one and you cannot suspend time. Time is one thing that we can never know for sure how much of it we do have and you cannot borrow time from someone. Why then would you waste any of your time? Use your time well so that you do not delay your healing. Be intentional in the management your time and wisely navigate your healing journey. Be advised that you cannot regain lost time.

THE WHOLE ARMOR

> ***Whoever dwells in the shelter of the Most High will rest in the shadow of the Almighty. I will say of the Lord, 'He is my refuge and my fortress, my God, in whom I trust*** (Psalm 91:1-2).

THE WHOLE ARMOR OF GOD: For this treacherous journey that you are on, you must be fully armed and protected by putting on the whole armor of God. You must be completely covered.

> *Therefore put on the full armor of God, so that when the day of evil comes, you may be able to stand your ground, and after you have done everything, to stand. v14 Stand firm then, with the belt of truth buckled around your waist, with the breastplate of righteousness in place, v15 and with your feet fitted with the readiness that comes from the gospel of peace. v16 In addition to all this, take up the shield of faith, with which you can extinguish all the flaming arrows of the evil one. v17 Take the helmet of salvation and the sword of the Spirit, which is the word of God. v18 And pray in the Spirit on all occasions with all kinds of prayers and requests. With this in mind, be alert and always keep on praying for all the Lord's people. v19 Pray also for me, that whenever I speak, words may be given me so that I will fearlessly make known the mystery of the gospel*
> (Ephesians 6:13-18).

You must put on the whole armor of God by seeking daily the anointed covering of the Holy Spirit without fail for He is your defensive shield. You must know the Word, live the Word, speak the Word and share the Word of God.

> **So shall they fear the name of the Lord from the west, and his glory from the rising of the sun. When the enemy shall come in like a flood, the Spirit of the Lord shall lift up a standard against him** (Isaiah 59:19).

HOPE

> **If in this life only we have hope in Christ, we are the most miserable of all men** (1 Corinthians 15:19).

> **Therefore my heart is glad and my tongue rejoices; my body also will rest secure, because you will not abandon me to the realm of the dead, nor will you let your faithful one see decay. You make known to me the path of life; you will fill me with joy in your presence, with eternal pleasures at your right hand** (Psalm 16:9-11).

> **Anyone who is among the living has hope, even a live dog is better off than a dead lion**! (Ecclesiastes 9:4).

HOPE: *el-pece/elpo* is Hebrew which is a primary word (to anticipate, usually with pleasure) expectation (abstract or concrete) or confidence: faith, hope, to expect or confide; hope for and trust. In the Old Testament the Hebrew word **batah** and its cognates (other words from the same origin) has the meaning of confidence, security, and being without care; therefore, the concept of doubt is not part of this word. In the New Testament, the word **hope** is the Greek *elpis/elpizo*. Therefore, biblical hope is a confident expectation or assurance based upon a sure foundation for which we wait with joy and full confidence. There is no doubt about it (*Strong's Hebrew & Greek Dictionaries*).

On this journey you must have sincere hope in Christ Jesus. When you have hope in Christ it is a feeling of great expectation and there is no element of doubt that a certain thing will happen for you. You can celebrate in advance since hope is a feeling of great expectation that Christ will see you through every step of the way with His provisions of grace that awaits you. To have hope is to have a positive and optimistic mindset for a positive desired outcome which brings you joy and assurance. Your love for Christ and the indwelling of the Holy Spirit is your source of hope. Faith and hope go hand in hand. With hope you believe something will happen even without you having tangible proof or evidence.

PATIENCE:

> "*Love is patient, love is kind. It does not envy, it does not boast, it is not proud*" (1 Corinthians 13:4).

"*Be joyful in hope, patient in affliction, faithful in prayer*" (Romans 12:12).

"*You too, be patient and stand firm, because the Lord's coming is near*" (James 5:8).

"*I waited patiently for the Lord; he turned to me and heard my cry*" (Psalm 40:1).

PATIENCE: For some wounded travelers limping along on this lonesome journey from brokenness of heart to healing and wholeness patience just might be in very short supply. Some travelers in surrender give up on themselves and stop by the way for they do not have the strength of will and the patience that it takes to keep going so they stop or they rest for a long while which is just as dangerous. While on the other hand, some travelers do not have the patience to travel in a watchful, careful and timely manner so they rush along in haste and this behavior is not advisable for it is just as dangerous.

Some travelers are so impatient that they rush along in haste without God and this is very life threatening. "***Wait on the Lord, be of good courage, and he shall strengthen thy heart: wait, I say, on the Lord***" (Psalm 27:14). Here we are advised to wait on the Lord and take courage while we wait. The wise traveler who has the desire to be successful on this journey will wait on God's perfect timing for while you wait God will supply you with needed strength for the continuation of the journey. The Scripture says that God will strengthen your heart while you wait. You wait for the Lord because you have patience and you are coura-geous enough to wait. It is during your period of waiting that the Good Lord will give divine strength to your heart to make your journey successful.

Patience should be considered a Christian virtue. Patience is one of the nine qualities of the Fruit of the Spirit therefore patience is of great importance to the child of God on this healing journey. There is an abundance of blessings to be obtained as reward when one exer-cises patience. "***Those who wait (hope) in the Lord will renew their strength. They will sour (mount up) on wings like eagles; they will run and not grow weary, they will walk and not be faint***" (Isaiah 40:31). It must be understood that patience in the Lord will produce strength of will; strength of Christian character; strength of purpose; and the strength of your love for God. Patience in the Lord produces supernatural spiritual strength.

The Word of God says that when you wait (patience) on the Lord your strength will be renewed and you will be strong enough to sour like eagles. With this supernatural strength that God blesses you with it enables you to suc-cessfully navigate your brokenness to wholeness journey. Your strength in all areas of your life will be renewed when you exercise patience and wait on God. Child of God, acti-vate your faith and put it to the test by waiting on God. You will be rewarded for your patience for God's Word is true and His timing is perfect. God will bless you with His divine grace which is the source of your strength for God's grace (strength) is made perfect in your weakness. "***But he said to me, 'My grace is sufficient for you, for***

my strength (power) is made perfect in weakness" (2 Corinthians 12:9).

SONGS OF PRAISE! HALLELUJAH!

SONGS OF PRAISE: On this journey of healing, songs of praise will fill your heart with joy. When you sing there is a freedom that you will experience in your spirit and you will be liberated from that which hurts your heart so deeply. Songs of praise activate the Spirit within you and brings you closer to the presence of God. There is a peace that sweeps over your soul when you sing and you feel a sense of hope. In addition to the many beautiful hymns of the church there are many great ones in Scripture some of which are provided for you here. King David encourages us from his personal experience to sing unto God praises for He has been wonderful and good to us. When we sing to God we are reminding Him of what He has done for us and we are telling Him how thankful we are. "**Sing of what God has done**" (Psalm 132:9). "**Sing to Him, sing praise to Him; tell of all his wonderful acts**" (Psalm 105:2). When we sing unto the Lord we are giving Him thanks.

> **Oh sing unto the Lord a new song; sing unto the Lord, all the earth. Sing unto the Lord, bless his name, show forth his salvation from day to day** (Psalm 96:1-2).

My lips shall greatly rejoice when I sing unto thee; and my soul, which thou has redeemed (Psalm 71:23).

And he hath put a new song in my mouth, even praise unto our God; many shall see it, and fear, and shall trust in the Lord (Psalm 40:3).

Speaking to yourselves in psalms and hymns and spiritual songs, singing and making melody in your heart to the Lord (Ephesians 5:19).

I hope that you are convinced that you truly need your survival kit and that every tool in your kit has a unique purpose and is very much essential for the success of your journey.

ENDURANCE:

"Not only so, but we also glory in our sufferings, because we know that suffering produces perseverance; perseverance, character; and character, hope" (Romans 5:3-4).

"But the one who endures to the end, he will be saved" (Matthew 24:13).

*"**Knowing that the testing of your faith produces endurance**"* (James 1:3).

*"**May the God who gives endurance and encouragement give you the same attitude of mind toward each other that Christ Jesus had**"* (Romans 15:5).

ENDURANCE: I call endurance spiritual stamina for this to me is strength of will, character and patience. "***But he that shall endure unto the end, the same shall be saved***" (Matthew 24:13). Although surmountable obstacles are placed in your path to derail you, with a high level of endurance you will persevere and overcome those obstacles. Jesus exercised a high degree of endurance when on His way to the Cross of Calvary. There is a hardship that accompanies endurance and this was evident as Jesus journeyed to Jerusalem to be crucified. In Jesus' case the weight and burden of His cross was very challenging and difficult to carry. Yet, Jesus endured the hardship of the heavy cross; the beatings; the mocking from the crowd; and the name calling. When you have endurance you courageously encourage and convince yourself that you have the ability to be strong enough to confront the challenges that you face. With an attitude of endurance you keep working on something that is difficult for you have hope in the outcome. Patience and endurance are intertwined for you must have patience if you are to endure, which is to labor and wait.

When you have endurance you do not give up you persevere and keep going because you are persistent. For this healing journey you will need a high level of endurance for there will come times when your ability to withstand the pain and agony of your journey from brokenness to wholeness will be put to the test. When you endure it means that you purpose in your mind that in the end of it all the benefits will be rewarding. Faith, love and hope undergird your endurance for to endure someone must believe in something and have an expectation that it will be so. "*We remember before our God and Father your work produced by faith, your labor prompted by love, and your endurance inspired by hope in our Lord Jesus Christ*" (Thessalonians 1:3). You cannot give up now so keep going for your healing depends on your willingness to endure. "*Being strengthened with all power according to his glorious might so that you may have great endurance and patience*" (Colossians 1:11).

Do you have the strength of will to produce the character that it will take to endure? It will take an unquestionable character to endure. When you have unshakable hope in the outcome it feeds your character and stabilizes your focus. With endurance you do not gaze at the struggles and obstacles instead you stay focused on the goal.

CHAPTER 2

Broken And Left To Die

"My spirit is broken, my days are extinguished. The grave is ready for me" (Job 17:1).

Dear friends, do not be surprised at the fiery ordeal that has come on you to test you, as though something strange were happening to you. But rejoice inasmuch as you participate in the sufferings of Christ, so that you may be overjoyed when his glory is revealed (1 Peter 4:12-13).

When you break a branch from the trunk (vine) of a tree and place it on the ground it will stay there and die. This is a sure thing! The death of this branch begins at the very moment it is detached from the trunk or vine although its death is not immediately visible for there are no signs. It will take a few days to notice that the leaves of that branch begin to wither. This branch is cut off from its life giving source leaving no hope of surviving. This disconnected branch is exposed to the scorching heat of the sun and has no source of life sustaining connection that would keep it alive. "**Reproach has broken my heart and I am so sick and I looked for sympathy, but there was none, and for comforters, but I found none**" (Psalm 69:20).

The same is true for the children of God who are disconnected from Christ who is our life giving source for without Christ we can do nothing.

> *I am the vine; you are the branches. If you remain in me and I in you, you will bear much fruit; apart from me you can do nothing. If you do not remain in me, you are like a branch that is thrown away and withers; such branches are picked up, thrown into the fire and burned. If you remain in me and my words remain in you, ask whatever you wish, and it will be done for you. This is to my Father's glory, that you bear much fruit, showing yourselves to be my disciples* ((John 15:5-8).

Heartbreak is an invisible wound and one causing intense inner emotional pain in your heart. Broken heartedness is an inescapable human condition and the root cause originated in the Garden of Eden when Adam and Eve disobeyed God's orders and instructions. The consequences of their disobedience resulted in their separation from God just like the branch that is separated from the tree. The human race has inherited this brokenness condition from our parents, Adam and Eve.

The health and wellness of the soul of man can only be realized when we honestly acknowledge our wrongdoing and go to God as we seek the cleansing, healing and deliverance that is found only in Christ Jesus. The inner healing of your heart and soul cannot be realized by therapists and physicians writing prescriptions and giving recommendations for medications that can only treat the physical body. It will take the Word of God to heal your heart and soul.

> ***For the Word of God is quick, and powerful, and sharper than any two edged sword, piercing even to the dividing asunder of soul and spirit, and of the joints and marrow, and is a discerner of the thoughts and intents of the heart*** (Hebrews 4:12).

I have come across many people in all areas of life including people within the church, the body of Christ, who have been hurt in various areas of their lives and need healing. Sometimes when people are hurt in the church to add to that problem of broken heart and pain, in many cases no one reaches out to show love and offer support or encouragement. That was exactly what happened in my experience. This is a typical example of being broken and left to die, thus, adding to the inner pain and suffering. You should not assume that everyone in the church is perfect although God calls us to be perfect because He is perfect. The Bible teaches that the wheat and tears must grow together until the day of harvest. As a result, you will find the good and the bad in the church just be sure that you govern yourself according to the Word of God for every person must give account unto God for himself or herself.

> *Let both grow together until the harvest: and in the time of harvest I will say to the reapers; First, gather together first the tares, and bind them in bundles to burn them: but gather the wheat into my barns* (Matthew 13:24-30).

Broken and left to die has been my own personal experience. I have had several experiences of heartbreak some average while others more severe and intense. Some examples of my heartbreak experiences include the fact that I have had several deaths of close members in my immediate family including grandparents, mother, father, uncles and a sister. I have also been through a divorce and more than one car accidents. Although these experiences of heartbreak were very painful they were somehow easier to manage because I had support in dealing with them for we grieved as a family supporting one another and that eased my pain to a great extent. To be frank, my severe wounded and heartbroken experience which I am writing about in this book took place in the church and that experience is the background for this book. To be broken and left to die within the church is most difficult psychologically and emotionally painful experience of heartbreak that I have ever had to deal with in my life. This broken heart experience was far more difficult than the others I mentioned because I suffered in silence with no support. It is God's intention that the church, His church, the body of Christ be a place of refuge, healing, deliverance, restoration, love and peace. Unfortunately we find that it is too often that the opposite takes place in the church. "***What is causing the quarrels and fights among you? Do not they come from the evil desires at war within you***?" (James 4:1). "***Where there is strife, there is pride, but wisdom is found in those who take advice***" (Proverbs 13:10).

From my own personal experience I can truly say that one does not have to do anything wrong or sinful to experience church hurt directed at them. This reality is what makes my heartbreak experience so extremely painful and very hard to comprehend. In this particular church I served God completely and sincerely; I committed my time and resources to the ministries of the church; I supported the ministries; I developed and launched ministries; I directed ministries; I served in various capacities whole heartedly; and I willingly did what I was asked to do whenever I was asked including preaching. It is not in this book that I will explicitly share my *church hurt stories*. Instead, my goal is to take you on the healing journey. "***But if we walk in the light, as he is in the light, we have fellowship with one another, and the blood of Jesus, his Son, purifies us from all sin***" (1 John 1:7).

There was one question that I kept asking myself and I still do ask that question. "*How can we say that we love one another and do the wrong things that we do to one another within the body of Christ, the church*?" **Broken and left to die** is when church leadership and in my case clergy abuse their role and selfishly make decisions by doing things to prevent you and you suffer alone for years. Be assured that no one can abort God's divine purpose that is in your heart, and so in the fullness of time, God's own set time He will bring to light for everyone to see. My heartbreak got more intense when no one reached out to me to show that they care about me or my spiritual wellbeing. This is heartbreak and agony! Let me say very clearly that I am delighted that I serve a God who knows how to mend the broken pieces of my heart and I trusted Him to take care of my heart in making it whole again.

"***The blessing of the Lord, it maketh rich, and he adds no sorrow with it***" (Proverbs 10:22). If you are broken and left to die you must seek healing for the wellness and wholeness of your own soul depends on being healed. You should not continue to suffer like this and you will know if God is involved in what is going on for He will make Himself known to you in some way and in His due time. Moreover, God will supply you with the needed grace to endure the struggles of your heart pain. God's grace and mercy brought me through my turmoil and He will do the same for you. In my dark and lonely days and there were many, God Himself performed a great work inside of my heart and soul thus preparing me with the tools, resources, testimonies, and messages to reach you and others. My mission is to provide help in guiding someone out of their brokenness state and into their God given intended wholeness and purpose.

From my experiences I can tell you that brokenness of heart will bring you to a place of humility where you are forced to look at yourself through the lenses and mirror of God's Holy Word and make the changes God points out to you through His Word. Many of us suffer heart break alone but by reading this book the Holy Spirit is ministering to you and through this book I am right there with you for support.

On my brokenness to wholeness journey there were many times when the thought came to me that I had wasted my time all those precious years in this particular church where I invested greatly of my time, finances, skills, resources, gifts, ideas and so much more. The pain in my heart would convincingly say, *"Oh what a loss, what a wasted period of your precious life and time."* There were times that I felt so unappreciated and disrespected by senior leadership (clergy) and like a lamb to the slaughter I humbled myself, observed carefully what was taking place and governed myself accordingly in wisdom. I thank God that I have a strong sense of self for whenever these feelings came upon me I did not linger in that negative state of mind for long but I called on the God within me for deliverance. Let me hasten to say that I give all glory to God for the Comforter the Holy Spirit who would quickly whisper to me the encouraging words I needed to hear. The Holy Spirit has assured me that those years were not lost or wasted for during those years God had a purpose which at the time was not clearly revealed to me.

Looking back I can clearly see how those years have prepared me for this amazing ministry which God has given birth to first in my heart. This very book "**Especially Chosen to be Broken for Purpose**" is one of the many fruits that are born out of those long and agonizing years of very painful heart experiences. Now upon reflection I truly praise God for those years of heartbreak and pain for from my experiences I get to minister to others from a compassionate heart full of love, humility and understanding. I am now in a place where God has proved me and He is satisfied that I am ready to "come up higher" for He can use me to fulfill the purpose He has for me in a different and enlarged territory.

> *To grant to those who mourn in Zion, to give them a beautiful headdress instead of ashes, the oil of gladness instead of mourning, the garment of praise instead of a faint spirit; that they may be called oaks of righteousness, the planting of the Lord, that he may be glorified"* (Isaiah 61:3).

God now calls on me and allows me to use my experiences to bless others. When as a shepherd David was in the field caring for his father's flock as difficult as those years were they were his years of preparation during which time God was grooming him to be the great king of Israel he later came to be. At the time David was in the field he did not know that some time in the near future he would become the great king of Israel. God's great plan for our future we will not fully know until He reveals and makes it clear to us. The story of David is a beautiful story for later the Prophet Samuel was sent by God Himself to Jesse's house to anoint David to be the next king of Israel who would succeed King Saul. David speaks from his own experience about his **weeping** which takes place at **night** but his **joy** he said comes in the **morning**. For you and me it is dark at night which means that we are hurting, praying and weeping in our private closets. The night is our secret and private space, which could be day or night for it is our dark moments of heart pain when we meet with Almighty God and share with Him the agony and emotional pain in our hearts as we pour out our hearts to Him. In the night God is preparing you for His divine favor upon your life and in the morning He will bless you for all to see. In due time, God will take our pain and agony and will replace them with joy in the morning for all to see while He God gets the glory.

The Parable of the Good Samaritan: Luke 10:25-37

In this lesson Jesus teaches about what it means to care for and be compassionate in treating others with love and respect when they hurt and the way we would want to be treated by others. If and when someone is broken and left to die our responsibility as Christians is to restore that person. In this story a man was travelling from Jerusalem to Jericho when he was attacked by rootless robbers. They stripped him of his clothes, beat him and went away leaving him to die, he was half dead. There were those who passed him by without helping including a priest and a Levite. Along came a Samaritan who was travelling on this same road also and when he saw the wounded and hurting man he had mercy on him and took time to help him. The Samaritan bandaged his wounds and poured in **oil and wine**. He then put the wounded man on his own donkey, brought him to an inn and took care of him before leaving. Prior to leaving the Good Samaritan paid the inn keeper to take care of the sick man. The Samaritan also promised the inn keeper that he would return to visit the sick man at a later time and if there were additional expenses he would cover those expenses as well (Luke 10:25-37).

Upon careful examination of this story it is clear to me that the Good Samaritan risked his own life to help someone, the half dead man who was a stranger to him. This was a dangerous road that was heavily trafficked by robbers who were ready to attack anyone they desire to steal from, kill or destroy. The intention of any person travelling on this road was to get off as quickly as possible, yet, the Good Samaritan stopped to help. It is clear to me that the Good Samaritan was not self centered and he was not thinking of his own safety instead he was thinking of and was concerned about the hurting man. I believe that those who passed by the wounded man without stopping to help were trying to protect themselves for their intention was to get off this road as quickly as possible.

One cannot deny that the behaviors in this story are realities that are practiced in our society today. Additionally, there are some church leaders and clergy members who behave much like the Levite and the priest by having no compassion to stop and help the hurting traveler but instead they passed by on the other side. The point I am making is that those church leaders who fall in the category of the priest and Levite they have no desire to support you in your purpose, your calling or even sometimes in your spiritual growth for they would rather see you in the condition like the wounded traveler on the Jericho road. Jesus requested from Peter specific treatment for His lambs and sheep. Church leaders and especially clergy do have a special responsibility from God concerning how they should treat His people.

> **The third time he said to him, 'Simon son of John, do you love me?' Peter was hurt because Jesus asked him the third time, 'So you love me?' He said, 'Lord, you know all things; you know that I love you.' Jesus said, 'Feed my sheep** (John 21:15).

In this story the Good Samaritan represents Jesus and the wounded man represents us. "*I am the good shepherd. The good shepherd lays down his life for the sheep*" (John 10:11). Jesus is the Good Shepherd and we are his sheep and the Good Shepherd lays down his life for his sheep. In my case, my heart was so shattered, wounded and sore I had to earnestly make a serious and urgent appeal to God to pour in some extra **oil and wine** in my wounded heart. Thank God for answered prayer! God in His faithfulness supplied my daily needs of extra **oil and wine** for I certainly needed extra. The **oil** represents the anointing of the Holy Spirit for the purposes of health, honor and consecration. The **wine** represents God's divine grace, His sustaining grace which is the source of our strength.

God surely does work through unexpected circumstances and I have learnt to trust and praise Him even during those difficult and very trying times. In my experiences of brokenness that I am writing about in this book, in my heart God took me to a place where only the anointing power of the Holy Spirit and His divine grace could have kept me there. In that deserted place God covered me; protected me; hid me; comforted me; encouraged me and supported me with all that I needed to survive spiritually. That was a very dark and lonely place but during that time God's purpose seed was growing in the womb of my heart and it was well nurtured by the Holy Spirit. Glory hallelujah to His precious name!

Jesus advises us that as children of the kingdom of God we too should do likewise for one another as the Good Samaritan did for the wounded stranger. As I examine my own experience I can safely say that there are clergy members who themselves abuse their authority. In so doing they behave like the "thieves" on the Jericho road by being the ones who inflict wounds and leave people half dead some of whom never recover. These unsuspecting "clergy" think that they can hijack you and rob you of your purpose, gifts and graces that God has ordained for you. What God has for you is for you and no one can take away what God has appointed. People of God, we cannot claim to be Christians and at the same time instead of giving to other Christians the support that they need from us we inflict wounds on them and leave them to die. We cannot behave like the robbers; or the priest; or the Levite in this story and at the same time claim to be children of the light. If we claim to be children of the light then we should walk in the light as Jesus did. We cannot walk in darkness doing the things that are not Christ-like and at the same time claim to love others as God requires.

It is a fact that the way we treat others will reveal if we are walking in light or in darkness. "*But if we walk in the light, as he is in the light, we have fellowship one with another, and the blood of Jesus Christ his Son cleanses us from all sin*" (1 John 1:7). Not only did Jesus walk in the light He was the light and still is the light and we are expected to follow His example. When the divine love of God saturates our hearts it will be easy to love others instead of hurting them. "*Again Jesus spoke to them, saying, 'I am the light of the world. Whoever follows me will not walk in darkness, but will have the light of life*" (John 8:12).

God has always had a perfect plan and a purpose for our brokenness and that is the reason why you were *Especially Chosen to be Broken* for that **Purpose** and I encourage you to find out what that purpose is and operate in it fully. "**All** *the trees of the forest will know that I the LORD bring down the tall tree and make the low tree grow tall. I dry up the green tree and make the dry tree flourish*" (Ezekiel 17:24). God will always turn things around on your behalf and for His glory if you obey Him and trust Him completely with all of your heart to fully implement His plan and purpose for you. Be encouraged that your situation will not be all doom and gloom for there will be joyful moments and in those times you should liberally praise God and give Him the honor due to His Holy name while you stay centered and hopeful. Let me remind you that God alone is the source of your life. God is the giver of life and He is the sustainer of life. You might be broken and left to die by others but you can count on God who will sustain and preserve your life for a greater purpose which He will make very clear to you in His appointed and perfect time.

CHAPTER 3

It Takes Courage

Be strong and of good courage, do not fear nor be afraid of them; for the Lord your God, He is the One who goes with you. He will not leave you nor forsake you (Deuteronomy 31:6).

G od told Joshua to be courageous and likewise He is telling us to be courageous. It takes courage to step out from our comfort zone and into the vast unknown. To be courageous you will need a strong faith to rely on. Courage [faith] is bravery and it is an attitude of determination which is what it will take to enter the unknown journey. I encourage and challenge you to visualize this unknown journey through your mind's eyes as entering a tunnel, a dark and unfamiliar tunnel. Tunnels are normally dark because the light cannot shine all the way through them. This experience is like an unknown journey which you have never taken before. Since you have never entered this tunnel before, you have no idea of the pitfalls or dangers that are lurking on the inside. I must admit to you that this is very scary just thinking of the unknown.

Moreover, no one ever goes through the tunnel and return to the entrance to tell their stories for they come out or exit on the other side and continue their journeys. Some people exit the tunnel feeling a bit defeated while others victorious. There is no one to brief you on what to expect when in the tunnel. It is therefore important to know that each person's journey experience is quite different. Therefore, it could be a blessing in disguise that no one returns to tell their stories for some stories might scare you away to the extent that you might give up on trying to enter the tunnel.

I want you to visualize yourself standing at the entrance of the tunnel and as you gaze inside you can only see darkness. This is indeed quite frightening! As you gaze inside the tunnel there is no sign of light in sight and there is no person to be seen for you to ask a question concerning what to expect in the tunnel. At the entrance of the tunnel it is darkness you see staring back at you. As you stand there at the entrance and gaze at the darkness, you have no knowledge of the distance of the journey through the tunnel that you are about to embark upon. You have no knowledge of how long it will take you to navigate your way through to the other side. You have no knowledge of the dangers that await you in the tunnel. You have no awareness of any likely support that will be available to you inside the tunnel. There is no doubt that it will feel like you are on your own.

As you stand there and contemplate the treacherous journey ahead, in that tunnel, you cannot help but also imagine how dangerous the journey might be. On the other hand, you cannot help but wonder and visualize what waits at the other end of the tunnel. The uncertainty is very intense. You want to think only positively that there may be victory and joy awaiting you on the other side. On the other hand, there are some negative thoughts and images creeping in your mind about how difficult the journey is going to be. The reality is that you cannot stand there at the entrance of the tunnel forever you have to do something. Be courageous and make a decision to keep moving forward. Here is a true story of **courage** from which you can take comfort and motivation.

> *Now there were four men with leprosy at the entrance of the city gate. They said to each other, 'Why stay we here and die?' If we say, 'We will go into the city, the famine is there, and we will die. And if we stay here, we will die. So let us go over to the camp of the Arameans and surrender. If they spare us, we live; if they kill us, then we die. At dusk they got up and went to the camp of the Arameans. When they reached the edge of the camp, no one was there! For the Lord had caused the Arameans to hear the sound of chariots and horses and a great army, so that they said to one*

another, 'Look, the king of Israel has hired the Hittite and Egyptian kings to attack us! So they got up and fled in the dusk and abandoned their tents and their horses and donkeys. They left the camp as it was and ran for their lives. The men who had leprosy reached the edge of the camp, entered one of the tents and ate and drank. Then they took silver, gold and clothes, and went off and hid them. They returned and entered another tent and took some things from it and hid them also (2 Kings 7:3-8).

This bold action of the four lepers is courageous and fearless faith at work. What a mighty God we serve who knows how to work miracles on the behalf of His children. Child of The Most High God, I encourage you to allow God to take your hand and lead you through this tunnel of brokenness to wholeness that you must travel through. Your healing and wholeness depend on it and your Great God cannot and will not fail you! Soon or late you will have to embark on your journey by going through the tunnel for there is no other way to get to the other end.

This beautiful picture of the lepers which I have painted is clearly saying that when our hearts are broken we cannot and should not ignore the situation causing our heartbreak and pain. However, in order for us to experience healing and wholeness we must go through the processes, and all the experiences along the way that will lead to healing though difficult they may be. Know that you are not alone! God Himself will go with you in the person of the Holy Spirit, the Comforter, who will never leave nor forsake you.

> ***Then your light will break forth like the dawn, and your healing will quickly appear; then your righteousness will go before you, and the glory of the Lord will be your rear guard,"*** (Isaiah 58:8). **This is assuring so, *"Fight the good fight of faith, and lay hold on eternal life*** (1 Timothy 6:12).

Child of The Most High God, It will require of you to fight a good fight and it is not a fight of flesh and blood for it is not physical. In this fight you fight against the forces of evil that have come to oppose you in your spiritual wholeness journey. Satan's plan is to steal, kill and destroy you (John 10:10).

> ***We fight not (struggle not) against flesh and blood, but against the rulers, against the authorities, against the powers of this dark world and against the spiritual forces of evil in the heavenly realms*** (Ephesians 6:12).

With the struggle, fight, and war of indecision going on inside of you, take courage and chose to embark on the journey of the unknown tunnel for you heard the voice of God saying to you, "*If anyone would come after me, let him deny himself and take up his cross daily and follow me*" (Luke 9:23). You have to put an end to this heartache, pain and suffering and this should be your goal.

Unwavering courage is what it takes to step in the "mouth" of this dark tunnel to embark on this unknown journey. You must be brave and travel in the strength and name of the Lord God of heaven. It is the strength of God's grace that will empower you on this faith walk. Your determination to get through and get to the end will propel you through the tunnel and to the other side where the "light" of God's healing and **wholeness** awaits you. At the end of the tunnel you will find God's angels waiting to minister to you as they did minister to Jesus.

After Jesus fasted for forty days and forty nights in the wilderness, He was tempted by the Devil, but in the end, angels came and ministered unto Him (Matthew 8-9). In like manner, God has a provision of blessings that await you at the end of the tunnel. In order for you to benefit you must go through the tunnel. There at the end of the tunnel you will receive abundance of God's grace; increased faith; renewed strength; greater power; renewed hope; and a desire to testify and tell what the Good Lord has done for you.

You have to endure your heartache though painful it may be. You must go through the tunnel and at the end of this segment of your journey you will be able to count it all JOY and you will be better for all the ups and downs of your challenges. With the help of the Lord you will come out as pure gold. "*But He knows the way that*

I take; when He has tested me, I will come forth as pure gold" (Job 23:10). This is your test and with God's help you will pass it victoriously.

Remember, everyone's tunnel journey experience is different. No two journeys are identically the same although there will be similarities and differences. At the same time, do not undervalue your tunnel experiences because they are different from someone else's. You must learn from the experiences of others and gain strength to support you as you keep moving forward on your own healing journey.

CHAPTER 4

Time To Embark

But before they embark, the newly liberated man begs to come along and join the band of disciples. No. Go home. Tell your people this amazing story about how much God has done for you (Luke 8:38-39).

"In all the travels of the Israelites, whenever the cloud lifted from above the tabernacle, they would set out" (Exodus 40:36).

"They have told the church about your love. Please send them on their way in a manner that honors God" (3 John 1:6).

You are about to embark on a unique journey of heart and soul healing. Your heart is already broken and you now seek to embark on this journey to restore your broken heart and make it whole again. Some people live the most of their lives with a broken heart. They suffer alone and silently because they believe that there is no one with whom they can share their story which to them is so personal, private and painful. On the other hand, it would seem that some people want to remain broken to bring attention to themselves by having everyone to feel sorry for them. This attitude is self destructive behavior.

It is not in the human nature to welcome inner suffering and brokenness of heart for it is not a pleasant experience for anyone to have to endure. How does one prepare for the brokenness to wholeness healing journey? Who wants to be broken hearted anyway? These are emotional, psychological, personal, social and professional brokenness and they are not welcomed in our lives. As a result of your broken heart which is like death, there lies the potential for abundant growth in those areas of your life that are broken. Take it from me, sometimes you just have to die a little on the inside in order to be reborn and rise again as a stronger, wiser, happier and healthier you. Get ready to replace your brokenness with healing and wholeness and fortify your soul! "*I tell you the truth, Unless a kernel of wheat (seed) falls to the ground and dies, it remains only a single seed. But if it dies, it produces many seeds*" (John 12:24).

The most sustainable preparation for your journey from brokenness is to fortify your soul with the Word of God. For this journey of heartbreak to healing you must build a spiritual wall of protection and defense. This wall of protection is your defensive shield to protect your heart, soul and body from and against all attacks of fear, doubt and discouragement. What are you protecting? You are protecting your territory. You are protecting your heart and soul. You are God's chosen and He has a way of protecting His very own so depend on God Almighty to build that wall of defense around you. "***When the enemy shall come in upon me like a flood, the Spirit of the Lord shall lift up a standard against him***" (Isaiah 59:19).

Going through your "tunnel" and coming out on the other end safely will take the divine covering of God Himself in the person of the Holy Spirit. Anything can happen in that dark and hazardous tunnel which is the journey of life. Please know that you are exposed to dangers of every kind and of varying degrees. It will take God, who knows the way to lead you safely all the way through your "tunnel." Jesus says He is the way so follow Him for this is a spiritual warfare and Satan's desire is to destroy you completely. "***The thief cometh not, but for to steal, and to kill, and to destroy; I am come that they might have life, and that they might have it more abundantly***" (John 10:10).

One cannot escape from the experience of broken heartedness for no one is immune to heartbreak but one can be prepared to deal with those situations if and when they happen. Take heed to the Word of God and build your "*wall of defense.*" This wall of defense means that you should put on the whole armor of God for you must be covered completely. You have your **Survival Kit** and you are courageous so you are more prepared for this journey more than you give yourself credit.

Stand therefore, having your loins girt about with truth, and having on the breastplate of righteousness; and your feet shod with the preparation of the gospel of peace; above all taking the shield of faith, wherewith you shall be able to quench all the fiery darts of the wicked. And take the helmet of salva-tion, and the sword of the Spirit, which is the Word of God; Praying always with all prayer and supplication in the Spirit, and watching thereunto with all perseverance and supplication for all saints (Ephesians 6:14-18).

Part Two
God's Great Work

Behind The Scenes

So I sent messengers to them with this reply: 'I am carrying on a great project and cannot go down. Why should the work stop while I leave it and go down to you? (Nehemiah 6:3).

"*To this end I strenuously contend with all the energy Christ so powerfully works in me*" (Colossians 1:29).

B ehind the scenes God is at work inside of your heart and soul. God wants to focus your faith; your heart; your service to others; your love for God; your love for others; your mind; and your witness to others about what God has done for you and on your behalf. "*For we are God's handiwork, created in Christ Jesus to do good works, which God prepared in advance for us to do*" (Ephesians 2:10).

God's great work on our behalf will reveal that He prepares us and expects us to do good works in His kingdom here on earth. Whatever works we do should be from the heart and done in sincere love. Our motives should not be for man to see and shower us with praises but for God to be pleased and get the glory while our brothers and sisters receive the benefits. Although brokenness results in our suffering, God will cushion our suffering with joy and He will reward us in His own way, publicly or privately. "***We work hard with our own hands. When we are cursed, we bless; when we are persecuted, we endure it***" (1 Corinthians 4:12).

God is right there with you and you have His full support. In due time, He will prepare a table for you in the presence of your enemies. During your time of heartbreak no one sees your tears, closet prayers, fasting, devotion, your time in the Word of God, and God's faithful supernatural work that is taking place within your heart. No one sees our travail in prayer before God for we travail in our private chambers. "***This is the confidence we have in approaching God: that if we ask anything according to his will, he hears us***" (1 John 5:14).

What is happening inside of your heart is private for it is just between you and God. It is not visible for anyone to see with their natural eyes. In complete surrender to God's will you are enduring your inner pain while God ministers to your heart and soul. God can now work fully and freely in your broken heart through the circumstances and restore you to wellness and wholeness.

CHAPTER 5

Rejoice When You Are Broken

Consider it joy, my brothers and sisters, whenever you face trials of many kinds, because you know that the testing of your faith produces perseverance. Let perseverance finish its work so that you may be mature and complete, not lacking anything (James 1:2-3).

"For His anger is but for a moment, His favor for life; Weeping may endure for a night, but joy comes in the morning" (Psalm 30:5).

The Scripture above encourages us and gives us good reasons why we should all rejoice in the Lord even in our difficult circumstances because God has a great reward that awaits us if we endure to the end of the test. *"Rejoice in the Lord always, and again I say, rejoice"* (Philippians 4:4). Sometimes our brokenness is self inflicted wounds and when that is the case we mourn in regret for we take no pleasure in what we did and so it is hard to rejoice. Hopefully your brokenness which you are experiencing right now or have experienced, are not self inflected. If by chance it is self inflected, God is forgiving and patient and He will forgive you and will sustain you with His grace and mercy. "**Call to me and I will answer you and tell you great and unsearchable things you do not know**" (Jeremiah 33:3). God has a path for you to take that will lead you through to complete healing and wholeness of heart to praise Him and rejoice in your salvation.

If and when you are broken you should rejoice in the Lord for this is a test to prepare you for your purpose. You may ask, how can I rejoice when I am broken and hurting? Well, the Bible teaches and encourages us saying, "**And we know that all things work together for good to them that love God, to them who are called according to his purpose**" (Romans 8:28). I must admit that it is hard to rejoice when your heart is broken and hurting. From experience I must also admit that when you rejoice in the Lord you gain strength and your spirit is encouraged. Also, when in your brokenness state it is a time for you to listen intently to God for He will be speaking. You should listen carefully to God's voice for your wholeness and purpose are knocking at your door. How quickly will you open the door and let them in?

Listen to God in obedience and do as your Heavenly Father desires that you do. God says, "**For the Lord disciplines those he loves, and he punishes each one he accepts as his child**" (Hebrews 12:6). Know that some of these brokenness experiences are part of God's divine plan for our lives and spiritual development. In this state of brokenness, rejoice that you have a God to call on for help. God says in His Word, *"It shall come to pass, that, before they call I will answer, and while they are still speaking, I will hear"* (Isaiah 64:24). God is constantly listening for your call. Child of God, I encourage you to be earnest, and repent. You may say, "I have done nothing wrong what should I repent for." Well, something was done to break your heart and healing from brokenness comes with sincere repentance.

> *Therefore, if you are offering your gift at the altar and there remember that your brother or sister has something against you, leave your gift there in front of the altar. First go and be reconciled to them, then come and offer your gift* (Matthew 5:23-24).

God is waiting for an invitation to enter in the picture of our circumstances. I submit to you that God could be waiting for one of two reasons. He could be waiting for His appointed time or he could be waiting on you for an invitation to come in. Let it not be that He is waiting on you. If you have completely yielded to God, then He is waiting on His appointed time. God always has a perfect time and He tells that to Jeremiah. *"I know the plans I have for you says the Lord"* (Jeremiah 29:11).

If and when you let God into your circumstances He will be the captain of your ship as you sail through these difficult storms of your broken heartedness to the calm shores of peace of heart and mind. So, relax and trust

God completely for He alone can do what you cannot. If you have never flown in an airplane the people who have must trust the pilot for a safe flight and landing. We board the plane and we sit and hope that the pilot lands the plane safely. The pilot knows what he or she is doing and as passengers there is nothing we can do to help but to follow the instructions that we are given. Likewise God is the pilot or captain of our souls and our lives so trust Him and follow His instructions.

I am reminded of the disciples as they sailed on the stormy Seas of Galilee that Jesus was available to assist and rescue them but He was waiting for them to ask. The seas were rough and although Jesus was not in the boat with them at that moment He was close enough to see what was taking place and He was on His way walking on the water to get to them. When they saw Jesus walking on the water they were terrified for they did not know it was Jesus. They were very fearful and Jesus had to speak to them assuring them to take courage. Jesus waited for the perfect time to help and rescue his disciples and He will do the same for you. When Peter called out to Jesus to help him Jesus was quick to assist Peter but no soon after Peter started to walk on the water he started to sink. Jesus asked Peter a thought provoking question, "**Why did you doubt?**" (Matthew 14:22-33). Do not doubt God, trust Him! It is important to know that an attitude of doubt will undoubtedly defeat you and your purpose.

Ask, and it shall be given unto you; seek and you shall find; knock, and it shall

be opened unto you. For every one that asketh receiveth; and he that seeketh findeth; and to him that knocketh it shall be opened" (Matthew 7:7-8).

Jesus came to their rescue at the perfect time and He spoke to the storm, "**peace be still**." Jesus knows the way, and with Him the glory lingers near. "**Jesus answered, 'I am the way and the truth and the life. No one comes to the Father except through me**" (John 14: 6). Jesus will speak peace to your storm. Oh yes, He will at the right time, His appointed time which will be good for you and will bring glory to His holy name. You are not alone for Jesus is watching out for you and watching over you. Let me encourage you to have faith in God as you go through your experiences. Trust God completely for He is your strongest defense.

CHAPTER 6

Brokenness Results In Suffering

Going a little farther, he fell with his face to the ground and prayed, 'My *Father, if it is your will [possible], let this cup pass from me, [be taken from me. Yet not my will, but as your will* (Matthew 26:39).**

"*If we endure, we will also reign with him. If we disown him, he will also disown us*" (2 Timothy 2:12).

J ob is a prominent Bible character who knows a great deal about being heartbroken for he experienced brokenness of heart in many areas of his life including losing his children. The Apostle Paul experienced brokenness repeatedly in many ways including being shipwrecked. Peter experienced brokenness for he was mistreated and imprisoned. David had his life threatened multiple times by Saul who pursued him to kill him because of jealousy. Each of these individuals encountered heartbreak and suffering and they never gave in instead they endured the suffering and heartbreak and their God rewarded them in due time accordingly. I encourage you to find strength in their experiences and keep moving forward.

When humanity decides not to obey God's instruction concerning what they can and cannot do they are indirectly choosing to be broken in many instances and areas of their lives. To disobey God is to directly or indirectly choose brokenness of heart and consequences. It is sin to disobey God, and God punishes sin. Disobedience to God will lead you into unchartered paths. When we disobey God we veer away from the path He has designed for us and by doing so we expose ourselves to serious danger like *The Lost Sheep* (Luke 15:4-7). The Word of God teaches, "***Trust in the Lord with all your heart; and lean not unto your own understanding. In all thy ways acknowledge Him, and he shall direct thy paths***" (Proverbs 3:5-6). God knows the way so allow Him to lead you. Allow God to order your steps and follow as He leads you. "***The steps of the good man/person are ordered by the Lord, and he delights in his way***" (Psalm 37:23).

Our first brokenness experience is in our relationship with God and this puts a direct strain on our fellowship with him. The first couple to experience brokenness in their relationship with God was Adam and Eve. Since God must punish sin, the consequences of their disobedience were very severe. How did they suffer? Well, they became aware that they were naked, afraid, exposed, vulnerable, and they lost their original fellowship with God then they hid themselves as a result. Their punishment was direct and severe. God chased them out of the Garden of Eden and their entire conditions of living changed. God had forewarned them and yet they were unprepared for the consequences that followed as a result of their disobedience and sins.

It is often that God warns us not to do something and we rebel and go in the opposite direction. To do this is "playing with fire." Do not play, God is serious. God cannot and will not go back on His Word. God hates disobedience and it is sin to disobey God. "***Thy word is true from the beginning: and every one of thy righteous judgments endures forever***" (Psalm 119:160).

CHAPTER 7

Church Hurt Is Real

On hearing this, Jesus said, 'It is not the healthy who need a doctor, but the sick. But go and learn what this means: I desire mercy, not sacrifice. For I have not come to call the righteous, but sinners (Matthew 9:12).

Not forsaking the assembling of ourselves together, as the manner of some is; but exhorting one another: and so much the more, as you see the day approaching (Hebrews 10:25).

The main function of a **hospital** is to provide medical care to people who are sick and are in need of such care. When someone is **admitted** to the hospital this person becomes a patient who is allowed to stay in the hospital for observation, investigation, treatment and care by the medical professionals. While you cannot stay in the hospital indefinitely you will be kept long enough under the care of the professionals until the doctors are satisfied that it is safe to discharge you to go home where your healing journey will continue. The church is considered a spiritual hospital that provides spiritual care for the souls of mankind.

The church which is the body of Christ is a universal group of people who believe in their hearts and confess with their mouths that Jesus is the Christ the Son of the Living God. By so doing these persons are saved and have become one in Christ united by the Holy Spirit and this makes us the church. *"And I say also unto thee, that thou art Peter, and upon this rock I will build my church; and the gates of hell shall not prevail against it"* (Matthew 16:18). The place where we assemble for worship to God and fellowship with one another is also called the church.

Christ intends for the church to be a place for healing and peace for His people. People come to the church because they are searching for hope. As an outsider, people see and perceive the church as a place of rescue and they come seeking a safe haven from the turmoil of their lives. They are here to seek refuge from the burdens of life and they are seeking peace for their souls. When they come to the church for love and guidance they come with open hearts expecting to experience these things. Sadly though there are too many people who experience the opposite of what they are looking for in the church. They soon find out that their hope is shattered for they are not fed the rich spiritual experience and the food of God's Word that they desire and crave for. Sometimes they observe the way some people behave and the way they treat others in unkind ways which they find to be disheartening.

Yes, pastors are humans too and they have their own needs that should be met. Some of these needs are spiritual, emotional, personal, and social, among other needs. We all do have the same basic human and spiritual needs. However, it does not excuse the fact that being the person who is the leader the pastor of God's people takes a special awareness to be compassionate and lovingly care for God's sheep even though you have your own needs. Therefore, pastors should care for their souls in order to be well enough to care for and nurture the souls of others.

We all should keep in mind that the pastor's work is very demanding and can be very stressful. The pastor not only preaches but is responsible for the success or failure of the day to day functions of the church. The pastor is responsible for and carries the burdens of individual members. As pastors they are ultimately responsible to and answer to God as God's under shepherd. Pastors are not only concerned about the members of the church but they also serve the larger community. There are "foundational members" in the church who can be and are resistant to the pastor and these members can cause much trouble for the pastor and the church. Periodically pastors should take time out for rest and counseling in order to refresh their bodies, souls and spirits. Pastors are not immune to mental illness but we find that the stigma associated with mental illness issues prevent faith leaders such as pastors from reaching out and getting help and support even when such help is available to them and can be easily accessible. It is important that you pray for the pastors.

The pastor operates in multiple roles which pull energy from him or her all the time. Some of the roles in which they function include counselor; mediator; comforter to distress families; they listen to the concerns of others all the time; they visit the sick and follow up with calls just to name a few. Pastors also need support to release and cleanse their thoughts to disconnect from some of the concerns they have heard from some of their parishioners. Some pastors become over burdened with concerns of the church and individual members that they themselves now feel that they cannot cope and so they become depressed which could after a while lead them to experience suicidal thoughts. There are some pastors who feel just too ashamed to seek for the help from others and some of these pastors end up committing suicide because their burdens are compounded and become too much to endure.

The most excruciating pain that a human being can experience is pain in the heart and emotional pain. Church hurt is mentally agonizing and very difficult for anyone to endure including members and pastors. This can be more difficult for younger Christians who are not yet well established in the Word of God. Church hurt can be so devastating to the extent that it could cause mental illness such as shame, stress, regret, depression, fatigue and it could even develop into serious mental illness. Church hurt can have long lasting effect on someone to the extent that this inner pain could affect other areas of a person's life. It would seem that no one saw the pain in these persons, no one noticed their hurt, or, they notice and do not know what to do and it could be that they know what to do but are afraid. Sadly enough for some reasons there are persons who because of severe church hurt they commit suicide.

There are pastors in recent times such as in the years of 2019 and 2020 who have themselves committed suicide. One can always speculate the reason(s) why a pastor or a member of the clergy would commit the act of suicide but the reasons are extensive ranging from personal reasons to church matters. Whatever the cause, something happened that negatively impacts one's emotional, psychological, and social wellbeing. We must be merciful in remembering that pastors are humans too and church hurt affects them too directly or indirectly.

If you are not careful church hurt can over time make you into a person whom you are not and have never been, or want to become. Church hurt comes in many forms some of which are noticeable while others are not. Church hurt could push you to become someone who feels devalued and less than who you really are. If you are not careful because of church hurt you could resort to treating other people the way you have been treated in the church. It will require God's grace and strength of will to confront the cause of your pain and encourage yourself in order to be released and set free from the entanglement of your heart pain in order to move on. You may not be able to overcome on your own and it is okay to seek help from others. You may need a professional counselor depending on the nature of what you are dealing with.

How do hurt people in the church behave? Whenever people in the church are hurt by someone in the church whether it is the pastor or another member this could be much more painful emotionally than the hurt directed by someone else outside of the church even if that person is a family member. We must admit that it is not everyone who goes to church has a personal relationship with God even though they believe in God. Some people go to church in search of healthy social and friendly relationships. Some of these individuals after a while end up accepting Christ as Savior of their lives so they join the church and this is great. You will find too that some of these people lead other family members and friends to the church as well. This is evangelism and the impact is church growth.

Some people come to the church already experiencing broken heart and deep hurt while there are people who get hurt while in the church. Many people do not share their experiences and heart pain for different reasons. Some of these people in the church who are hurting do not share with anyone what they are going through and this sometimes is because of privacy. Although these individuals hurt badly they still seek to protect the church because of their love and respect for God and the church. On the other hand, there are those who experience church hurt and they will tell their stories to anyone who will listen to them.

People who get hurt in the church may begin to attend church irregularly; their attitude to worship may change; they may withhold their giving; they may participate less in social events; and they may speak less of their church. You may find that in the church pastor hurt members; members hurt members; and members hurt pastors too. Some pastors are hurt by their overseers and supervisors. It is clear that people within the church hurt people within the church and no one is immune to having church hurt directed at them for any day it could be the next person. Members of the pastor's family including spouse and children are at times subjected to church hurt. Whenever people in the general community find out about the hurt that some people within the church experience it negatively impacts the relationship between the church and the community.

There are those in the church who seem to forget the Word of God which instructs that we must bear one another burden and fulfill the law of Christ (Galatians 6:2). "***Come unto me, all you who are weary and burdened, and I will give you rest***" (Matthew 11:28). Whenever our hearts hurt deeply we should not hurt others but instead we should take our burdens to the Good Lord and He will supply us with His Grace to strengthen us to endure and He will give us wisdom to handle the situation. I know deep within my heart based on my own experience what it means to be wounded and hurt in the church by those you love and whom you expect to love you in return according to the Word of God. "***My command is this: Love each other as I have loved you***" (John 15:12). I found out that the most severe wound(s) are those inflicted upon you by fellow Christians especially if it is by your shepherd the pastor. Church hurt wounds could be the hardest to be healed but they can be healed if we apply God's principles.

Some clergy and ministry leaders in the church hurt people: There are pastors and church leaders who do not hurt people. Most pastors have the heart of a servant and they treat people kindly, respectfully, compassionately and with love. Unfortunately there are those who will be jealous of your gifts and potential and they will throw stumbling blocks of various kinds in your way. There are leaders in the church who intentionally hurt people because of their own heart pain and insecurities. If only these leaders who mistreat God's people knew of the purpose seed that they carry inside of their hearts they would fear God and treat these persons differently and not mistreat them. No one should be mistreated especially by a clergy member in the church. "*If anyone causes one of these little ones, those who believe in me, to stumble, it would be better for them to have a large millstone hung around their neck and to be drowned in the depths of the sea*" (Matthew 18:6).

There are clergy members who at the beginning of their ministries operate from a place of humility and compassion. Unfortunately after some time when their congregations have grown to a large number or they feel that they are now well established in years at that church and in their social circles they seem to change. After a while some seem to forget that God called them to serve his people and they are accountable to God but instead they become indifferent and sophisticated in their behaviors. Some of these pastors now have no time to talk to you for they cannot be reached and you only see them when they get in the pulpit to preach. "*Just as the Son of Man did not come to be served, but to serve, and to give his life as a ransom for many*" (Matthew 20:28). Considering how these pastors conduct themselves they show that by their actions they have lost sight on what the Bible teaches about humility. **"Be completely humble and gentle; be patient, bearing with one another in love"** (Ephesians 4:2). It would seem as if they have replaced humility with pride. In their behavior and attitude they seem to treat God's people with disdain without realizing how devastating heart pain is to the individual to whom their behavior is directed. There are pastors and church leaders who do things and pull different strategies to hold certain people back by not giving them opportunities to operate in their God given gifts because they feel threatened by the gifts and graces of these individuals.

These pastors fail to understand that they cannot suppress the purpose seed that God has planted inside of your heart. To their surprise God will find creative ways that are more grandiose to elevate you far beyond what they withheld from you. God has a stage for you and it is a solid stage that cannot crumble for man did not build it God built it Himself and no man can prevail against it. God will always take you higher because He placed greatness within you. You must have unwavering faith in God for He will not fail you. God will place people in your path to support you. If these clergy and church leaders have a clear understanding of God's principle they would understand that whatever they do to support you God would bless them abundantly in return.

Generally speaking when people begin to notice that something is not right and they ask questions of these pastors they will cover their misdeeds by misrepresenting the truth. When the clergy misrepresents the truth about what happened this will add to your heart pain. It is a prideful heart that prevents them from being honest enough to admit their wrong, apologize and ask for forgiveness. Some of these pastors use their power to undermine and belittle those who outshine them instead of working with them as a team for the edifying of the body of Christ. Church members respect and honor their pastors for it is the right thing to do and the Bible also requests it so they should do it. As a result they are more likely to believe their pastors and church leaders over the hurting parishioners. Members within the church can do things to cause hurt for other members and the clergy may have to council and mediate. If it is perceived that the clergy takes sides this too will cause church hurt. The Bible calls on pastors to be wise. King Solomon asked God for wisdom and God was pleased with Solomon and granted his request.

> ***Behold, I give you a wise and discerning mind, so that none like you has been before you and none like you shall arise after you. I give you also what you have not asked, both riches and honor, so that no other king shall compare with you, all your days*** (1 Kings 3).

God's principle of healing teaches that in order to be forgiven we must first be willing to forgive others in order to receive God's forgiveness and healing. It is important that you forgive others even if they did not request from you to forgive them. Some people leave that church where they got hurt for there was none including clergy to facilitate the restoration of their souls. Sometimes people can be so hurt in the church yet they are not feeling safe or comfortable enough to share their experiences with anyone. Things sometimes get bad enough and out of control to the extent that people do not feel happy at this church anymore and they do not feel that they are part of that church family, instead they feel like an outsider. When this happens the feeling of rejection sets in and one may eventually leave the church. Sometimes the entire family and or friends may also leave the church. This is a lonely place to be emotionally for you are feeling empty inside considering that you gave so much in so many ways to the church. You want to be free from heart pain but when you leave that church with the unresolved matter you leave with the pain and recovery could take a longer time.

Individuals in the church who experience and suffer broken hearts because of people in the church have many questions for which they want answers. Why do you look at me and not see the pain in my eyes? How could you listen to me speak and not hear the pain in my voice and in my heart? Why do you look at me and not notice the hurt in my attitude or behavior? Do you not see or hear any difference in my laughter and smile? Why do you not care enough to do something about that which you have noticed? This is a precious life that you are dealing with and not an ordinary person. All of God's children are very special and no one is ordinary for we are all fearfully and wonderfully made by God. Every person has a divine purpose seed planted on the inside by God Himself. Pastors and church leaders should look beyond the surface and acknowledge and support the God and purpose seed inside each person.

CHAPTER 8

Spiritual Abortion

"Before I formed you in the womb I knew you, before you were born I set you apart; I appointed you as a prophet to the nations" (Jeremiah 1:5).

"So God created mankind in His own image, in the image of God he created them; male and female he created them" (Genesis 1:27).

Naturally speaking, **pregnancy** is the term used to describe the period in which a fetus develops inside a woman's womb or uterus. Pregnancy usually lasts about 40 weeks, or just over nine months. Health care providers refer to three segments of pregnancy, called trimesters. An abortion is the removal or expulsion of an embryo or fetus from the uterus or womb resulting in its death. Abortion is when a woman decides to prematurely end the pregnancy which is the deliberate and forced termination of the (fetus) baby. Abortion is a procedure that is taken to end a pregnancy; this abortion is the forced removal of the pregnancy; abortion is when the woman ends the pregnancy so that it does not result in the normal birth of the baby; abortion is to get rid of the baby's life before it is time to give birth to the baby.

Spiritual pregnancy: *Spiritual pregnancy* as revealed to me by the Holy Spirit is very profound and thought provoking requiring me to think deeply. Based on my insight through the revelation of the Holy Spirit, spiritual pregnancy means that God Himself has planted a "seed" which is His divine purpose for you, in the womb of your heart. That seed will stay there in your heart and develop until it is God's appointed time for that purpose to be publicly manifested and goes into full effect for the changing of lives. Unlike the pregnancy of a woman that lasts for nine months, your spiritual pregnancy could last for less or more than nine months. Your pregnancy will last for as long as it will take for God's purpose in your heart to be developed. As revealed to me, **Spiritual abortion** is to ignore your purpose by doing nothing to nurture the seed God placed in the womb of your heart and so that seed which is your purpose becomes dormant but not dead for God controls the life. God is loving, patient, and faithful, so He is waiting on you to take appropriate action.

God told the Prophet Jeremiah that before he formed him in the womb He knew him and that He had set him apart and appointed him a prophet even before his birth. This declaration from God applies to us as well for before we were formed in our mothers' wombs God who is the source of life knew us and had a very special purpose for our lives. During my youthful years God protected

78

His purpose within my heart by watching over me and allowing His purpose to grow within my heart and as I grew I grew to love that purpose. In my teen years I was operating in my purpose and gifts at some level but I did not clearly know at the time for I was not then fully aware of God's call on my life to ministry. In my young adult years I sensed God's call on my life and over the years God strategically positioned me to fulfill His purpose.

> *For you created my inmost being; you knit me together in my mother's womb. I praise you because I am fearfully and wonderfully made; your works are wonderful, I know that full well. My frame was not hidden from you when I was made in the secret place, when I was woven together in the depths of the earth. Your eyes saw my unformed body; all the days ordained for me were written in your book before one of them came to be* (Psalm 139:13-16).

Accidental abortion: If and when a woman experiences the abortion of her baby by accident this could happen in a number of ways such as a slip and fall or an illness. An abortion can be a very traumatic experience for any woman who has to experience such heartbreak. There are many other circumstances causing abortion such as domestic violence or spousal abuse under which conditions a woman may experience the abortion of her baby.

Spiritual abortion: There are several ways in which a Christian could encounter what I call a "***spiritual abortion.***" Please know that both men and women experience spiritual abortion for this is not in the physical but in the spiritual. The Bible teaches that in the spirit realm we are neither male nor female but spirit, for we are all spirit, we possess a soul and we live in a body. "***There is neither Jew nor Gentile, neither slave nor free, nor is there male and female, for you are all one in Christ Jesus***" (Galatians 3:28). Spiritual abortion by external forces could be caused by the discouragement you encounter from others who are aware of God's call and purpose for you and they do everything to cause hurt and hinder you. These individuals want you to doubt your calling and they question if you are sure because they want to plant the seed of doubt in your heart and mind. External forces causing spiritual abortion could also mean that you receive little or no encouragement or support from your family, friends, church family or Christian leaders. These external forces could also be in the form of lack of opportunity to nurture your purpose. The Holy Spirit reveals to me what I call "***self imposed***" spiritual abortion which is when a Christian is fully aware of God's call in his or her heart but they avoid responding to the call and doing what God desires and requires.

Discouragement: When someone is discouraged that person is no longer interested, confident or enthusiastic about something. If and when discouragement takes hold of you it could be an onslaught of discouraging words descending upon you by a large or small number of people who are probably close to you making it difficult for you to cope with what they are saying and at the same time stay focused on your divine purpose. These are some of the same people in your close circle and now you are torn between listening to them and listening to God and your purpose. You should not forget that people in general including some who are close to you can be cold and insensitive and some will even plot against you to steal, kill and destroy your purpose. "*The thief comes only to steal and kill and destroy; I have come that they may have life, and have it to the full*" (John 10:10). Stay close to God for He is the only one who can and will protect and defend you and the purpose seed that is developing on the inside of your heart.

Discouragement can cause the *spiritual abortion* of your purpose for if one is discouraged and unmotivated to engage in his or her calling then one will be reluctant or uninterested in engaging in such gifting. If you are not careful discouragement can creep into your heart when you receive no support or encouragement from those on whom you depend. Instead of encouraging you some will seek to find a way to abort your purpose God planted inside of you. The cares of life itself can cause your purpose to be aborted for you could be so consumed and overwhelmed with life issues and all kinds of worries and if you are not careful these things can pull you away into distractions to the extent that your purpose becomes dormant. Do not allow this to happen to you! Protect your baby! Protect your divine purpose.

Spiritual miscarriage: Naturally, when a woman unfortunately experiences a miscarriage it means that her pregnancy prematurely ends and she had no control to prevent it from happening. This could be that she accidentally fell and lost her baby or for some medical or physical reasons she had a miscarriage and her pregnancy ends prematurely. A *spiritual miscarriage* on the other hand, I believe happens when leadership within the church or Christian community tries to talk you out of your purpose. You must protect your purpose from these individuals and from miscarriage. These types of leaders will notice that you are pregnant with purpose and they will see the reservoir of substantive gifts that you carry and have to offer and they will wish that you have a miscarriage. Remember Daniel was thrown in the lion's den not because he did wrong but because those close to him were jealous of the anointing upon him for they could clearly see his potential and they knew of his character (Daniel chapter 6). You are the one who should be fully persuaded of what is on the inside of your heart. This should be between you and God until you reveal your "*spiritual pregnancy*" to others and the larger community. "*But Mary treasured up all these things, pondering them in her heart*" (Luke 2:19). Like Mary the mother of Jesus, you should keep your purpose in your heart secret, until it is fully developed and you are persuaded that it is time before you launch out fully and reveal what God is doing in your heart which is His divine purpose plan for you.

Be courageous and take the responsibility to nurture your God given purpose inside of you to full maturity which will be the time when your purpose is fully developed and made perfect in you. Many will try to pull you down and pull you back as you seek to move forward in your purpose and they see what God is doing in your life and ministry. These people will stop at nothing to make sure that you have a full *spiritual miscarriage*. This is why you must fight with the Sword of the Spirit which is the Word of God and prayer and ask God to build a wall of defense and protection around you. The Christ like discerning leader will see God's hand upon you and will provide you with nurture and support. Make no mistake God will place the right people in your path who will add value in helping to get your task done. "*For I, said the Lord, will be to her a wall of fire round about, and will be the glory in the middle of her*" (Zechariah 2:5). "*Those who live in the shelter of the Most High will find rest in the shadow of the Almighty*" (Psalm 91:1). God Himself is sending you help.

Child of God, those who lay wait to relish in the miscarriage of your purpose will be sorely disappointed for they will first have to deal with God to get through to you. Be assured that God will stop at nothing to protect and defend His purpose in you. Remember that Satan had to first get God's permission before he could approach Job. "*Have you not put a hedge around him and his household and everything he has? You have blessed the work of his hands, so that his flocks and herds are spread throughout the land*" (Job 1:10). The enemy cannot get to you unless God gives permission and if God does give permission it will be a test and if you are steadfast you will be victorious in passing the test for God will help you.

Samuel as a child was called by God when he was with Eli the Priest for training. Samuel remained with Eli until he was well prepared for the task to which he was called "*The boy Samuel ministered before the Lord under Eli*" (1 Samuel 3:1). "*And the Lord said to Samuel: 'See, I am about to do something in Israel that will make the ears of everyone who hears about it tingle*" (1 Samuel 3:11). "*The Lord was with Samuel as he grew up, and he let none of Samuel's words fall to the ground. And all Israel from Dan to Beersheba recognized that Samuel was attested as a prophet of the Lord*" (1 Samuel 3:19-20). Notice that Samuel first had to be mentored and nurtured by Eli the priest and as the Lord was with Samuel as he grew up so will He be with you through to the spiritual maturity of your purpose.

Celebrate the fact that you are pregnant with your God given purpose and this is your baby which no one on their own can take away from you so you must fight the good fight in order to protect that purpose seed in you. The power of the Holy Spirit is with you so do not give anyone the opportunity to cause your purpose to be aborted. Remember that you are accountable to God to protect this purpose on the inside of you therefore you must be wise. You must be brave and you must be fearless. Like Solomon you should ask God for wisdom and discernment (1 Kings 1-15). Your strength and commitment got you through to this point and every struggle, test, disappointment and challenge you have faced have served to strengthen your will. Your tears will now be tears of joy and praise for you are at a place now where you can see quite clearly in the spirit.

Full term pregnancy and birth: In real life every mother is overjoyed to give birth to her full term baby. She delivers and welcomes her baby into the world and introduces her baby to family and loved ones who had been waiting for the arrival of this precious human being full of life and great potential for the future. In the spiritual sense once you carry your *spiritual pregnancy* to full term this means that your purpose is now fully developed in your heart and spirit and it is ready to impact the world. This means that in your heart you are fully persuaded that this is what God wants you to do and you are ready, prepared and delighted in the Lord to embark and walk in the steps He has ordered for you. Once you say, *yes Lord I am ready*, God has the right people lined up and the right platforms waiting to receive you and the message you bring. "*A man's gifts opens doors for him, and brings him before great men*" (Proverbs 18:16). God will organize and set things in order for you in such a way that people will seek after you for what you are anointed to do and do so very well with the help of the Holy Spirit.

By reading this book of healing instructions which is an anointed ministry in itself you will without doubt gain enough insight and wisdom to finally reach a turning point in your brokenness to wholeness journey. This is the place where you make a conscious determination that you must nurture your purpose to full term and a victorious birthing. This birthing is when you launch out into the unknown in your purpose and reach out to the human race and minister to them making a difference in the area to which God has called you. "*When he had finished speaking, he said to Simon, 'Now go out where the water is deeper, and let down your nets to catch some fish*" (Luke 5:4).

As Jesus told His disciples so likewise He is also telling you to trust Him and step out into the deep unknown and fulfill your God given purpose. If your purpose is in full term, the third trimester, you cannot hold it in any longer you have to give birth whether or not you are ready. In the natural when it is time for a woman to give birth to her baby, ready or not that baby is going to leave the womb and come forth. When your purpose is fully mature in your heart it must come forth and with your willingness and God's help everything will fall perfectly into their rightful places. If it is time you must go right ahead and give birth and do not allow God to force it out of you for He can do that too if He chooses that route.

Affirmations:

1. God has a unique purpose for me to accomplish
2. God Himself planted the purpose seed in my heart
3. God Himself cares for and nurtures my purpose
4. God will protect His purpose seed in my heart
5. God will defend His purpose seed in my heart
6. God will establish His purpose and use me
7. God will sustain me as I operate in my purpose

CHAPTER 9

Awareness Of Brokenness

"*The woman said to Him, 'Sir, I perceive that You are a prophet*" (John 4:19).

"*Then the eyes of both of them were opened, and they knew that they were naked; and they sewed fig leaves together and made themselves loin coverings*" (Genesis 3:7).

W e cannot be healed and grow into wholeness until we have recognized or identified our brokenness state and take ownership of it. One must have a desire to be true to one's self and be honest about the root cause of the heartbreak in order to move away from the **broken condition** and overcome it. This is necessary so that you can begin to heal and grow into wholeness of heart and soul. Seek help if you must for your soul's healing and wholeness is the goal so you must do whatever it takes.

Jesus asked the lame man at the Pool of Bethsaida a very important question. "*When Jesus saw him lying there and learned that he had been in this condition for a long time, he asked him, Do you desire to get well?*" (John 5:6). The lame man did not take responsibility for not getting in the pool. Instead, he made an excuse saying, "*Sir, the lame man replied, 'I have no one to help me into the pool when the water is stirred. While I am trying to get in, someone else goes down ahead of me*" (John 5:7). In dealing with my own broken heart I discovered that even though others had done me wrong I had to do the work to heal my own broken heart. We cannot wait around for other people to do what they should such as apologize and ask for forgiveness. Some people are very cold at heart and they are not thinking about your wellbeing so do not wait for them to ask for your forgiveness. It is very sad to say but this happens inside the church too for that was where my heart got broken and shattered to pieces. Sadly enough, no one asked for forgiveness or apologized to me and no one seemed to care about my spiritual wellbeing. I will encourage you to take care of yourself and move on, move forward, for there is no time to stand still and wait for apologies which may never come. Forgive them and move forward.

Adam and his wife Eve hid themselves when they heard God walking in the garden. They knew that they were broken. So too you should admit that your precious heart is broken and take ownership and face the situation that hurts you so badly. Facing the situation and taking ownership does not mean blaming yourself it means that you acknowledge your hurt and you are aware that you need healing. It means that you will not hide from what happened for hiding and avoidance cannot and will not solve the problem or change the situation that concerns you.

As in previous times, God took a walk in the garden to commune with the couple. Adam was so broken he could not face his maker so he hid himself. This type of behavior seems typical of mankind who tries to avoid someone when there is brokenness in the relationship. Some individuals stay away from church if there is brokenness in communication, shortcomings or experiences that lead to their heartbreak and hurt. Church hurt is when someone within the church hurts you and the hurt is even greater felt and more painful when it is caused by someone in leadership especially clergy. As we overcome our brokenness we grow into wholeness and the further removed we are in overcoming our brokenness it is the more growth experiences we have in growing into our wholeness and purpose. As we move further away from one we move closer towards the other.

There are lessons to be learned in your brokenness state and if you learn the lessons and govern yourself accordingly it will serve you well. The sooner you understand and learn is the faster you will move on to the next stage of your healing and wholeness journey. The most important question you must ask God as you go through these difficult times should be, "***My Lord and my God, what is the lesson or lessons that you want for me to learn as I go through these difficult situations***? As you journey through your experiences these are times for you to listen to God's still small voice for He will seek to communicate with you. Be assured that He will direct your path through the good and the difficult times.

As you go through your valley experiences, if you learn your lessons you will be transformed spiritually and personally, becoming wiser, stronger, more caring and sympathetic towards others. Additionally, you will have your testimonies and opportunities to share them knowing that someone out there somewhere is desirous of a helping hand and you just might be the person to help. The scripture teaches that, "***They triumphed over him by the blood of the Lamb and by the word of their testimony; they did not love their lives so much as to shrink from death***" (Revelation 12:11).

Where are you now on your journey from broken-ness to wholeness? Remember that your goal is to be whole again. Each stage of the journey will be deemed as successful, difficult, or failure, as well as it may be a combination of experiences. Please know that your brokenness could be allowed or permitted by God for in that state of brokenness of heart he tried you; groomed you; trained you; equipped you; anointed you; prepared you; armed you; and humbled you for His divine pur-pose and His maximum usefulness. Therefore, live fully in the state that you are in right now and make every moment count.

Part Three
The Tunnel: Pruging

IMPURITIES MUST GO!
Stations Along The Way

"Purge me with hyssop, and I will be clean; wash me, and I will be whiter than snow" (Psalm 51:7).

Now no chastening for the present seemeth to be joyous, but grievous: nevertheless afterward it yieldeth the peaceable fruit of righteousness unto them which are exercised thereby" (Hebrews 12:11).

A passenger or freight train has several tunnels that it must travel through along the way to the intended destination. The distance of some tunnels are long while others are short. When a passenger train enters the tunnel it is a dark place and you wish for that segment of the journey through the tunnel to end quickly for you do not like the darkness. For this segment of the journey you have some degree of trust in the train engineer and conductor so you stay on the train. If you were to exit the train by jumping out you knew that would not be safe but quite dangerous. This purpose journey that you are on I encourage you to be in it for the long duration even during the dark and difficult times. God Himself will be with you to the very end and you must trust God completely for He is your spiritual engineer on this journey to wholeness and purpose.

Are you ready to purge yourself of those unhealthy impurities? This first tunnel that you must go through is the tunnel of *purging* and it is not a physical but mental and spiritual one. The hurts inflicted on your heart and soul left wounds and infections that must be healed. This journey is your life's lonesome journey that you must take. Going through this tunnel is a spiritual purging and cleansing process. In the physical (natural) there are various cleansing remedies that we take to purge our bodies from impurities that seem to negatively impact the health and proper function of our bodies. Likewise in the spiritual we must purge ourselves of unhealthy thinking, behaviors and emotions by taking heed to the Word of God and practice daily healthy spiritual disciplines. "*For whom the Lord loves he chastens, and scourgeth every son whom he receiveth*" (Hebrews 12:6).

The stages in the **Brokenness to Wholeness** journey are very real and I call them **stations along the way**. These stations are grouped in two categories which I have named tunnels. The first tunnel is "**purging**" with fifteen *stations* namely *Brokenhearted; Detour; Shock; Denial; Anger; Bitterness; Grief; Fear; Guilt; Pride; hate and jealousy; discouragement; ask for help; Acceptance and repentance.* Our hearts and souls must be purged of the toxicity that hinders us from being healthy and whole. Each toxic emotion is unhealthy and we must seek to get rid of each one by purging ourselves if we are to have a successful Christian life's experience and journey.

In life, and in the natural human experience, when we go on a journey from point A to point B, there are always stations along the way regardless of how we travel. For example, if we take a long road trip, we have to stop at different places along the way for different reasons. Sometimes we stop for fuel, food, rest, or to use the restroom. The same is true for our spiritual journey which I call "**stations along the way**." For the fortification of our souls we must stop at these stations for a fresh supply of God's love, humility, forgiveness, grace and mercy among other spiritual nutrients.

I will sincerely and patiently walk with you as you embark on this unknown journey. Each station is very critical and mastering the lessons learned at each will set the stage for your success or failure at the next station. Each station serves as a building block on which all other stations must stand therefore, build a solid foundation that cannot be shaken or crumble. The Bible tells us about the wise man who built his house on the rock. The rain came down, the streams rose, and the winds blew and beat against that house; yet it did not fall, because it had its foundation on the rock. Jesus said that everyone who hears His words and does not put them into practice is like a foolish man who built his house on the sand. The rain came down, the streams rose, and the winds blew and beat against that house, and it fell with a great crash. (Matthew 7:24-27). We all should build wisely to secure our sure foundation in

Christ Jesus. There is light at the end of each tunnel of your journey. Jesus is the light of the world so He is the light at the end of your tunnel waiting for you and this should give you great hope to keep pressing forward.

CHAPTER 10

Brokenhearted

Broken For Purpose

*"**The Lord is close to the brokenhearted and saves those who are crushed in spirit**"* (Psalm 34:18).

*"**Do not let your hearts be troubled. You believe in God; believe also in me**"* (John 14:1).

M any life experiences can cause heartbreak. For some people the cause of heartbreak could be a divorce, death in the family, illness, domestic violence just to name a few (see the introduction). Whatever the cause, heartbreak should be taken very seriously for it can lead to intense sorrow, grief, and emotional pain. Intense heartbreak if not healed could lead to many forms of emotional and or physical complications. Sometimes when something is broken it is also shattered, ruined, destroyed, and become inoperable. Something happened to have caused the brokenness experience and condition of your heart. At times we are caught off guard in an unexpected situation and things are thrown off balance. Your whole routine is disrupted and your smooth life is derailed. It could be personal illness or sickness of a loved one, a bad marriage, loss of a job or any number of things or experiences in one's life. In this time of heart brokenness, your peace of mind is attacked and this I know quite well.

Such experiences take us out of our comfort zone and we end up in an emotional unknown environment that seems unsafe, untested and we think that our life is ruined or so it seems to be. We feel helpless, hopeless, and unprepared and we become bewildered and feel that our dreams are destroyed forever.

Something happened to throw us off balance and slow us down. Our peace of mind is replaced by worry and doubt. The experience could be very complex and frightening. Sometimes it is at this place that God gets our undivided attention! Some of us are extremely stubborn while others are extremely too busy with our own agendas thus preventing God from getting through to us. Some of us are both busy and stubborn, thus, making it difficult for God to speak to us using His "still small voice."

God will not fail to use extreme situations and conditions to grab and hold our attention so that He can speak to us and have His purpose known. God is jealous so give Him your full attention and hold on to His promises. *"I will not die but live, and will proclaim what the Lord has done. The Lord has chastened me severely, but he has not given me over to death"* (Psalm 118:17-18). Believe me, like others you will live to tell your extraordinary story.

God frequently used extreme situations to get the attention of His beloved people. God says, "**Be still and know that I am God**" (Psalm 46:10). If God cannot get us to be still so that He can speak to us He will take extreme measures and do radical things to get and hold our attention. In the case of Saul now Paul, when on his way to Damascus to persecute the Christians God stopped him and called him in a dramatic way. Saul was close to Damascus when suddenly a light from heaven flashed around him and he fell to the ground during which time he heard a voice say "Saul, Saul, why do you persecute me?" When Saul eventually got up from the ground he could not see for God had blinded his eyes. God sent him to the house of Judas where he would meet Ananias. During his encounter with Ananias he regained his sight after three days and he was told what his assignment would be moving forward. As a result of that experience Saul became one of the greatest apostles, Apostle Paul (Acts 9).

Our brokenness state is a period of darkness and most times or sometimes we cannot see or envision the light at the end of the tunnel. Let me assure you that out of your darkness will come light. After the storm there will be the calm. Your steps are ordered by the Lord so trust Him. If God takes you to the storm He will take you through it and to the other side where your "calm" awaits. "**Weeping may endure for a night but joy comes in the morning**" (Psalm 30:5). God knows for sure what the outcome will be for He knows the future. Your purpose is already ordained except that it is not yet for you to know or see clearly and fully understand everything.

When God reveals the outcome and the full reason of your brokenness is manifested you will delight yourself in the Lord and thank Him for the experiences you went through. Your testimony will be intensely powerful and you will be anxious to share it and help someone else. You will say with a heart full of gratitude "I will praise thee my God." Thank you God for these experiences I am truly a better person. David says:

> *Even though I walk through the valley of the shadow of death, I will fear no evil, for you are with me; your rod and your staff, they comfort me… Surely goodness and mercy/love will follow me all the days of my life, and I will dwell in the house of the lord forever* (Psalm 23:4 & 6).

Think about these self reflective questions for a moment. Do you truly know who God is from a personal relationship experience? Do you truly believe that He will bring you out? Do you believe that God can and will take you safely through your brokenness situation to your wholeness? To doubt God is sin and without faith is impossible to please God so I trust that you have unwavering faith in Him.

God will not give you more than you can bear and He will always make a way of escape for you. God's time is perfect so be patient and wait on God for He will bring you out of any situation. Nothing is too hard for God! Remember to use the tools in your **survival kit**, see chapter one. You need these tools at every point of your journey.

CHAPTER 11

Detour

Broken For Purpose

"Though I walk through the valley of the shadow of death, I will fear no evil, for Thou art with me, Thy rod and staff they comfort me" (Psalm 23:4)

A detour may be a long or roundabout route that is taken to avoid something or to intentionally visit someone or somewhere along the way. Some detours are planned while others are unplanned. On a long road trip you may plan to stop somewhere for a sightseeing of a special landmark or to see a special friend or relative. Unplanned detours could be a road sign warning you to take another way. Another example of a detour could be that you got lost. Whichever it is a detour takes you off course and out of your way.

You are suddenly faced with an unexpected reality and your first thought is to wish for a detour to escape from the situation. We can trust God in the detours of our lives for God has a reason for every detour. During this period things may appear to be confusing but we must continue to seek God and trust Him for this is a time to learn about God's purpose for us. Detours can become our biggest blessings at times when our full dependence is on God. In avoidance you try not to deal with the situation by pretending that it did not happen and it does not exist. This is a defense mechanism while in detour you find and take another way out.

Oh how I wished there was a detour on my brokenness to wholeness journey for it is indeed a lonesome and difficult journey. Along this brokenness journey there is no detour from any of these stations for we must pass through everyone. In my own brokenness experience when the emotional pain got so difficult for me I wished there was a detour which would be a way to avoid the pain. My longing for wholeness was real as I wished for the kind of detour that could be a way to escape from the emotional pain and agony of my broken and wounded heart. My wait for deliverance seemed very long and like forever.

On this spiritual journey, even on a detour, one must fuel daily with God's grace, faith, and the Word of God. If one fails to fuel, one will not have the fortitude to endure the attacks of the enemy along the detour. Your experience of a victorious journey depends on daily and consistent fuel using the tools in your **survival kit**.

At each station there are valuable lessons to be learned in order to move on successfully to the next station. Lessons missed and or not mastered could undoubtedly hinder the success of your continued journey from this station to the next. Although this is a detour you must be aware of your location and not be distracted. Be intentional and determined to stay focused to learn and understand the lessons at each present station. These are lessons that will help to build your foundation for your continued journey to be successful. The longer it takes you to learn the lesson or lessons at each station, is the longer that it will take you to move on through this tunnel.

To successfully navigate your way to the next station you have to willingly and fully surrender yourself to God and grasped the lessons at the current station. The strength of your desire and commitment to move on to the next level of your journey will motivate you as you seek to learn your lesson at the present station, detour. Yes, you truly need God's divine help and strength for this journey for it will take much more than you expect it will.

> *"I will lift up my eyes to the hills, from whence cometh my help. My help comes from the Lord, who made the heaven and the earth"* (Psalms 121:1-2).

Jonah intentionally took a detour and boarded a ship to avoid God's purpose for him to go and warn the people of Nineveh. That did not work out well for Jonah for God took extreme action to stop him and Jonah ended up in the belly of a whale. This to me is what it means to be broken and shattered for Jonah was bewildered. However, God in His mercy had the whale took Jonah to the shores of Nineveh thus giving Jonah yet another chance to fulfill God's divine purpose. Eventually Jonah had no choice but to go to Nineveh and fulfill God's purpose and warn the people to repent (Jonah 1). What will you do? I do not know the reason for your broken heart but God does and He is the one who can and wants to heal your heart. "***He heals the broken hearted and binds up their wounds***" (Psalm 147:3).

CHAPTER 12

Shock (Trauma)

Broken For Purpose

*"**But whoever listens to me will dwell secure and will be at ease, without dread of disaster**" (Proverbs 1:33).*

S hock is a very strong emotion that springs upon you without any notice. Any critical incident such as an accident or death can cause someone to experience shock. Some statements we make when we are shocked are- "I cannot believe this is happening to me!" I am in disbelief! I am frightened! At this time of shock we begin to think that what has happened will go away but only to feel devastated that it just might not be going away anytime soon. We say things like- "I am bewildered and my world is turning upside down and spinning out of control." We are consumed with shock and disbelief. Shock is an unconscious state of awareness and acceptance. This is a time when one questions if the event is really happening or did ever happen. The result of shock is emotional imbalance.

Depending on the degree of shock one could be consumed to the extent of being depressed and quit trying to do anything about the current situation or move on forward with normalcy.

When one experiences shock it throws one in a state of **disbelief** and **distress**. Broken heartedness in any area of our lives can cause **devastation** to the mind. Someone can be held captive emotionally and psychologically due to one's brokenness experience and state of shock. Sometimes this will require help of some kind from others and some may require professional help such as counseling.

Our Lord Jesus experienced great depth of heart brokenness that was quite severe. Jesus' brokenness gripped Him emotionally as He journeyed to Jerusalem to offer His life for our redemption. Jesus was very broken by the weight of what awaited Him at Calvary that He stopped in the Garden of Gethsemane to pray. **"Going a little farther, he fell with his face to the ground and prayed, My Father, if it is possible, may this cup be taken from me. Yet not as I will, but as you will"** (Matthew 26:39).

In shock something serious and unexpected happened that demanded your attention and you could not even believe it was happening. Sometimes there are no warning signs and so we think that the experience happened suddenly. Sometimes the warning signs are there but we just did not notice them. What do you do at this point? This is when you seek God in prayer and wait on the Lord and be of good courage (Psalm 27:14).

Each person will handle shock differently. Some will pray, cry, tell someone, become withdrawn, feel defeated and the list goes on. With the power of the Holy Spirit you will overcome this if you rely on God and follow the direction of the Holy Spirit.

CHAPTER 13

Denial

Broken For Purpose

"But Anyone who denies me here on earth will be denied before God's angels" (Luke 12:9).

"Then He said to them all, 'If anyone desires to come after Me, let him deny himself, and take up his cross daily, and follow Me" (Luke 9:23).

D enial is a coping mechanism that gives you time to adjust to the challenging circumstances you are facing. Denial is the action of refusing or an unwillingness to accept or not declaring something to be true. A practical example of denial is a spouse who cannot cope with and will not admit that his/her spouse has left the marriage. In denial you are trying to protect yourself by refusing to accept the truth about something that is happening in your life. To linger in denial is not emotionally healthy.

Our hearts can be broken to the extent that we deny our brokenness and pain. The pain in our hearts can be so severe that we become emotionally numb at the thought that it is there. Someone who refuses to accept or agree with what has taken place and is taking place is in denial. Sometimes the pain in our broken heart may be so severe it is hard to reject it so some of us curse and rebuke it instead of dealing with it head on. We need time to process what has happened and so we pretend that it happened.

Denial is a coping mechanism which means that you are trying to figure things out while you are at the same time trying to find a way to cope. However, prolonged denial can cause serious emotional hurt and damage to your hurting heart. During denial you are trying to adjust to this situation that has crept up on you. You should not stay here in denial for too long for it could be detrimental. You have to, and you must move on. Since denial is one of the stations along your journey from brokenness to wholeness you must pay close attention. At this station you have to dig deep within and find the strength to face and defeat this emotion and then acquire the skills necessary that will take you successfully to the next station in this tunnel "**purging**.

You cannot deal with something if you deny its existence. Tackle the challenges of your brokenness for to stay at this particular station of denial for too long will delay your healing. To be frank, since we are all different, each person's time spent at any given station will be different. You should not move on to the next station until you have learnt the lessons at this current station.

Focus on the lessons and master them sufficiently enough before moving forward for this "load" denial is too heavy to carry.

Denial is very emotionally harmful! Denial will compound your current situation. Whenever we deny a problem that does not make it go away. Instead, we become distracted and cannot focus fully on any other tasks on hand. To deny our circumstances is to cause other essential areas of our lives to suffer. This suffering includes our personal, social, emotional and spiritual wellbeing. All areas of our lives can be affected by our attitude of denial if we lose control.

Keep in mind that denial could also mean that others have denied you in various ways. Denial could be that some people have overlooked you; ignored you or pretended that you do not exist. People will have different reasons for denying you which can also be due to their own jealousy for different reasons that can include their own insecurities. Your very God given gifts and graces that God has blessed you with may have others to be jealous of you and as a result deny you access and opportunities. Since you have no control over what other people do, you cannot control them denying you. Your responsibility is to love these persons anyway as God requires of you and pray for them; wish them well; and be a godly example to them. Be assured that in due time God will turn things around on your behalf and for His glory alone.

CHAPTER 14

Anger
Broken For Purpose

"Refrain from anger and turn from wrath, do not fret, it leads only to evil" (Psalm 37:8).

"Beloved, never avenge yourselves, but leave it to the wrath of God, for it is written, 'Vengeance is mine, I will repay, says the Lord" (Romans 12:19).

"Be angry and sin not" (Ephesians 4:26).

Anger is an emotion that every human experiences at some point in time. Anger prevented Moses from entering the Promise Land Canaan. As the Children of Israel journeyed from Egypt to Canaan they got to Zin and there was no water and God told Moses to speak to the rock but instead, out of anger he struck the rock. As a result of his disobedience God did not allow Moses to cross over to the Promise Land Canaan (Numbers 20:1-13). Intense anger leads to sin and the sin of Moses was disobeying God. Moses was overcome with anger and as a result, he probably forgot God's instruction. If and when intense anger leads to rage you cannot be rational and this could lead you to engage in unacceptable behavior that grieves God. Seek God's divine help and remember to use the tools in your **survival kit**.

It is advisable to purge yourself of anger. Do not allow your anger to consume you to the extent that you cannot be rational. Anger experts describe this emotion as a primary and natural emotion which has evolved as a way of surviving and protecting oneself from what is considered a wrong doing. Anger could be a good thing because anger is part of the healing process. When someone is angry there is a certain amount of strength and energy that goes with it and you are driven to do something by taking action and hopefully the right action. Sometimes we become so angry that we blame others instead of dealing with the cause of our anger. Other people sometimes become so angry and uncontrollable that they hurt themselves and sometimes hurt others verbally or physically.

It is okay to get angry for even Jesus got very angry! For example, when Jesus entered the Temple in Jerusalem, He found the money changers and people buying and selling in the Temple. This behavior was misuse of the Holy Temple and as a result, Jesus got very **angry** and He turned over their tables and chased the people out of the temple. This Bible story is called, *The Cleansing of the Temple*- "*It is written,*" *He said to them, "My house will be called a house of prayer, but you are making it a den of robbers*" (Matthew 21:13).

Although it is a natural human emotion to be angry, it should be dealt with in a positive way. Anger, if goes unchecked could lead to frustration, resentment and aggression. If not controlled anger can lead you to do things that you may regret later. Uncontrolled anger can lead to physical aggression, verbal abuse or any other negative and unacceptable behavior. You should deal with what is causing you to be angry and heal yourself.

I believe that anger is a corrosive emotion that if allowed can arrest and hold captive your mental and physical health. Anger is an intense emotional state of mind. Jesus warned against becoming too angry for this could lead someone to commit sin and even murder. The Word of God says, "***Be angry, and sin not: let not the sun go down upon your wrath***" (Ephesians 4:26). The lesson is clear and it is that we should control our anger by depending on the Holy Spirit who is our helper to help us get rid of anger. In our society today we see people become so very angry with one another that they cannot rationally settle their dispute. Sometimes they inflict verbal and physical hurt on their opponent and sometimes some people go to the extreme by committing murder.

Ask God to help you with an abundance of His grace and mercy in dealing with your broken heart so that you do not express your anger in ways that will hurt you or anyone. Different types of anger and different degrees of anger affect people differently and will manifest in different signs. Some signs that may signal anger include one's tone of voice, body language, and other non-verbal cues, such as staring, frowning, among other signals. Some people have anger management issues to the extent that they have to seek medical help and also professional counseling intervention. There are people who will hurt you in ways that break your heart and cause you to be angry but, you must still take the time to forgive, heal yourself of anger and move on.

Child of the Most High God let me encourage you to avoid severe anger which could lead to emotional illness and physical illness such as high blood pressure. You must fight to get rid of this anger regardless of its degree. "*Fight the good fight of faith, lay hold on eternal life, whereunto you are also called, and hast professed a good profession before many witnesses*" (1 Timothy 6:12).

While all stations on your journey from "*brokenness to Purpose*" are very important points along the way, you must not allow yourself to be consumed with anger. If you do, you will be trapped here at this station and become stagnant. God may not allow you to move on with anger in your heart for it is a load too heavy to carry. Purge yourself of anger and protect yourself from doing the things that could cost you your blessing.

CHAPTER 15

Bitterness

Broken For Purpose

*Behold, it was for my welfare that I had great bitterness;
but in love you have delivered my life from the pit of
destruction, for you have cast all my sins behind your back*
(Isaiah 38:17).

*"Looking carefully lest anyone fall short of the grace of God;
lest any root of bitterness springing up cause trouble, and
by this many become defiled"* (Hebrews 12:15).

So much hurt that we go through in our experiences can be detrimental to our souls. These hurtful experiences leave infections in our souls. Child of God, this is a warning about bitterness! *"**Bitterness is a state of mind and heart which feeds on angry feelings.**"* It is a sure thing that a bitter root will produce a tree with bitter fruits. The root of the tree is underground and the tree gets its nutrients from the root and the root gets nutrients from the soil. So likewise, no one can see or tell if a person's heart is bitter until that person speaks or behaves a certain way. Do not allow bitterness to contaminate your heart and life so try your hardest to purge your heart of any bitterness.

> **Let all bitterness, wrath, anger, clamor, and evil speaking be put away from you, with all malice. And be kind to one another, tenderhearted, forgiving one another, even as God in Christ forgave you** (Ephesians 4:31-32).

Bitterness of heart leads to wrongful intentions to do evil. If bitterness is in your heart it cannot be concealed for too long for it will be exposed in your words and or in your actions. Bitterness is a root that should be rooted out and destroyed. Bitterness causes pain, great emotional pain. It should be replaced with love for love conquers all. If you are not careful your broken heart can take you to a place of bitterness and leave you there. Bitterness is like a cancer that if not checked and removed it could become deadly by growing into a condition resulting in corruption which will devour and destroy your heart and your very soul.

Purge yourself of bitterness for if allowed it will corrode your soul. As you deal with your heartbreak situation do not ignore your emotions. Bitterness is emotionally toxic and you do not want to entertain this toxicity so deal with it and be healed from it. This bitterness if allowed will entangle your soul and suffocate you! It will pull every life out of you and leave you emotionally and spiritually hopeless and in the end it will leave you lifeless spiritually.

Through the eyes of the Spirit I see bitterness and it is like a suction tube. It will gradually pull out of you all of your joy; all of your hope; all of your faith; all of your courage; all of your strength; all of your desires; all of your peace; your salvation and your very life. In the end it will leave you empty and dry like the dry bones in the valley (Ezekiel 37:3-4). God asked the Prophet Jeremiah if the dry bones in the valley could live and Jeremiah responded saying, "**Lord you do know**." God has not given up on you and He will not give up on you. God is the source of divine healing and you can be healed of your broken heart. Some people may even insult you and reject you and these experiences could frustrate you and if you are not careful you may feel like you are a failure and your life has no meaning and so you become bitter. Please know that there is hope for you because God can breathe new life into you as He did for the dry bones in the valley.

The Bible warns against bitterness of the heart. The Word of God says that a bitter heart is a "bitter root." "**See to it that no one falls short of the grace of God and that no bitter root grows up to cause trouble and defile many**" (Hebrews 12:15). In the Hebrew culture, poisonous plants were called "bitter." The metaphor points to that which could bring harm to a Christian and to the church, the body of Christ. In the Old Testament, the "*bitter poison*" is idolatry in the rebellion against the covenant between God and the Israelites.

Make sure there is no man or woman, clan or tribe among you today whose heart turns away from the Lord our God to go and worship the gods of those nations; make sure there is no root among you that produces such bitter poison (Deuteronomy 29:18).

You cannot afford to poison your soul with the spirit and attitude of bitterness for bitterness if not dealt with can become a "*root of bitterness*" in your heart. This root of bitterness will take grip of your heart making it more difficult for you to deal with the hurt of your broken-ness. Eventually, this will make it more difficult for you to forgive others of their wrong doing towards you and receive your healing and wholeness of heart.

Remember to use the tools in your **survival kit**, personal choice, prayer, the Word of God, faith, trust, humility, time, the whole armor of God, hope, songs of praise, patience and endurance (See chapter one). You need these tools at every point of your journey and you need them now more than ever before. What you are going through may not be good in your judgment but God knows how to make your bitter to become sweet. God knows how to turn things around. In my own experience, as I was going through my heartbreak and pain I had to make a daily and conscious effort not to be bitter. I had to ask God for extra grace and mercy.

Do not stay here in this situation (condition) of bitterness of heart any longer for God wants you to move forward to your new life and experiences of healing and wholeness. From a heart full of compassion I encourage you to treat the root of the tree (your heart) and purge it from this bitterness so that your heart becomes healthy again and healthy enough to produce healthy fruits so that those around you could eat and be satisfied. "*Let your light so shine before men, so that they may see your good works, and glorify your Father which is in heaven*" (Matthew 5:16).

CHAPTER 16

Grief

Broken For Purpose

"For godly grief produces a repentance that leads to salvation without regret, whereas worldly grief produces death" (2 Corinthians 7:10).

"The Lord is close to the brokenhearted and saves those who are crushed in spirit" (Psalm 34:18).

At this station called "grief" you grieve the loss of something or someone you love and consider to be precious to you or it could be that you grieve because of some wrong that have been done to you. Grief is a natural human emotional condition and we all grieve at some time whenever we experience loss or hurt. As a natural part of life we grieve because we are okay. When we grieve deeply the people around us suffer with us as well. The degree and intensity of our grief will depend on the value we place on that which we have lost. Grief is deep sorrow which one might not be able to fully explain. Along your healing journey this station which is called grief is accompanied by a pain that is very deep and sometimes unbearable. "***Surely he took up our pain (grief) and bore our suffering, yet we considered him punished by God, stricken by him, and afflicted***" (Isaiah 53:4). Whenever our hearts are broken and we grieve our spirit cannot soar because our spirit is broken as well and is held captive. Grief brings negative energy to our hearts and souls and we must work through that which is causing us to grieve.

Some people move away from grief which means that they try to suppress their grief instead of dealing with the cause. Some people move towards their grief by working through their pain. It can be hard to let go of grief and move on for you are hurting deeply inside. Some examples of situations causing grief could be the death of a family member; the serious illness of a family member or friend; an accident; retirement, unemployment; a marriage going bad; children getting in trouble with the law; internal illness; family disagreements can be bad enough that it cause grief; sibling rivalry and ongoing quarrels can cause grief. Distant relationships with family members can also cause grief. The loss of anything special and dear to you can cause grief. A situation that causes grief for one person may not be for another.

Although this emotion called grief is a human condition if it is allowed unchecked it could cause you deep sorrow and misery of heart and soul. God is your healer so call on the Good Lord for help. He is waiting for your call. It is okay to grieve but at some point we have to seek divine healing in order to let go and move forward. Sometimes in our grief we are not ready to share our experiences with others for we may just want to be alone but we can talk with God in our secret closet and tell Him all about our heart's concerns.

> **Hear my cry, O God; listen to my prayer.**
> **From the ends of the earth I call to you,**
> **I call as my heart grows faint, lead me**
> **to the rock that is higher than I. For you**
> **have been my refuge, and strong tower**
> **against the foe** (Psalm 61:1-3).

Although there is no time limit on how long one should grieve for about something you should try to monitor yourself. You should not linger here at this place of grief for too long but you must take action that will help you to overcome this grief. Grief recovery helps the soul to heal and soar so do not ignore your grief deal with it in a timely way. You must forgive and release yourself to move on to the next station. Remember that the goal is your complete healing and wholeness from your broken heart. There is no detour at this point so you have to go through this station and your healing is depending on your decision to keep moving. You must go through the entire tunnel to purge yourself in order to reach your goal of healing and wholeness.

Whatever is causing you to grieve take courage in taking "baby steps" towards dealing with the situation and give yourself permission to heal and become spiritually healthy, free, and whole again. Treat your grief like an onion and peel each layer away until you get to the core or cause of your grief.

CHAPTER 17

Fear

Broken For Purpose

"Be strong and of a good courage, fear not, nor be afraid of them: for the Lord thy God, he it is that doth go with thee; he will not fail thee, nor forsake thee" (Deut 31:6).

"The name of the Lord is a strong tower: the righteous runneth into it, and is safe" (Proverbs 18:10).

"I sought the Lord, and he answered me; he delivered me from all my fears" (Psalm 34:4).

What is fear? *"For the Spirit God gave us does not make us afraid, but gives us power, love and self discipline"* (2 Timothy 1:7).

Some types of fears are fear of failure; fear of pain; fear of the present; fear of nature; and fear of the unknown. Fear is intimidating and it will have a threatening effect on your mind, attitude, emotion and the choices that you make. In psychology it is said that fear is directed towards an object or situation that does not present a real danger. In spiritual terms fear is a spirit and negative fear, I believe, will arrest your thoughts and make you become a negative thinker. When fear causes one to think negatively one will respond to situations negatively in their choices and emotions. Fear is a cognitive and emotional experience and if negative fear dominates your thoughts this will affect the way you handle situations. In addition, fear is a distressing emotion that will cause us to respond to perceived or impending danger, evil, or pain in ways we would not normally do whether the threat is real or imagined. Sometimes the situation or experience could be a positive one that generates fear in that you may be fearful that it is more than you can handle and you "fear" the success or failure of the outcome.

The New International Version of the Bible sometimes replaces the word "**fear**" with "**reverence**". It can also mean fear of God's judgment. In Proverbs 15:33, the fear of the Lord is described as the discipline" or "instruction" of wisdom. Fear is an emotion that can make you anxious and afraid while the opposite of fear is to be curious, trusting, or courageous. In the Bible fear is also a good thing which has a positive purpose. The purpose of fear towards God is to get us to act by doing as God requires. There is a certain amount of emotional energy that is aroused in someone when fear sets in due to the circumstances that this person is faced with.

Instead of being a positive thinker negative fear will make you doubt God but God has not given us negative fear. The spirit God gives us is power, love and a sound mind (self discipline). "***For God hath not given us the spirit of fear; but of power, and of love, and of a sound mind***" (2 Timothy 1:7).

If you focus on the problem due to fear, this will be self defeating. You should focus on God who has the solution and not on the problem. When you magnify the problem you discredit God and what He can and wants to do on your behalf. Trust God and be fearless. Sometimes we fear people because of the position they hold; the influence they have; and the doors that we believe that they can open or shut. Sometimes we find ourselves being intimidated by their "power" and what we think they could do to hurt us professionally, socially or otherwise. Remember who is in control, God. "***Cast all your burden upon the Lord, and he shall sustain thee; he shall never suffer the righteous to be moved***" (Psalm 55:22).

We should only fear God who can destroy both body and soul. "***Do not be afraid of those who kill the body but cannot kill the soul. Rather, be afraid of the One who can destroy both soul and body in hell***" (Matthew 10:28). Be bold and persistent! Rely on the power of God, the Holy Spirit who is within you and operate in that power. Do not allow fear to control you for you can defeat fear with love, power and the sound mind that God has given you.

Purge yourself of fear and give birth to your purpose for you are accountable to God! The harsh reality is that some of those who are in authority over us in the Christian community will do everything to prevent us from stepping out into our God given purpose. As a result, instead of supporting, encouraging, or provide guidance to us some will set traps of varying sorts to trip us up and have us fall by the wayside. Unfortunately some of these leaders will even try to redirect us away from the purpose and calling they can see that God has placed upon us. It is important that you are clear about the seed that you know God Himself has planted inside of your heart.

Child of God, I speak from my own personal experience that because of **fear** sometimes we operate from the vantage point of respect to our leaders because they have authority. Sadly enough, some of us follow along without fully realizing that some of them mean us no good. When God reveals to you what their intentions really are you should rejoice and step out boldly into your God given purpose without holding grudges for what "they" have done to you. You must forgive them and count that which had taken place all joy and blessings for you and keep moving in the new path that God has created and made clear for you. In the natural sometimes we have to literally move away from that physical environment that is causing us to **fear** and doubt for this can and will lead to stress. God does not want us to stress He desires for us to be excited about our God given assignment and purpose.

> *Many have become my enemies without cause; those who hate me without reason are numerous. Those who repay my good with evil lodge accusations*

against me, though I seek only to do what is good (Psalm 38:19-20).

If deep in your heart you know without doubt that God has planted a purpose seed inside of your heart you should nurture that seed and be ready to give birth to your purpose in the fullness of time when it is to be delivered. You cannot make room for **fear** or leave any opportunity for fear to creep in your heart and soul unde- tected. You must intentionally examine all areas of your life and make the necessary tough changes that you must make to fulfill your purpose. Some of the necessary changes could include change of environment, people, approaches, mindset, or fear of retaliation. The goal is to get from where you are to where God has called you to be and that place (not necessarily physical) is where you will grow, operate and flourish in your God given purpose. Fear cannot and will not take you there instead fear will cripple and prevent you from getting there so purge yourself of this monster that is fear.

Fear has the capacity to cause the death of your purpose: Do not try to keep holding on to that which God has already released you from because of fear. Your fear of the unknown can cause you to freeze right where you are. Your fear of what people will say about you and they do have a lot to say, could prevent you from acting. Fear of how you will be perceived by others could keep you standing still in a place where God has longed wanted you be released from. God has released you so do not keep holding on to that situation which is "**poisonous**" while you are suffering alone on the inside of your heart and soul. The **fear** of letting go has you hanging on because of your respect, obedience, humility, or loyalty to those to whom you look for support. What will you do when the "brook" is dried up and there is no more sign of water? Remember that you cannot survive for long or live without water. Even when the "brook" is dried up it is hard for some of us to let go and move on. If you do not let go you will stay there and die for there is no more water to keep you alive. **Purge** yourself of **fear** and follow God's plan for your purpose. "*I sought the Lord, and he answered me; he delivered me from all my fears*" (Psalm 34:4). Let go of fear and step out into your calling with confidence and in the authority of the Holy Spirit with nothing to fear.

CHAPTER 18

Guilt

Broken For Purpose

*"**For my iniquities have gone over my head; like a heavy burden, they are too heavy for me**"* (Psalm 38:4).

*"**The times of ignorance God overlooked, but now he commands all people everywhere to repent**"* (Acts 17:30).

Guilt is real and sometimes we feel guilty even when someone else has done us wrong. Sometimes we feel guilty if we believe that there is something that we could have done differently. Feeling guilty for our own actions is self-guilt. Severe self guilt could lead to depression or self-condemnation. Guilt is a cognitive or an emotional experience that is taking place in your mind. Guilt as an emotion can be a negative feeling. Negative guilt feeling will not motivate you to do something positive instead it may urge you to do or say something negative. On the other hand, positive guilt could prompt you to do something positive. Positive guilt is that "inner voice" speaking to you to take action and do something in a given situation.

Too much guilt can cause you agony, loneliness and grief. Some guilt can cause someone to experience a feeling of shame. Some people have a way of acting in ways that make other people feel guilty. Such behaviors reflect more on the person who is projecting a behavior to make someone feel guilty. Instead of dealing with the cause of guilt some people resort to aggressive behavior and blame. Additionally, guilt is a complex emotion which can cause a feeling of anxiety and unhappiness that you have done something wrong. You should take action and correct the situation that has caused you guilt feeling and which might have caused loved ones emotional harm as well.

In light of our relationship with God the guilt of sin and shame are real because we have sinned against God. It is God's desire that we acknowledge our sins and ask His forgiveness. "***In Him we have redemption through His blood, the forgiveness of sins, according to the riches of His grace***" (Ephesians 1:7). God in His mercy will forgive us and we will be redeemed and be set free from the guilt of sin and shame. "***For I will be merciful to their unrighteousness, and their sins and their lawless deeds I will remember no more***" (Hebrews 8:12).

Should your broken heart cause you to feel guilty in any way you are encouraged to identify the specific reason or cause of your guilt feeling or thinking and find the courage to address the situation for the sake of your inner healing and emotional well being. If you have to ask someone to forgive you for something you said or did you should take the courage and be bold enough to ask others for their forgiveness, forgive yourself and ask God for His forgiveness and free yourself then celebrate your freedom from the bondage of guilt.

CHAPTER 19

Pride

Broken For Purpose

"But he gives us more grace. That is why Scripture says: 'God opposes the proud but shows favor to the humble"
(James 4:6).

"Pride goes before destruction, a haughty spirit before a fall"
(Proverbs 16:18).

"When pride comes, then comes disgrace, but with humility comes wisdom" (Proverbs 11:2).

Pride is considered an emotion which could be positive or negative. Whenever pride is negative it is the opposite of humility. Pride in Latin is (***supervia***) and is considered a deadly sin from a biblical perspective. To be prideful could be detrimental and the Word of God has a lot to say about pride. Negative pride is when a person behaves in ways that are considered to be self-conceited or self-glorification. Prideful persons speak of themselves and their achievements in a bragging way which could be due to poor self-worth. "**He who exalts himself shall he humbled and whoever humbles himself shall be exalted**" (Luke 14:11). God will bring the proud person to his or her senses in His own way and time. In pride you elevate yourself while you put others down. God resists the proud but He gives grace and favor to the person who is humble. Pride is one of the seven deadly sins of the Bible and there are several examples in the Bible of the downfall of prideful people. Take the wise advise to purge yourself of any and all prideful spirit for the spirit of pride is detrimental to the health of your soul.

> *There are six things the Lord hates, seven that are detestable to him: haughty (arrogant) eyes, a lying tongue, hands that shed innocent blood, a heart that devised wicked schemes, feet that are quick to rush into evil, a false witness who pours out lies and a person who stirs up conflict in the community* (Proverbs 6:16-19).

The Dangers of Pride (2 Kings 5): The account of Naaman's healing from leprosy is a vivid illustration of how pride can be a stumbling block in someone's own way and delay or prevent them from having the healing they really want. Naaman was a commander of the army of the King of Aram. The king considered Naaman a valiant soldier but Naaman had leprosy. There was a young girl who had been taken captive from Israel and she was maid to Naaman's wife. This young girl told her mistress that if Naaman would see the prophet in Samaria he would cure him of his leprosy. Naaman asked permission of King Aram to allow him to go to Samaria to seek healing. King Aram not only gave his permission but he sent a letter to the King of Samaria on Naaman's behalf.

The King of Samaria was not pleased with King Aram for having sent him a letter and he admitted that he cannot heal anyone. The prophet Elisha heard about the king being upset and instructed that Naaman be sent to him. When Naaman got to Elisha's house Elisha did not go out to meet him and he did not take from Naaman the gifts he had brought for him. Instead, Elisha sent him a message that he should go and wash himself seven times in the Jordan River and his flesh would be restored and he would be cleansed

Pride filled Naaman's heart to the extent that he went away very angry and he complained that there were better rivers that the prophet could have sent him to wash in. One of Naaman's servants spoke to him and encouraged him to do as the prophet had instructed. We find that sometimes a little encouragement from others goes a long way. Naaman had a change of mind and he did as the prophet had commanded. "*So he went down and dipped himself in the Jordan seven times, as the man of God had told him, and his flesh was restored and became clean like that of a young boy*'" (2 Kings 5). After being cleansed Naaman showed gratitude of heart and he went back to the man of God, prophet Elisha and testified saying, "*Now I know that*

there is no God in all the world except in Israel" (2 Kings 5:15).

My encouragement to you is that you should be very careful not to allow pride to get in the way of your divine healing and blessing. Naaman was prideful to the extent that he stood in the way and delayed his own healing from leprosy. I imagine Naaman thanked God that he had a servant with him who was brave enough to approach him and encouraged him to do as the prophet had instructed. God still cares for His children including those with prideful hearts and He desires the best for them all. "***The Lord is not slow in keeping his promise, as some understand slowness. Instead he is patient with you, not wanting anyone to perish, but everyone to come to repentance***" (2 Peter 3:9). You must do everything possible to avoid negative pride.

Pride is not always negative for it could also be a positive trait that expresses good positive attitudes and emotions. In the positive sense, pride is someone having a feeling of being good and worthy with self respect. When someone sets a goal and works very hard to achieve that goal one celebrates with pride. Someone who practices a high standard of moral living and is consistent uses the attitude of pride to maintain that standard. Pride is feeling good about yourself by having a positive self concept of who you are. Positive pride will motivate you to be morally good and practice good deeds but negative pride you must avoid.

CHAPTER 20

Hatred And Jealousy
Broken For Purpose

"Anyone who hates a brother or sister is a murderer, and you know that no murderer has eternal life residing in him" (1 John 3:15).

"Love must be sincere. Hate what is evil; cling to what is good" (Romans 12:9).

"Anyone who claims to be in the light but hates a brother or sister is still in the darkness" (1 John 2:9).

The wrong that some people do to us can cause our hearts to be broken to the extent that if we are not careful and stay prayed up hatred could enter our hearts. Hatred and jealousy are deadly combinations and they must be **purged** from one's heart and soul. You do not want to be associated with these emotions for they will destroy you without mercy. Do not allow any room in your heart for hate or jealousy.

Although your heart is broken do not allow hatred or jealousy to take root in your heart. If and when someone mistreats you by God's grace you should love them anyway and seek to do the opposite (Matthew 5:44). It is possible for you to do this with the help of the Good Lord who supplies the grace. You cannot fight hatred or jealousy by yourself but with God's grace you can and for the sake of your inner healing and wellbeing you should work things out and reconcile with others and become free. Do not allow what hurts you in the past or today to control your future. Remember that you cannot change people but you can ask God to change them while you work on your own heart and pray for those people. The heart of man is concealed from others but God reads (knows) the heart and He possesses the power to change them if they desire to be changed. While insecurity and fear can cause someone to be jealous, hate can be more intense. To hate someone is to despise them intensely and this is due to an unforgiving heart. It is important to keep in mind that love supersedes hate and jealousy.

Hate is a cruel emotion. The Bible tells us that Saul's heart was consumed with hate towards David to the extent that he was obsessed in wanting David dead. Saul's hatred for David was extremely intense in that he began to make it known that he wanted David dead. He unsuccessfully tried multiple times to kill David himself but failed. In contrast, David was respectful to King Saul and served him well even though he knew that Saul was trying to kill him. Love defeats hate!

Jealousy generally refers to the thoughts or feelings of insecurity, fear, and concern. Jealousy is different from envy and it can cause serious problems. Jealously can be a negative state of mind and can cause the person who is jealous to experience low self-esteem and or feelings of inadequacy. It is very important that you understand that the person's jealousy is not about you but rather about them. When you become aware of someone's jealousy of you be very careful in how you deal with that person and be sure to stay prayed up. You should work on yourself at all times and walk in the precepts of God's Holy Word in order to be protected from hatred and jealousy. You should try not to be suspicious but at the same time you must use wisdom an avoid situations that are likely to cause arguments or disagreements with people whom you know are jealous of you.

Jealousy in (Hebrew is *qana*; Greek zeloo) is an emotion that emerges in response to a perceived disloyalty or rivalry as hatred and envy of others. God calls Himself jealous. "***For you shall worship no other god, for the Lord, whose name is Jealous, is a jealous God***" (Exodus 34:14). We belong to God for He made us and owns mankind. When God made man He breathe life into man and he became a living soul. God desires man's faithful service to Him for we are His own. "**And the Lord God formed man of the dust of the ground, and breathed into his nostrils the breath of life; and man became a living being**" (Genesis 2:7). "***Or do you think Scripture says without reason that he jealously longs for the spirit he has caused to dwell in us***?" (James 4:5).

God's jealousy is His zeal towards His people and His passionate desire for faithful relationship with us. God does not want us to serve Him and at the same time be unfaithful and serve other gods. When we come to know and love God as our Heavenly Father we too are zealous of Him. The more time we spend with God is the more we get to know Him as the Lord of our lives, and the more we know Him is the more we become zealous for Him. This jealousy or zealousness is more about being earnest towards God in love, service and worship which is a good thing.

This zeal is different from jealous emotion. Our zeal for God is not an emotion but rather a deep passionate love of the heart which is expressed in our faith, love, and worship in serving God. God requires that we be zealous of Him as His Word teaches. "***Love the Lord your God with all your heart and with all your soul and with all your strength***" (Deuteronomy 6:5). "***You will seek me and find me when you seek me with all your heart***" (Jeremiah 29:13). "***Even now, declares the Lord, return to me with all your heart, with fasting and weeping and mourning***" (Joel 2:12). "***Trust in the Lord with all your heart and lean not on your own understanding***" (Proverbs 3:5). "***Blessed are they who keep his statutes and seek him with all their heart***" (Psalm 119:2).

Child of the Most High God, do not be overcome with the emotion of jealousy or hate but rather may your heart be consumed with zeal for God. Jesus is our perfect example of this zeal and the prophet Isaiah spoke of the zeal of Jesus saying, "***He put on righteousness***

as his breastplate, and the helmet of salvation on his head, he put on the garments of vengeance and wrapped himself in zeal as in a cloak" (Isaiah 50:17). In the New Testament Gospels John wrote, "**His disciples remembered that it is written, "Zeal for your house will consume me**" (John 2:17). Allow the Holy Spirit to minister to you as you examine yourself through the lenses of God's Holy Word and purge yourself of hatred and or jealousy.

CHAPTER 21

Discouragement

Broken For Purpose

"Do not let your hearts be troubled. You believe in God, believe also in me" (John 14:1).

"Give thanks in all circumstances; for this is God's will for you in Christ Jesus" (1 Thessalonians 5:18).

Discouragement is a temptation common to everyone. When someone is discouraged that person is experiencing loss of confidence or enthusiasm. Discouragement can lead to despondency, doubt, hopelessness and despair. When someone is discouraged that person may not want to try anymore. Do not allow discouragement to entrap you for it will kill your desire, dream, vision, and it may even weaken your faith. Discouragement will strip you of your passion and purpose.

No temptation has overtaken you except what is common to mankind. And God is faithful; he will not let you be tempted beyond what you can bear. But when you are tempted, he will also provide a way out so that you can endure it (1 Corinthians 10:13).

"*The Lord is good, a refuge in times of trouble. He cares for those who trust in him*" (Nahum 1:7). You are reminded to use the tools in your **survival kit** such as songs of praise that will serve you well when you feel somewhat discouraged for singing songs of praise to God will lift your spirit and set you free.

One who is discouraged needs support and encouragement. At other times one may need a little toughness and a little push. Jesus does not want us to be discouraged for discouragement could lead us to give up on ourselves instead of trying harder. This is a time when you should not give up but must fight for your spiritual survival. "*Submit yourselves, then, to God. Resist the devil, and he will flee from you*" (James 4:7). Try not to spend much time with people who discourage you by their words or actions. Confide in someone with whom you can be honest in sharing only as much as you wish to share concerning what is causing you to be discouraged.

It is God's desire that you have peace of heart and soul and to be discouraged does not bring peace. "*I have told you these things, so that in me you may have peace. In this world you will have trouble. But*

take heart! I have overcome the world" (John 16:33). Here are some things that you can do to overcome discouragement including thinking about your past victories; singing songs of praise; read your Bible; pray and build your relationship with God. "**Do you not know that in a race all the runners run, but only one gets the prize? Run in such a way as to get the prize**" (1 Corinthians 9:24).

There is one weapon that Satan successfully uses if he is given the chance and it is that of discouragement. Severe discouragement could lead to stress and depression especially when people who you believe should be supporting you try to prevent and deny you. Keep fighting and do not be discouraged for this is about the healing of your heart and soul. You must do what it takes to purge yourself of this unhealthy emotion and pursue a life of vibrancy in Christ.

CHAPTER 22

Ask For Help

Broken For Purpose

Whatever you ask in my name, this I will do, that the Father may be glorified in the Son. If you ask me anything in my name, I will do it (John 14:13-14).

When all your people Israel pray and ask for help, as they acknowledge their intense pain and spread out their hands toward this temple, then listen from your heavenly dwelling place, forgive their sin, and act favorably toward each one based on your evaluation of their motive (2 Chronicles 6:29-30).

It is a sign of strength to recognize that you need help and to ask for help. *My help comes from the Lord, who made heaven and earth* (Psalm 121:2). You should purge yourself of the thought that you can manage and do this on your own and all by yourself. If and when God allows you to be in a situation that you cannot manage on your own it means that in such situation He wants you to ask for His help and sometimes for the help of others. Everyone at some point in life will need the help of someone else for some reason or another because we cannot always do everything on our own. There is absolutely nothing wrong in asking for help from others who can help you and are willing to help. Christians are expected by God to ask for His help daily for it is only with His divine help that we will be victorious in any and all of our circumstances. When we ask people for help it is God who inspires them to provide the help that we need at that moment in time. Sometimes we desperately need help but we feel that we do not want to burden others with our concerns. No one sets out with a desire to fail but failure could be the experience if we believe that we can do everything on our own.

It is a wise person who recognizes that help is needed and it does not mean that one is weak in asking for help but it means that one is wise, strong and insightful. Continue to ask the Lord for help and strength daily realizing that it is impossible to live a victorious Christian life without His help. Moreover the Good Lord encourages us to ask for His help. "***Ask, and it will be given to you; seek, and you will find; knock, and it will be opened to you***" (Matthew 7:7). Whenever we ask God for His help we show to Him that we are dependent on Him to do what He promises in His Word that He will do. "***So do not fear, for I am with you; do not be dismayed, for I am your God. I will strengthen you and help you; I will uphold you with my righteous right hand***" (Isaiah 41:10).

Like a parent who protects and provides for a dependent child so likewise the Good Lord protects us who are His children. A non-adult child depends on his or her parents to supply his or her every daily need. So likewise as Christians we too must fully rely on God for His divine help. *"The name of the Lord is a strong tower, the righteous run into it and are safe"* (Proverbs 18:10). First and foremost we should seek God's help and secondly we should seek to obtain help and wise counsel from others with the desire and capacity to help.

No one can do anything of great spiritual value if you are unhealthy in heart and soul. We will all experience pain and tragedy at some time in our lives and we may better serve ourselves when we share our pain, tragedy, challenges and stories with others who are willing to listen and give some encouragement. Emotion and tension that are held in for a long time are released when you let go and share with someone. Do not be afraid when seeking help from others although you should be very careful in knowing what to look for in the person you choose to share with. Seek help from people who love and serve God fully and these people do not have to be pastors.

You are not alone in needing help for even pastors from time to time will need the help of others to support them in their difficult circumstances. Pastors can be broken too for many reasons and will need others to help them carry their burdens. *"Bear ye one another's burdens, and so fulfill the law of Christ"* (Galatians 6:2). Pastors have to manage the operations of the church and manage people some of whom do not want to be managed but instead want to do their own thing and have their own way. Pastors are accountable to God for the people who are placed in their pastoral care by God. Pastors have to manage their personal lives, their homes, their children, and their marriages. The cares and concerns of church members can become personal for pastors and they labor in prayer before God on the behalf of their members. In addition to all these concerns, some pastors have jobs in the private sector as well in order to supplement their salaries from the church. My point is that everyone needs help from someone for one reason or another.

When you ask for help you are intentionally taking care of your mental health. Some situations that you have to deal with you can just talk with a trusting friend about it while there are other situations for which you may need professional help such as the help of your pastor or a certified Christian counselor. Going to see a mental health professional does not mean that someone is mentally ill. What this means is that you are seeking clarity in dealing with your difficulties and seeking help in resolving conflicts and needing direction and support for your life and well being. Sometimes the pastor's schedule can become very busy and at such times the Christian counselor can do much to make the job of the pastor easier for the pastor cannot do everything since they too have limits. Moreover, some people may not be ready to talk with the pastor just yet, and so talking to someone else may be their preference especially if it is not a grave situation.

Jesus is our perfect example of one reaching out for help. When Jesus was on earth He constantly called on His Heavenly Father to ask for help for different reasons. For example, when Jesus was on the Cross to be crucified on our behalf He desperately called on His Father to help Him for He could not endure the suffering all by Himself. "***About three in the afternoon Jesus cried out in a loud voice, 'My God, my God, why have you forsaken me?***" (Matthew 27:46). In this life there are some experiences we will have, many of which we will have no control over and will not be able to change them. Some of these experiences will be more than we can manage on our own and it is at these times that we should call on God like Jesus did and without doubt God will give us the sustaining grace that we need to overcome those situations. In addition, I will recommend that you have a few trusted individuals in your circle that you can call on for help and moral support.

Asking for help is not always easy to do and this is the reason why many people need help but they do not ask. Some people do not ask for help because they are too prideful. Others do not ask for help because they are ashamed. Some do not ask for help because they blame themselves believing that it is their fault why this is happening to them so they feel guilty. There are those who do not ask for help because they feel intimidated and feel afraid to approach the person whom they believe may be able to help them. These individuals suffer in silence and sometimes hope for someone to reach out to them.

As children of God we should be alert and be able to recognize when someone is in need of help and extend a helping hand. There are those who can help but have no desire to help others. There are many reasons that are unknown to us why some people are reluctant to reach out and provide help to others. Some reasons could be that these people do not have a kind heart; they might be waiting to be asked; they have no compassion; their hearts may not be saturated with the love of God. It is very important to have the spirit of discernment to see and understand when someone is in need of help. Someone could be very desperate but fail to ask for help because of pride, shame, intimidation or anything else. There are people who are not in need of help but they pretend in order to prey on other people. You must be careful and watchful of these people and this is also why it is important to have the spirit of discernment. God is counting on us to help others who are in need and to also ask for help when we are in need. For our own emotional, psychological and social wellbeing and spiritual development we should seek help when it is needed.

CHAPTER 23

Acceptance

Broken For Purpose

*"**In everything give thanks; for this is the will of God in Christ Jesus for you**"* (1 Thessalonians 5:18).

With an attitude of acceptance you recognize the reality of the situation but this does not mean that you approve what took place. Acceptance is one of the first steps towards healing. This acceptance means that you have decided to see things as they actually are. In acceptance you acknowledge that your heart is broken and you let go of denial. In acceptance you are ready to purge your mindset from the thought that it did not happen.

Job accepted his brokenness condition and this was evident when his dear wife told him to curse God and die. Job responded to her saying that she was speaking like a foolish woman (Job 2:10). Job also said, *"**Though he slay me, yet will I trust in him: I will surely maintain mine own ways before him**"* (Job

13:15). Job truly experienced broken heartedness when his children died; he lost his property; his animals and all other possessions and then his wife tried to encourage him to curse God. Job instead choose to accept his fate and learnt his lessons. He was a quick learner for he did not become angry with God or become discouraged instead he accepted his circumstances and trusted God to bring him out of the situation. His focus was on God whom he knew could and would deliver him out of his broken hearted circumstances in due time. Job took the right approach by relying on God for help and he did not blame God or anyone else. God will give you the courage, grace and the wisdom to do the same as Job.

If you are not careful, heartbreak will get you to do quite the opposite of what you really want to do and should do. To accept what caused your heart to be broken is to acknowledge that the problem does exist. In acceptance you recognize that there is nothing that you could have done differently and even if there were some things that you could have done differently those are now in the past and you cannot go back in time to fix that so move forward.

Something happened to break your heart and hurt your soul for a reason and a purpose. "*In everything give thanks; for this is the will of God in Christ Jesus for you*" (1 Thessalonians 5:18). Acceptance is for your healing and for you to operate in your purpose. Even in this circumstance that break your heart give God thanks and trust Him that it will in the end be for your good and His glory to be fulfilled in you. Do not be afraid to accept what has happened for acceptance does not mean that you approve what happened instead it means that you acknowledge that it happened.

You are not alone for God is right there with you and He will see you through to the very end for He is working on your behalf. At some time in our lives each of us experience a broken heart to some degree for no one is immune to heart break. Do not blame yourself if you did not do anything to cause others to inflict hurt upon your heart. God cannot help you unless you allow Him to help you for God gives you freedom to choose. Trust God and allow Him to help you purge and cleanse your heart and soul of these impurities. Inner hurt which is heart brokenness results in deep pain that one must be healed and delivered from.

Emotional heart pain does cause some people to resort to self destructive behaviors such as bad eating habits; poor social behaviors; poor performance on the job among other unacceptable behaviors. Inner pain can be intense to the extent some people engage in physical harm of various sorts and these could also lead to stress if not treated. Without "**purging**" it becomes difficult to move on and grow in the spiritual things of God or grow in other areas such as professional, personal or social life. These impurities you read about in Part Three will harm you so it is not profitable for you to hold on to them. In the name of Jesus Christ your Lord, you must purge yourself of these impurities.

CHAPTER 24

Repentance

Broken For Purpose

Therefore, if you take your gift to the alter, and there remember that your brother has something against you, leave your gift there before the alter, and go your way. First be reconciled to your brother, and then come and offer your gift (Matthew 5:23-24).

"Repent of your sins and turn to God, for the Kingdom of Heaven is near" (Matthew 3:2).

Y our journey through *the tunnel purging* had been a very long and challenging one. Anyone including yourself who attempted and successfully traveled through this tunnel purging all the way and emerged on the other end should be celebrated. The stations along this tunnel purging are many and each station has its own sets of difficulties. The key to success is endurance and a high level of patience that are required of everyone travelling through this tunnel to tackle the severe hardships on this journey. The ultimate goal of this journey is **soul care healing** which can only be realized by faithfully going through every station. The traveler going through this tunnel must utilize every tool provided in the survival kit in order to emerge victoriously on the other end of the tunnel. The goal is to be thoroughly purged of all impurities. "***Purge me with hyssop, and I shall be clean: wash me, and I shall be whiter than snow***" (Psalm 51:7). "***Unless you repent you will all likewise perish, said Jesus***" (Luke 13:3). All the impurities from which you had to purge yourself in this tunnel were not easy to let go of for they all required of you much focus, determination and diligent hard work which you were willing to do.

A Time for repentance: Now that you have emerged on the other end of the tunnel purging this is a wonderful time and place to **repent** and ask God to forgive you for having had all or some of those impurities in your heart. **Repentance** involves recognizing that you have thought wrongly in the past or have acted wrongly and you are now making a decision to think differently and rightly in the future. To repent means that you have a change of heart and mind and this should result in behavior and attitude change as well. In the New Testament Gospel, John the Baptist warned the people to turn from their evil ways and repent and demonstrate in their behaviors that they have changed. "***Produce fruit in keeping with repentance***" (Matthew 3:8). Repentance and faith produce forgiveness and salvation. Not only do we ask God for His forgiveness when we repent but we also must ask the forgiveness of others whom we have wronged.

The (Hebrew word for repentance is **shub**, the Greek word is **metanoia**; and the Latin word is **poenitentia**). Biblical repentance means that one is remorseful and as a result engages in the act of expressing contrition or sorrow and penitence of sin. *"First to those in Damascus, then to those in Jerusalem and in all Judea, and then to the Gentiles, I preached that they should repent and turn to God and demonstrate their repentance by their deeds"* (Acts 26:20). It is a conscious decision one makes to repent and ask for forgiveness then change the course of his or her behavior.

Repentance is an inward (or internal) and external act of godly sorrow for wrong behaviors or attitudes. The outward expression of repentance first begins inwardly in the heart with an acknowledgment of the wrong done and a desire to make that wrong right by repenting which is asking for forgiveness and making necessary changes. It is God's requirement that we all repent and He punishes those who do not repent. *"In the past God overlooked such ignorance, but now he commands all people everywhere to repent"* (Acts 17:30). God does not and will not force anyone to repent instead He graciously makes the opportunity possible for everyone to repent. *"This day I call the heavens and the earth as witnesses against you that I have set before you life and death, blessings and curses. Now choose life, so that you and your children may live"* (Deuteronomy 30:19).

> *He told them, 'This is what is written:*
> *The Messiah will suffer and rise from*

the dead on the third day, and repentance for the forgiveness of sins will be preached in his name to all nations, beginning at Jerusalem (Luke 24:46-47).

The Great Renewal: After a godly sorrow and sincere repentance one enjoys the feeling of liberation for repentance is freedom from guilt! Genuine repentance liberates you from the impurities of heart and soul. "***Old things are passed away; and behold, all things are become new***" (2 Corinthians 5:1). My vessel is cleansed and it is emptied of the old wine and is ready for the new wine. Upon repentance, one has a new vessel which is a clean and new heart one that is ready for the pouring in of "**new wine**" to replace the **impurities** that have been cleansed and removed from your heart and soul. In Scripture "**wine**" represents healing, transformation, joy and the power of God's grace and these are what you received upon repentance. The message and foundation of the Christian faith is repentance. This is the message that John the Baptist and Jesus preached and it is **The Great Commission** of Jesus to His disciples and to us today. If and when someone is guilty of any sin that person must confess in order to receive atonement and forgiveness from God. When other persons are involved we must also ask those persons for their forgiveness. The genuine act of saying the words "I am sorry please forgive me" followed by a change in behavior is repentance. David prayed a beautiful prayer of repentance in Psalm 51 and I encourage you to read his prayer.

Daily prayer of repentance: Dear God, my Heavenly Father, thank you for your daily provision of forgiveness of my sins and wrong doings. Today I repent and ask for your forgiveness. Thank you for not giving up on me when I do make mistakes, but instead you reach out to me and seek to bring me back to the fold, your fold of forgiveness, mercy and safety. Thank you, Lord, for your great love to me and all mankind. Thank you, Lord, for your grace and mercy in Jesus' name. Amen.

REFLECTIONS

The Tunnel: Purging

*"The Lord is my light and my salvation whom shall I fear?
The Lord is the stronghold of my life of whom shall I be
afraid'* (Psalm 27:1).

Upon reflection, when you consider the hazardous journey that you travelled through in the tunnel of purging to get to this place, the end of the tunnel, you cannot help but being amazed that you actually made it through. Glory to God! Your tunnel of purging is where you were tested and tried. That was also your time of preparation for the journey ahead of you for the journey continues. You do have much to show as fruit or evidence for your suffering and growth. The fruit(s) of your labor is your powerful testimony of what the Lord has done along the way on your behalf and how He brought you out of the tunnel victoriously. Going through the purging process you learnt to believe and trust God with no shadow of doubt. As dark as the tunnel was you could see clearly through your eyes of faith that God keeps His Word without fail for He was always present with you. "***It is the Lord who goes before you. He will be with you; he will not leave you or forsake you. Do not fear or be dismayed***" (Deuteronomy 31:8).

You are proof that God can and will turn the plan of the enemy to nothing. When your enemies and foes teamed up against you still you trusted God for He could not, did not and will not fail you. God will give you the grace to fulfill what He has called you to do. As you prepare and move forward on the next leg of your journey take courage and go with confidence knowing that the Good God who brought you this far will guide you to the very end.

> "***I remain confident of this: I will see the goodness of the Lord in the land of the living. Wait for the Lord; be strong and take heart and wait for the Lord***" (Psalm 27:13-14).

Now that you have purged yourself of the impurities in the tunnel purging you are now ready to embark on your journey through tunnel healing. The victories you experienced and the lessons you learned in tunnel purging should support you going forward.

Part Four

The Tunnel: Healing

The Power Stations

But you shall receive power when the Holy Spirit has come upon you; and you shall be witnesses to Me in Jerusalem, and in all Judea and Samaria, and to the end of the earth (Acts 1:8).

And said, If thou wilt diligently hearken to the voice of the Lord thy God, and wilt do that which is right in his sight, and wilt give ear to his commandments, and keep all his statues, I will put none of these diseases upon thee, which I have brought upon the Egyptians; for I am the Lord that healeth thee (Exodus 15:26).

This is **tunnel healing**, the second of two, and it consists of the power stations that will facilitate your healing. Now that you are purged from the impurities you read about in tunnel one purging, you are now ready for your broken, wounded and sore heart to be divinely healed. This is your divine inner healing of heart and soul. At this stage in your journey as you travel through the power stations you can anticipate the joy that you will experience when in the end your heart is healed from all the hurt inflicted on it for a long time.

The **Power Stations** are obedience, forgiveness, God's inner work, healing, peace, wellness and wholeness, rest, love, humility, grace and mercy, nurture your soul, the Fruit of the Spirit and integrity. I call these the **Power Stations** because they are the foundation on which you must build your spiritual fortitude. Without these spiritual qualities in your heart and life you cannot and will not be successful on this your spiritual journey. These stations are not optional and they can be quite challenging. Please remember that you have a **Survival Kit** and you still need every tool in your survival kit all along this journey and through every station in Tunnel Two (See chapter one).

Child of the Most High God, you are now in a wonderful place for you have purged and cleansed your heart and soul of the unhealthy emotions that captured your heart and held it hostage for a long time. The experiences that you had to go through in your **Tunnel One** journey were very real and quite difficult! You should know that everyone who experiences heartbreak goes through most or all of these emotions and each person will deal with and process them differently because we are all different.

Your complete healing will depend on your willingness to allow the Holy Spirit to do his great work within your heart. "***Restore unto me the joy of thy salvation; and uphold me with thy free spirit***" (Psalm 51:12). The open wound in your heart and soul must be healed and those impurities you removed must be replaced with the joy of your salvation and gently nurtured by the care of the Holy Spirit.

CHAPTER 25

Obedience

Growing Into Wholeness

"If you love me, you will keep my commandments"
(John 14:15).

"As obedient children, do not be conformed to the passions of your former ignorance" (1 Peter 1:14).

"If you are willing and obedient, you shall eat the good of the land" (Isaiah 1:19).

W hen a child does as the parents instruct or request that is obedience. An employee obeys the rules and protocols of the workplace by putting them into practice. As children of God we demonstrate obedience when we follow the laws and instructions given by God. Obedience is of extreme importance to God and obedience is what He requires of His people since the beginning of time. God promises that if we obey his voice by doing as He commands we will be His treasured possession. "***Now therefore, if you will indeed obey my voice and keep my covenant, you shall be my treasured possession among all peoples, for all the earth is mine***" (Exodus 19:5). In order for God to lead you successfully through all the stations in this **tunnel healing** you must trust Him completely with your healing process and follow as He leads you all the way through. The stations in this tunnel are many and you cannot avoid going through any of them. Every station is mandatory and each teaches specific lessons that will facilitates your growth in various areas of your spiritual, personal, social, and professional life and importantly your purpose.

Obedience to God has the benefits of great blessings. God does not dictate how one should choose but He lovingly advises how one should choose and what the result of each choice will be. "***This day I call the heavens and the earth as witnesses against you that I have set before you life and death, blessings and curses. Now choose life, so that you and your children may live***" (Deuteronomy 30:19). God gives specific and very clear instructions and He desires and expects that we will obey them. Once we are clear about what God wants us to do we should obey Him and not do our own thing. "***And Samuel said, Hath the Lord as great delight in burnt offerings and sacrifices, has in obeying the voice of the Lord? Behold, to obey is better than sacrifice, and to heed than the fat of rams***" (1 Samuel 15:22).

Disobedience to God's instruction and request is never a wise thing to do for to disobey God comes with a heavy price. To disobey God comes with a curse and not a blessing so I advise that you obey God (Deuteronomy 11:28). When God made Adam and then his wife Eve and placed them in the Garden of Eden He gave them specific instructions concerning the tree that they could or could not eat from. God gave to Adam and Eve the power of personal choice to make their own decisions. We too have that power of personal choice. However, God expects us to choose wisely by doing as He instructs us to do.

"*Obey and you will be blessed, disobey and you will be cursed*" (Deuteronomy 11:26-28). The options are very clear and it should be clear that you have the power of free choice since God has given you the power to choose by the free will He has given to you. Your choice to obey God must be grounded in your love for Him and you cannot love God and at the same time not obey Him. Your faith in God and your love for Him undergird your attitude of obedience to Him. I sincerely encourage you to be obedient to God, the Holy Spirit, your spirit and your divine purpose. Abram obeyed God and his obedience was rewarded to him as righteousness. "*Surely God is my salvation; I will trust and not be afraid. The Lord is my strength and my song; he has become my salvation*" (Isaiah 12:2). When we trust and obey God there is no need to be afraid of the outcome for God Himself is our strength, shield and deliverer. Obedience and trust are intertwined. When we trust God we will obey Him and walk in obedience even when we do not fully understand the task He wants us to do. God in His perfect timing will make everything clear to us.

Test of obedience: An example of a true test of obedience is found in Genesis chapter 22 when God tested Abraham's faith, love and obedience. God's test to Abraham came when God instructed him, "*Take your son, your only son, Isaac, whom you love, and go to the region of Moriah. Sacrifice him there as a burnt offering on one of the mountains I will tell you about*" (Genesis 22:2). Abraham's obedience was mixed with faith and love for God as he faithfully embarked on the journey to do as God instructed him. On the journey, Isaac asked his father, where was the lamb for the sacrifice and in an act of unquestioned faith Abraham responded, "*God Himself will provide the lamb for the burnt offering, my son*" (Genesis 22:8). Abraham prepared his son for the sacrifice and as he was about to slay his son the angel of the Lord called out to him from heaven and instructed him not to harm his son. Abraham looked up and there in the thicket (bushes) he saw a ram for the sacrifice. "*I swear by myself, declares the Lord, that because you have done this and have not withheld your son, your only son, I will surely bless you and make your descendants as numerous as the stars in the sky and as the sand on the sea-shore*" (Genesis 22:16-17). By this time I hope that you are fully persuaded to obey God completely for it will be in your best interest. Be confident in the fact that God keeps His Word.

In this story, Abraham's obedience was the fore-shadow of the ultimate obedience found in Jesus Christ who obeyed His Father God in offering His own life on the Cross of Calvary to redeem mankind from sin. "***God made him who had no sin to be sin for us, so that in him we might become the righteousness of God***" (2 Corinthians 5:21). God is truth and wisdom knowing everything and all things and so it is always better to obey God. "***But Peter and the apostles replied, 'We must obey God rather than any human authority***" (Acts 5:29). Obey God and allow Him to lead you all the way through to your complete healing, wholeness, and purpose.

CHAPTER 26

Forgiveness

Growing Into Wholeness

*"**For thou, Lord, art good, and ready to forgive; and plenteous in mercy unto all them that call upon thee**"* (Psalm 86:5).

For if you forgive other people when they sin against you, your heavenly Father will also forgive you. But if you do not forgive others their sins, your Father will not forgive your sins (Matthew 6:14-15).

No station on this journey is more powerful than the **power station of forgiveness**. Forgiveness is the foundation of our salvation and it is rooted in God's love. Jesus gave His disciples specific instructions and guidelines for praying. "***And whenever you stand praying, if you have anything against anyone, forgive him, that your Father in heaven may also forgive you your trespasses***" (Mark 11:25). True forgiveness is the key that will unlock the door to completely move you forward in accepting that you are not in a dream but that which did happen actually happened. Your heart is broken and now you are to forgive and move forward in your pursuit of wellness and wholeness of your own heart.

At the forgiveness station of your journey you are ready to let go of the past and purge yourself of any and all impurities such as bitterness, denial, anger, fear, among other heart and soul impurities. At this stage of the journey you need to fully realize that forgiveness is a divine cleansing that is taking place in your heart, soul, body and life. This act of forgiving you cannot do by yourself for it is the work of the Holy Spirit when you give Him permission to do this work in your heart. In your attitude towards people in general there should be a willingness to forgive and be at peace first with God, with them and with yourself. Inner peace comes with forgiving yourself and others even when they did not ask for your forgiveness.

From my own healing journey experience and the insight given to me by the Holy Spirit I have come to realize that it is not humanly possible to forgive but rather it is in our hearts by the indwelling presence of the Holy Spirit that we are able to forgive. Forgiveness does not take place in our minds for it is more than words and more than mere emotions and actions. Forgiveness is a divine action of love from the heart and it comes with a desire to want to forgive. This is why we can forgive and be free within even when others did not ask for us to forgive them of the wrong that they had done to us. Forgiveness is an attitude of the heart and to forgive is an intentional act.

When you forgive you do not dwell on the former things. True forgiveness does not mean that you cannot recall in your mind what was done for it is not in your mind that you forgive it is in your heart that you forgive and you have no desire for revenge. When you forgive you do not hold grudges. "*Forget the former things; do not dwell on the past*" (Isaiah 43:18). God alone can help you make the way in your heart to forgive. Learning the lesson of forgiveness in forgiving those who wronged us is extremely important in understanding our own need for forgiveness, cleansing and healing. Job who had a heart full of love and compassion forgave his friends and prayed sincerely for them. God was pleased with Job to the extent that He praised Job and blessed him with a double portion of wealth (Job 42:10). Additionally, God was so pleased with Job He added years to his life. "*After this, Job lived a hundred and forty years; he saw his children and their children to the fourth generation*" (Job 42:16).

When we fully understand the principles of forgiveness we do not wait for apologies from others before forgiving them. Apologies may never come for some people will never admit their wrong doing. Some people are too prideful to ask for forgiveness. To wait for apologies would be to slow down and prolong the process of our own healing and wellness, so, forgive and move forward. "*Forgive us our debts, as we also have forgiven our debtors*" (Matthew 6:12) "*For if you forgive men when they sin against you, your heavenly Father will also forgive you*" (Matthew 6:14). There is no limit to the number of times that we should be willing to forgive someone who wrongs us.

> *Then Peter came to Jesus and asked, "Lord, how many times shall I forgive my brother when he sins against me? Up to seven times? Jesus answered, "I tell you, not seven times, but seventy seven times* (Matthew 18:21-22).

Forgiveness is a wonderful experience of God's mercy and love for us and towards us. Therefore, it is important for all believers to forgive others as Christ has forgiven us. God requires us to forgive; He expects us to forgive; and He is depending on us to forgive. Jesus told his apostles, "**Whose sins you shall forgive they are forgiven**" (John 20:23). You must have a desire to forgive and it should come from your heart and not just your words.

Forgiveness matters because the consequences of not forgiving are enormous. When we fail to forgive others we place a stumbling block in our own way on our journey to wholeness. Some people run out of time and they lose their opportunities to forgive others in that the person dies or they die or move away to a faraway place such as a town or country. "**If I did know**," as many of us sometimes say is just a little too late. Therefore, do not be unwilling to forgive, instead be bold and be strong enough to forgive. Do not allow your heart to be so hard and cold towards forgiving others but know that to forgive takes desire and effort. Moreover, we cannot fully enjoy our salvation and fellowship with God with unforgiveness in our hearts.

When we forgive we pardon and excuse the offender the person who hurts us. In forgiveness we release and let go of the wrong they have done to us and we reconcile our differences. Forgiveness means that we have resolved the problem with the person and it is settled. In a case where the person does not want to work with you forgive that person anyway and move on. Now we are ready to be **reconciled** to God and to one another. Our reconciliation to God involves the exercise of His grace and the forgiveness of our sin. The result of Jesus' sacrifice on the cross is that our relationship with God has changed from hostility to friendship. "*I no longer call you servants. Instead, I have called you friends*" (John 15:15). In like manner our relationship with the person who wronged us should be changed from enmity to peace, respect, and fellowship.

Christian **reconciliation** is a glorious truth and experience for the forgiven! We were God's enemies but now we are His friends. We were in a state of condemnation because of our sins but we are now forgiven. Once we were at war with God but now we are at peace with Him. "*The peace of God that transcends all understanding and will guard our hearts and minds in Christ Jesus*" (Philippians 4:7).

Without **forgiveness** and **reconciliation** the conflict continues and even though it may be dormant if it is left unresolved it could resurface again and in some situations could become a feud. It could even escalate into something big and harmful such as inflicting hurt verbally or physically on the next person. The Bible says that Christ reconciled us to God and so likewise we must be reconciled with one another. To follow through takes a heart of love and a desire to forgive.

> ***Therefore, if you are offering your gift at the altar and there remember that your brother has something against you, leave your gift there in front of the altar. First go and be reconciled to your brother; then come and offer your gift***" (Matthew 5:23-24).

The fact that we needed **reconciliation** means that our relationship with God was broken. Since God is Holy, we were the ones who strayed away from His presence. "***All we like sheep have gone astray, we have turned everyone in his own way***" (Isaiah 53:6). It is our sin that alienated us from God and the Bible says that we were enemies of God: "***For if, when we were God's enemies, we were reconciled to him through the death of his Son, how much more, having been reconciled, shall we be saved through his life***!" (Romans 5:10). (2 Corinthians 5:18 & Colossians 1:20-21).

Self forgiveness is a crucial step in the cleansing and healing of our hearts and souls and we should also learn to forgive ourselves. To be transparent, I found that it can be harder to forgive myself and easier to forgive others. Believe me, your broken heart needs your forgiveness in order to recover and heal so forgive yourself.

To recover from heartbreak is very difficult to do and can be dramatic. This is emotional hurt and it takes time, so, be patient with yourself while being intentional about your healing. Our human nature is to seek revenge and not forgiveness but that is not what God requires and that behavior does not lead to healing. God calls upon us to have the mind of Christ (1 Corinthians 2:16) and with the mind of Christ it becomes easier for us to forgive. Forgiveness is a Christ like desire and as children of God we operate in the Spirit and not the flesh. Since we are spirit it is in the spirit that we forgive. The Holy Spirit dwells in our hearts through faith in God who gives salvation.

> *Forbearing one another, and forgiving one another, if any man have a quarrel against any; even as Christ forgave you, so also do you* (Colossians 3:13).

> *Judge not, and you shall not be judged; condemn not, and you shall not be condemned; forgive, and you shall be forgiven* (Luke 6:37).

You must forgive others the way God forgives and you must love others the way God loves. Some people will not forgive you even when you ask for their forgiveness. You should try not to be that person. For the well-being of your own soul be quick to forgive others even when they did not request your forgiveness. If you ask someone for forgiveness and they choose not to forgive

you, go ahead and forgive them anyway, forgive yourself and move forward into your divine healing knowing
that you have the forgiveness of Almighty God Himself.
"*For thou, Lord, art good, and ready to forgive, and
plenteous in mercy unto all them that call upon thee*"
(Psalm 86:5).

CHAPTER 27

God's Inner Work

Growing Into Wholeness

He who dwells in the secret place of the Most High; Shall abide under the shadow of the Almighty. I will say of the Lord, 'He is my refuge and my fortress; My God, in Him I will trust' (Psalm 91:1-2).

"When the enemy shall come in like a flood, the Spirit of the Lord shall lift up a standard against him" (Isaiah 59:19).

After you have forgiven those who have inflicted hurt upon your heart ask God for a new and clean heart to start loving again. During this period of healing the Holy Spirit is doing a great **inner work** inside of your heart and this is the **fortification** of your heart and soul taking place! Invite and allow the Lord to build a strong tower of protection around your soul. You alone know that God is doing a great work on the inside of your broken heart. This is the power and presence of the indwelling Holy Spirit who is keeping watch over your soul. This tower of protection does not mean that you will never be hurt again but it does mean that you will be better prepared to deal with whatever the circumstances are in the spirit of love and forgiveness.

After we forgive, truly forgive, then comes the period of advance level inner work in our hearts. This is when the Holy Spirit repairs our hearts from the damage it encountered. This is a time of reassurance and comfort by the Holy Spirit and it is refreshing. Remember that during the beginning and earlier stages of your broken-ness journey you went through a period of dormancy. At this station, you are also experiencing a period of dormancy for God is doing His inner work in your heart and no one can see it. This ***inner work is a quiet and reflective time***. Here we look back from whence we came and the experiences we encountered along the way. We meditate and thank the Almighty God for the experiences and the person we have become and con-tinue to become as a result of those experiences. In this place of dormancy we can envision the place of **whole-ness** with zeal and the person we will become when we reach that place of complete healing and whole-ness from our broken hearts. ***Overcoming Brokenness Growing Into Wholeness*** is a very meaningful journey. Glory hallelujah to God be the glory! You should take some well deserved time to shout for joy!

This is a wonderful and powerful period in the journey when you feel that you are heading in the right direction. No one can see with the natural eyes the great work that is taking place on the inside of your heart but at the same time this great inner work should be reflected in the spirit that you carry. New life and renewed hope are given birth on the inside of your heart and your inner man is being fortified.

Testify with confidence and tell everyone who will listen what the Good Lord has done for you! Be courageous and tell them: *I am in my right season in the cycle of my change for God is doing a great work inside of my heart!* So often change in our season of life can cause broken heartedness that even our spirit can be broken because we are afraid of the change that the new season brings but be reminded that this can be a great period but you must see it through your eyes of faith. This period of change is a time to regroup and prepare for your new season and purpose. This is a season of abundance in terms of what is taking place inside of your heart.

Yes Lord I get it! At this place in my journey I am spending much more time with God and enjoying His presence. I am flourishing like the tree planted by the side of the river (Psalm 1). A wonderful birthing is taking place and about to come forth in my springtime. Hallelujah! This was my experience and it was refreshing and comforting. This is the experience that is available to you by the help of God.

As someone who loves gardening I will use my perennial plants to illustrate this point. During the fall and winter these beautiful plants fade away and eventually disappear completely from the surface of the ground. In early and middle spring they begin to burst through the ground into new life and they grow quickly with new attitudes of readiness for the spring and summer conditions.

When they bloom they add such colorful beauty to my garden. During the time of dormancy these plants are nurtured and fortified underground in preparation for the next cycle of their lives. Likewise in your period of brokenness you are fed and nurtured by the Holy Spirit and the Living Word of God.

In our spiritual dormancy the enemy might assume that we are defeated but we are not defeated we have food to eat which they know not of. "***In the mean while his disciples prayed him, saying, Master, eat. But Jesus said unto them, 'I have meat to eat that you know not of***" (John 4:31-32). We will emerge from dormancy with great desire and determination to operate in our purpose.

CHAPTER 28

Healing

Growing Into Wholeness

So he cried out to the Lord, and the Lord showed him a tree. When he cast it into the waters, the waters were made sweet. There He made a statue and an ordinance for them, and there He tested them, and said, 'If you diligently heed the voice of the Lord your God and do what is right in His sight, give ear to His commandments and keep all His statues, I will put none of the diseases on you which I have brought on the Egyptians. For I am the Lord who heals you (Exodus 15:25-26).

G od delights in our healing both physical and spiritual. *Confess your trespasses to one another, and pray for one another, that you may be healed. The effective, fervent prayer of a righteous man avails much* (James 5:16). The greatest healing is that of our hearts and souls and this is far more valuable than the physical healing of the body. The body is material and temporary while the soul is immaterial and eternal. When our hearts are healed we are released from the entanglement of the circumstances that affected our relationship with God and others. The healing of the physical body is very important because our bodies are temples of the Holy Spirit and therefore they should be healthy. Also, God desires that our bodies be in good health.

To honor God in our bodies we must take care of our physical bodies in order to be healthy. Although physical health and wellness are important God is more deeply concerned about the healing of our souls and the cleansing of our hearts. "*Dear friend, I pray that you may enjoy good health and that all may go well with you, even as your soul is getting along well*" (3 John 1:2).

Getting over heartbreak to a place of healing is a serious fight that you have to engage in and this is not a physical fight it is spiritual. "*For we fight not against flesh and blood, but against principalities, against powers, against the rulers of the darkness of this world, against spiritual wickedness in high places*" (Ephesians 6:12). This is the fight of your life and this fight requires your strongest weapons. These weapons of your warfare are the Word of God and prayer among others. Revisit chapter one for the tools in your **survival kit** for you need them at every point of your journey. These are the weapons with which you will fight. Sometimes you will have to resort to prayer and fasting. At one point Jesus told His disciples that some things will only happen because of prayer and fasting. "*But this kind does not go out except by prayer and fasting*" (Matthew 17:21).

Some situations will call for you to labor before God for a long period of time in prayer and fasting.

Heartbreak causes grief and this could be a complex social, emotional or psychological experience that impacts us in multiple ways. When our hearts are broken they leave a void that is full of pain and hurt. This void must be cleansed and healed by the blood of Jesus. We must replace that pain with spiritual nutrients in order to repair and heal our hearts. We must feast on spiritual food. This food is called The Fruit of the Spirit. *"But the fruit of the Spirit is love, joy, peace, long-suffering, gentleness, goodness, faith, meekness, temperance: against such there is no law"* (Galatians 5:22-23). This is the food for the spirit and the soul and nothing else will satisfy.

The soul cannot be healed with the physical things that are needed to heal the physical body. God alone can heal the soul and it takes the cleansing blood of Jesus to heal the soul. Since our bodies are temples of the Holy Spirit we must be intentional about caring for our bodies. Likewise, our hearts must be cleansed for the Holy Spirit to dwell there. To maintain a healthy heart your heart must be saturated with the presence and indwelling of the Holy Spirit. A healthy heart thinks on certain things:

> *Finally, brethren, whatsoever things are true, whatsoever things are honest, whatsoever things are just, whatsoever things are pure, whatsoever things are lovely, whatsoever things are of good*

report; if there be any virtue, and if there be any praise, think on these things" (Philippians 4:8).

We must be mindful of our well-being and take care of the whole person including the body, soul and spirit in order to maintain a good balance between our soul health and our physical health. There is a connection of the body and soul "**Soul Care and Self Care.**" Soul care benefits self care and self care also benefits the soul directly or indirectly for when our bodies are well and our mind is at peace we are freer to worship God. We could be taking care of our physical bodies yet, neglect to care for our souls and this would not be wise. Although they both have different needs things go on in our bodies that affect our souls and things go on in our souls that affect our bodies. The body and soul are interrelated and interdependent on each other and they have an effect on each other.

In society there are many programs that focus on healthy practices for the maintenance of proper self care while not much attention is paid to soul care. Let me recommend that there are practices that we can and should engage in for proper soul care.

Self care is physical practices that include but not limited to- physical exercise, healthy diet, adequate sleep, relaxation, rest, reading, drinking water, nature walk, medical exams, proper hygiene, music, time with family and friends, laughing and so much more.

Soul Care is spiritual practices which mean that we live our lives with God by doing what He requires of us. He is our Good Shepherd and we are His sheep so we must trust His caring for us and His tending to our souls. God nurtures, corrects and guides us in the paths of righteousness for His name sake. Soul care practices are spiritual disciplines and they include but are not limited to- repentance, prayer, forgiveness, meditation, solitude, songs of praise, study of the Word, worship, fasting, serving others, music and other disciplines. With these practices you will be able to "**Stand fast therefore in the liberty where Christ has set you free, and be not entangled again with the yoke of bondage**" (Galatians 5:1).

Inner healing means that we practice spiritual disciplines and train our hearts and minds into these new habits and we allow God to reign fully in our hearts. When these practices become our daily habits it will be natural for us to live out our lives manifesting the qualities of the Fruit of the Spirit. Glory to God Almighty! Our goal is to be transformed into the image of Christ and having the mind of Christ. We should be patient and consistent for this is a long process which should be our daily lifestyle. Along the way our Heavenly Father will fill our hearts with joy to the overflowing and He will give us a song in our hearts to sing and a daily Word to empower us in our daily walk.

To maintain your status of being healed is a daily effort and so I suggest and highly recommend that you begin each day with your devotional time and this you will find make a very big difference in your spiritual growth and development. By so doing, your day will be rich with peace, joy, and songs of praise in your heart.

CHAPTER 29

Peace

Growing Into Wholeness

"Let the peace of Christ rule in your hearts, since as members of one body you were called to peace. And be thankful"
(Colossians 3:15).

"Make every effort to live in peace with everyone and to be holy; without holiness no one will see the Lord"
(Hebrews 12:14).

During your healing process there is a peace that will flood your soul and you will want to rejoice. *"Thou wilt keep him in perfect peace, whose mind is stayed on thee: because he trusteth in thee"* (Isaiah 26:3). Here you are like a sunbeam and a bright shining star for you will glow and shine with such radiance because of the settled peace in your heart. The hurt in your heart is subsiding and the peace of your soul is shining through. Having purged your heart and soul of anger, grief, denial, bitterness, fear, and guilt, your hurt begins to subside and is replaced with forgiveness and the peace of your heart and mind increases.

Everyone who enters your presence can sense that there is a unique and special spirit residing inside of you that cannot be ignored. It is the presence of God that resides in your heart in His fullness in the person of the Holy Spirit. This is a peace that no one but God can give. It is a peace that anchors your soul for it gives you strength and makes you able to cope with and handle the cares and stressors of life.

The power of the Holy Spirit is always your support. "***So he said to me, This is the word of the Lord to Zerubbabel: 'Not by might nor by power, but by my Spirit' says the Lord Almighty***" (Zechariah 4:6). You do not feel overcome and defeated anymore because you have the power of the Holy Spirit dwelling inside of you. Oh yes, you are on your journey to complete healing and wholeness and you will get there by the power of God. "***Peace I leave with you; my peace I give you. I do not give to you as the world gives. Do not let your hearts be troubled and do not be afraid***" (John 14:27).

You can now sing the beautiful hymn of the church, "*When peace like a river attends my way, when sorrow like sea billows roll, whatever my lot thou has taught me to say it is well, it is well with my soul.*" You can sing this hymn because you entered and went through the "***tunnel of purging***" where you washed and cleansed yourself from those impurities and with the help of the Holy Spirit you patiently pushed your way through to the end of that tunnel. Presently you are travelling through the "**tunnel of healing**" and you are at that place in your journey where you can see some sign of light at the end of the tunnel. As you get closer to the end of the tunnel the light will be brighter and the complete deliverance and restoration of your soul will take place and you will receive great rest and greater peace. This is not a physical rest but rest from spiritual warfare. At the end of this tunnel liberation awaits you so pursue it with vigor and excitement!

THIS IS A WONDERFUL PLACE TO BE!
HALLELUJAH!

"*If it is possible, as far as it depends on you, live at peace with everyone*" (Romans 18:18).

"*Let us therefore make every effort to do what leads to peace and to mutual edification*" (Romans 14:19).

CHAPTER 30

Wellness And Wholeness

Growing Into Wholeness

"Be perfect, therefore, as your heavenly father is perfect"
(Matthew 5:48).

"Seek good, and not evil, that you may live; and so the Lord,
the God of hosts, shall be with you, as you have spoken"
(Amos 5:14).

"Because it is written, 'You shall be holy, for I am holy"
(1 Peter 1:16).

Wellness and wholeness are your ultimate goal which you are pursuing. It is your desire to overcome your brokenness and grow into your wholeness and purpose. That which caused your heart to hurt is now in the past and does not have control over your heart and soul anymore. You have confronted the source of your pain and broken heart for you spoke 'death' to that thing. By God's grace that situation is now trampled under your feet by the power of the Holy Spirit and so you declare it dead.

God calls on us to be holy for He is holy and since we are His people His desire is that we be well and whole in our hearts, souls and bodies. There is a moral perfectness that God expects us to live up to and if the Holy Spirit dwells richly within our hearts it will be by His strength that we are able to live the life God requires of us to live. The Word of God says that no sin can enter heaven and so we have to practice holy living here in this present life if we intend to make it to heaven. "*If we confess our sins, he is faithful and just to forgive us our sins and to cleanse us from all unrighteousness*" (1 John 1:9). God calls us to righteous living, which is godly Christian living. "*Be holy, because I am holy*" (1 Peter 1:16).

God has a standard of moral living with which we must comply. God does not have double standards and therefore everyone must comply and practice God's standards. "*Not everyone who says to me, 'Lord, Lord,' will enter the kingdom of heaven, but the one who does the will of my Father who is in heaven*" (Matthew 7:21).

Wellness is your healing and it means that you are in good health which is the state of your physical, mental, and social well being and you are also making healthy life choices.

Wholeness on the other hand, is the complete and harmonious whole of your spirit, soul, and body. Wholeness means that your heart and soul are purged, cleansed, restored and transformed to the wholeness state that God intended in His original plan. Adam and Eve were first whole which means they were without sin but after they disobeyed God they became broken and sinful. Sin crept into their hearts and they were no longer whole but God in His loving mercy restored them. Through God's plan of salvation He has redeemed us back to himself. God is calling us to wholeness and as He did for Adam and Eve by giving them a choice, so likewise, He gives us the free will to choose.

Wholeness is not a destination it is a daily journey. When you get to the wholeness stage of your journey you are at a new and quite different dimension of your spiritual development in Christ your Lord. This is a place of great joy and fullness of joy. Your journey takes on new experiences including some challenges as well. At this point you are not a babe drinking and requiring milk anymore but you are eating the meat of the Gospel which is the Word of God. "*Like newborn babies, crave pure spiritual milk, so that by it you may grow up in your salvation, now that you have tasted that the Lord is good*" (1 Peter 2:2-3).

Wholeness is life in its fullness in Christ and it is a way of daily godly living. Jesus says, "*If any man will come after me let him deny himself, take up his cross daily and follow me*" (Luke 9:23). Be aware that this wholeness is a state of heart and mind and not a destination where you lay all your armor down. This is a daily journey so fight on and keep fighting. Jesus says, "*My yoke is easy and my burden is light*" (Matthew 11:28). This is a time when your entire being comes into new life and God's desire is that your soul prospers. The

Word of God says, "***Dear friend, I pray that you may enjoy good health and that all may go well with you, even as your soul is getting along well***" (3 John 1:2).

Brokenness brings grief and pain but wholeness brings joy and peace in the Holy Spirit. At this stage of your journey with the peace God gives and the help of the Holy Spirit you are better prepared to deal with the challenges of life. Please know that your journey continues so journey on Child of the Most High God and be confident that victory is yours in the name of Christ Jesus.

CHAPTER 31

Rest

Growing Into Wholeness

"Truly my soul finds rest in God; my salvation comes from him" (Psalms 62:1).

"Come unto me, all ye that labor and are heavy laden, and I will give you rest" (Matthew 11:28-29).

It is time for you to take a deep breath and rest. After labor comes rest, and after a long and hard day's labor, we all seek rest for our bodies. *"And he said, My presence shall go with thee, and I will give thee rest"* (Exodus 33:14). To prepare for our physical rest we take a shower; eat a meal; relax; sleep and replenish the physical body and rest mentally for the next day's work. On this spiritual healing journey you have labored through your **tunnel purging** and you are now cleansed and ready for rest from those things that were of concern to you. What a relief knowing that it is time to rest! You have come a long way by God's grace. By your determination you are navigating your way through the **Tunnel Healing** and you have now arrived at the station of rest. Going through the "Power Stations" brings great hope and soul rest! This is the rest of your soul from all the difficult things it encountered that are not soul friendly or soul healthy.

> ***And it shall come to pass in the day that the Lord shall give thee rest from thy sorrow, and from thy fear, and from the hard bondage wherein you were made to serve*** (Isaiah 14:3).

Now you have the peace of God and the Holy Spirit is in full control of your heart. "***For I do not do the good I want to do, but the evil I do not want to do, this I keep on doing***" (Romans 7:19). The Holy Spirit is your helper and you must be strong in the Lord and the power of His might to maintain this rest of your soul. Here at this station your soul is not restless anymore. Instead, your soul is at rest in peace with God as you stand courageously by God's grace to enter the rest only God provides.

At this stage your soul is liberated and you are free to worship God to the fullest in Spirit and in truth. Here at this station along your journey your heart, mind and thoughts are centered on loving, serving, pleasing and praising God. "***God is a Spirit: and they who worship Him must worship Him in spirit and in truth***" (John 4:24). God has called us to rest and this is the rest of our souls and this is rest from sin and worry. This is rest from anything that stands in your way preventing you from freely worshipping and praising God. This rest is liberation of the spirit from all that could cause emotional pain and heart hurt.

Here at this station rest, you give all worries up to God for He alone has all the answers and you have labored long and hard enough. You have fought a good fight for your healing and you deserve to be healed and experience rest for this is God's desire for you. Enjoy your well deserved rest!

CHAPTER 32

Love

Growing Into Wholeness

A new command I give you: Love one another. As I have loved you, so you must love one another. By this everyone will know that you are my disciples, if you love one another (John 13:34-35).

"And over all these virtues put on love, which binds them all together in perfect unity" (Colossians 3:14).

W hat is love? *"Above all, love each other deeply, because love covers over a multitude of sins"* (1 Peter 4:8). God is love and in Him there is no wrong doing. Love is not a word it is action. Love is a way of life and this means that we do what is right by making good choices. We must love God deeply and completely without reservation. If we love God the way He requires us to love then we will be able to love others the way we should according to what God requires. God demonstrates His love to us by His plan of salvation in sending Jesus His Son to die on the Cross of Calvary in our place.

We cannot say we love God and not treat others in love and kindness. *"Whoever claims to love God yet hates a brother or sister is a liar. For whoever does not love their brother and sister, whom they have seen, cannot love God, whom they have not seen"* (1 John 4:20). It is not humanly possible for us to do the things God requires unless the love of God is shed abroad richly in our hearts. Our hearts need to first be saturated with the love of God if we are to love others as God requires. God loves us unconditionally and He expects us to love Him unconditionally. *Love the Lord your God with all your heart and with all your soul and with all your mind and with all your strength"* (Mark 12:30).

It is in our hearts that we love and not with our words only. When we love in our hearts we will speak it, live it, and sincerely show it in our actions. If love is not in our hearts we will speak it but there will be no evidence for our actions will be the opposite of what we say. Child of the Most High God, with your heart healed you are ready to love sincerely even those who have hurt you.

"Do everything in love" (1 Corinthians 16:14).

"Dear children, let us not love with words or speech but with actions and in truth" (1 John 3:18).

"***Whoever does not love does not know God, because God is love***" (1 John 4:8).

Love is patient, love is kind. It does not envy, it does not boast, it is not proud. It does not dishonor others, it is not self seeking, it is not easily angered, it keeps no record of wrongs (1Corinthins 13:4-5).

CHAPTER 33

Humility

Growing Into Wholeness

"Humble yourselves before the Lord, and he will lift you up"
(James 4:10).

"Humility is the fear of the Lord; its wages are riches and honor and life" (Proverbs 22:4).

H umility is a sign of good character and humility is not weakness but it is wisdom and a great Christian quality. *"Be completely humble and gentle; be patient, bearing with one another in love"* (Ephesians 4:2). Humility is a condition or attitude of the human heart. Humility of heart means that one has a sincere heart that is compassionate and kind. Someone with a humble spirit has a humble heart and does not go around boasting or humiliating other people. It will not be difficult to identify someone who is humble for humility is a behavior and an attitude that is coming from the heart. I believe that humility is a virtue of the heart and I also believe that it is hard to be humble by human effort. It is the power of the indwelling Holy Spirit in our hearts who enables us through His power to be humble.

Jesus Christ is our perfect example of what humility should be when He washed His disciples' feet. Jesus showed humility when He rode on a donkey. When Jesus left His splendor of heaven and came to earth this demonstrates His humility. "*The Word became flesh and made His dwelling among us. We have seen his glory, the glory of the one and only Son, who came from the Father, full of grace and truth*" (John 1:14). Jesus' ultimate humility was His death on the Cross of Calvary for the sin of the world. Someone who is humble is not prideful or self centered. It is in humility that we serve others with an attitude of love.

> "*For the Lord takes delight in his people; he crowns the humble with victory*" (Psalm 149:4).

> "*Before a downfall the heart is proud, but humility comes before honor*" (Proverbs 18:12).

> "*He guides the humble in what is right and teaches them his way*" (Psalm 25:9).

CHAPTER 34

Grace And Mercy

Growing Into Wholeness

"Let us then approach the throne of grace with confidence, so that we may receive mercy and find grace to help us in our time of need" (Hebrews 4:16).

Three times I pleaded with the Lord to take it away from me. But he said to me, 'My grace is sufficient for you, for my power is made perfect in weakness (2 Corinthians 12:9).

God's Divine Grace: The word grace originally meant "God's favor or help." God's grace gives you strength to endure trials and resist the temptation to do that which is wrong. By His grace God gives you and me that which we do not deserve because of our sinfulness. Our loving Heavenly Father gives us grace through His Son Jesus Christ. Through this grace we obtain spiritual power and healing.

God's divine Mercy: God in His mercy withholds from us the punishment and judgment (condemnation and death) which we deserve. This grace that God has given us imparts strength within us to endure trials and resist temptation. Grace (Greek *charis, charitoo*; Latin *gratia*; "favor." "kindness") unmerited favor.

Through the work of God's grace in Christ our sins are forgiven and our relationship with God is restored. Ephesians 1:6 tells us that by God's grace (unmerited favor), God "made us accepted in the Beloved." "***God made him who had no sin to be sin for us, so that in him we might become the righteousness of God***" (2 Corinthians 5:21). With God's divine favor upon your life this is supernatural blessing from God Himself in any and all areas of your life as God pleases. God's grace is His divine favor that gives you supernatural ability to operate in your purpose. This grace gives you favor with God and with man. With God's grace and favor upon your life this is your seal of protection.

As long as you obey God's Word and follow His instructions He will show you favor and place people in your path to assist you in your purpose. God chose you and extend His grace to you giving you divine favor because you proved yourself to be faithful, obedient, gentle, kind, humble and trusting. Deep in your heart you are sincere and committed to the task to which God has called you. God's favor upon your life is for His divine purpose in using you to make a difference in the lives of many in bringing to them the Gospel of Salvation. When God anoints you with His divine favor this means that He can trust you for He knows your heart.

To keep me from becoming conceited because of these abundance of great revelations, there was given me a thorn in my flesh, a messenger of Satan, to torment me, lest I should be exalted above measure. Three times I pleaded with the Lord to take it away from me. But he said to me, 'My grace is sufficient for you, for my power is made perfect in weakness.' Therefore I will boast all the more gladly about my weaknesses, so that Christ's power may rest on me. That is why, for Christ's sake, I delight in weaknesses, in insults, in hardships, in persecutions, in difficulties. For when I am weak, then I am strong (2 Corinthians 12:7-10).

God's amazing grace towards us is due to His divine love for us. "*For God so loved the world, that He gave His only Son, that whosoever believes in him should not perish but have everlasting life*" (John 3:16). It is by God's grace that we are saved. God wants us to come boldly to the throne of grace. "*My grace is sufficient for you.*" God said it to you, to me, to everyone, and to whosoever will. This is true today and will always be true for God's Word does not change and He does not and will not change.

How should we come before God? Come boldly to the throne of grace without doubt, and without fear. As you come it requires that you have trust. Come in faith believing and trusting God completely.

Where should we come? God said, come boldly to the throne of grace. **What is the object that we seek**? The object that we seek is grace, God's amazing grace. Through grace God gives us what we do not deserve which is His forgiveness, and His saving grace. God extends to us his mercy by not giving us what we deserve which is punishment, and condemnation, instead He gives us forgiveness. This is God's redeeming grace. If you are not saved you need God's **redeeming grace**. If you are saved you need God's **sustaining grace**.

When should we come? We should come right now! When God calls it is now. He says, "Today is the day of Salvation." We should come because we need God's sustaining grace for strength to sustain us in time of need. He told Paul, "*My grace is sufficient for you.*" God's grace is greater than all of your circumstances for His *amazing grace gives us power*. We should rejoice in God's grace. David says it best, "***Enter into his gates with thanksgiving and into his courts with praise. Be thankful unto Him and bless His name***" (Psalms 100:4).

I am inviting you to picture a very serious storm: When a serious storm is approaching we are warned by the meteorologist and the weather reports are relentless, warning us to prepare for the storm. We are given warnings and instructions on- [1 places to avoid; [2 supplies that we should store; [3 how to protect our property such as our houses, cars and pets; [4 the types of food to stock away; [5 bottled water; [6 self protection by having a place to hide or an evacuation plan. We do all these things to prepare and be ready for the storm in the natural and those who prepare are likely to save themselves from disaster.

Often times there are those who do not heed the warnings and when the storm is in full effect they are caught unprepared so they seek refuge on the roof of a house then they are trapped and surrounded by water with no way of escape. Some climb in a tree, and eventually they are carried away by flood waters downstream. This is the result of not preparing! Well, likewise in the spiritual we need to prepare for warfare, attacks and the storms of life of every kind. You will receive sufficient grace at the throne of God to prepare and shield you during your trials.

For the benefit of our spiritual growth we need to do as God commands. God's grace is available to everyone who seeks for it. This grace is God's provision and yours for the asking. "***Ask and it shall be given unto you, seek and you shall find, knock and it shall be opened***" (Matthew 7:7). People of God we need to be ready for the storms of life. We need to fortify our souls with God's amazing grace and God's sustaining grace. God is the one we are approaching for our supply of grace and He is the one who occupies the throne of grace.

Allow me to engage you: I want you to think for a moment of a court case. It could be a Federal case, state case or county case. In any of these cases there is a judge who presides over the case. As the defendant and his or her attorney approach the bench, sometimes they have no confidence that the judge who presides over the case will be just and fair to their case. Sometimes the attorney may request that a particular judge recuses or removes himself or herself from the case for reasons of bias. The Bible calls such a judge an unjust judge.

Well, as children of God, we too have a judge who presides over our cases and this judge is God Himself. The throne of grace is occupied by God himself and He is God Almighty; the Righteous Judge; the giver of life; He is your heavenly Father; our compassionate God; the maker of heaven and earth; He is the God of Abraham, Isaac and Jacob. Glory hallelujah! Child of God, you are not approaching the judgment throne, you are approaching the throne of grace.

As you approach the throne of grace you must consider who is sitting on the throne. Think for a moment when we invite people to church we say to them "come as you are." However, after they come it is our responsibility to teach them what God expects of them. They cannot remain the way they are. There must be some transformation of heart, attitude and behavior.

As you approach God the Righteous Judge who occupies the throne of grace here are some things that you cannot take with you.

1. You cannot take **fear**: Fear is not of God. *"God has not given us a spirit of fear; but of power, love and sound mind"* (2 Timothy 1:7).
2. You cannot take **doubt**: *"But when you ask, you must believe and not doubt, because the one who doubts is like a wave of the sea, blown and tossed by the wind. That person should not expect to receive anything from the Lord"* (James 1:5-8).

3. You cannot take **pride**: "God looks at the proud from a distance" (Psalm 138:6).
4. You cannot take **un-forgiveness**: *"But if you do not forgive others their sins, your Father will not forgive your sins"* (Matthew 6:15).
5. You cannot take **unbelief**: *"See to it, brothers and sisters, that none of you has a sinful, unbelieving heart that turns away from the living God"* (Hebrews 3:12). *"Can God really prepare a table in the wilderness?"* (Psalm 78:19).
6. You cannot take **disobedience**. *"It is better to obey God rather than man"* (Acts 5:29). *"So whoever knows the right thing to do and fails to do it, for him it is sin"* (James 4:17).
7. There are a host of other things that you cannot take with you when you approach the throne of grace to face God.

These are the instructions on how you are expected to approach the throne of grace and they are not optional.

1. Approach **boldly in faith**- come boldly unto the throne of grace (Hebrews 4:16); Come in faith and with confidence and full assurance for without faith it is impossible to please God (Hebrews 11:6).
2. Approach **with prayer**- and come rejoicing. *"Rejoice always, pray without ceasing, give thanks in all circumstances; for this is the will of God in Christ Jesus for you"* (1 Thessalonians 5:16).

3. Approach **in fasting**- "*This kind does not go out except by prayer and fasting*" (Matthew 17:21).

4. Approach **with praise**- "*I will bless the Lord at all times, His praise shall continually be in my mouth*" (Psalm 34:1).

5. Approach **with love**- "*Love the Lord your God with all your heart, with all of your soul and with all your mind*" (Matthew 22:37).

6. Approach **with patience**- "*Wait on the Lord, be of good courage, and he shall strengthen your heart*" (Psalm 27:14). "*They that wait on the Lord shall renew their strength ...*" (Isaiah 40:31).

7. Approach **with humility**- "*Humble yourself in the sight of the Lord and he will in due time lift you up*" (James 4:10).

8. Approach with **rejoicing, thanksgiving and praise**- "*Enter into his gates with thanksgiving and into his courts with praise, be thankful unto him and bless His name for the Lord is good*" (Psalm 100:4).

As you move forward in approaching the throne of grace, you must bear in mind that God is the righteous judge and His word is final. God has said it and it is so. "***I am the Lord and I change not***" (Malachi 3:6). "*So shall my word be that goeth forth out of my mouth; it shall not return unto me void, but it shall accomplish that which I please, and it shall prosper in the thing whereto I sent it*" (Isaiah 55:11). People of God, use God's Word to your advantage and bring glory to His name. God's Word is alive, active and it is powerful! Man cannot live by bread alone (physical), but by every Word that comes from the mouth of God (we need bread the Word of God for the soul) (Matthew 4:4). God says that we should remind Him of His word. "***Put me in remembrance: let us plead together: declare you, that you may be justified***" (Isaiah 43:26).

Whatever your thorn may be, do not pray asking God to remove your thorn, instead ask God for grace to endure your thorns. God will give you power, the power of the Holy Spirit to overcome any and all of your circumstances. God's grace is power to save and power to keep you from failing or falling. ***Three times Paul prayed asking God to remove his thorn*** but God said no, my grace is sufficient for you and my strength perfect in your weakness (2 Corinthians 12:8-10). There are many speculations concerning what Paul's thorn might have been. Paul did not say what the thorns were therefore it is not for us to know.

What we do know is the reason for Paul's thorn which I find to be more important. Paul knew why the thorn was given and he said, "*To keep me from becoming conceited, due to powerful visions and revelations I was privileged to have there was given to me a thorn in my flesh*" (2 Corinthians 12:7).

This reminds me of Peter. When Jesus asked his disciples, "Who do men say that I the Son of Man am? They all gave various answers but Peter said, "*You are the Christ, the Son of the Living God*" (Matthew 16:16). Jesus confirmed Peter's response by telling him that he was right but he did not know this on his own it was God who revealed it to him. "*My Father in heaven has revealed this truth to you*" (Matthew 16:17). Then Jesus warned Peter that he should not become boastful or conceited because he received the revelation from God.

The qualities of God's grace cannot be compared:

- **God's grace is reliable**. "God remains the same, yesterday, today and forever more.
- **God's grace is dependable**- it cannot and will not fail, it never has.
- **God's grace is sufficient**- it is enough for you to endure your thorn
- **God's grace is divine favor**- this is God's kindness to you
- **God's grace is universal**- it is for whosoever will. It is available to everyone
- **God's grace is effective**- in those to whom it is given there will be results
- **God's grace is powerful!** It is the power of God to save and keep

The character of our God cannot be questioned! He is God Almighty and by his grace we are always victorious. God's grace is power, the same power that raised Christ from the dead. God's strength is made perfect in your weakness and in your weakness if you allow God He will activate His power inside of you. Anyone or anything that rises up against you cannot stand for the power of God that is inside of you is greater. Activate the power of God's grace that is in you and let it work on your behalf! God your Mighty Conqueror dwells inside of you in the person of the Holy Spirit and you will not be defeated! God told Moses, "*I Myself will go with you*" (Exodus 23).

As I meditate on God's amazing grace I have come to realize how inadequate my grasp of God's amazing grace is. We cannot fully comprehend the power of God's grace but we can understand enough to go boldly to the throne of grace to obtain our daily supply. Amen!

We cannot talk about God's grace in isolation of his love and mercy. With such great love God is merciful towards us. God's Mercy is his tender heart, and loving compassion. And so, *God extends to us his grace, his unmerited favor, giving us what we do not deserve. It cost God the ultimate price, His Son Jesus who became sin for us so that we may become the righteousness of God* (2 Corinthians 5:21). The thorns and circumstances that we face in life are to prevent us from relying on ourselves and instead rely on God divine strength.

Do you have God's grace stored up in abundant supply for your time of need? Remember, you cannot exhaust the source for God is the source of your grace. If you store away a limited supply you may have a problem in your time of need when you realize that you run out or you do not have enough. The more time you spend in the Word of God and in prayer is the more you will increase in the things of God and in faith. You must grow in grace and in the knowledge of God! God's grace has empowered us to do what we cannot do by ourselves. Why then in the midst of our thorns and snares we falter and fail? It is because we lack awareness and complete dependence on God and we fail to ask for His grace.

Since God's grace is so powerful instead of asking God to remove your broken heart (your thorn), ask him for enough grace to endure that which you are going through. It takes the power of God's grace to resist the devil and have him flee from you. The power of God is the Word of God. Therefore you should study and know the Word of God and use it. The Word of God is your greatest weapon. Jesus used the Word to defeat Satan and all those who opposed Him. Who can stand before us when we call on that great name, the name of Jesus? Remember that God's grace is enough for you and so you are not alone for God is right there with you and I am also.

God expects you to be generous in extending grace and mercy to others. Therefore, be compassionate towards others, be kind, forgiving, helpful and gentle. Consider God's grace and mercy towards you and do likewise to others.

CHAPTER 35

Nurture Your Soul

Growing Into Wholeness

"Gracious words are a honeycomb, sweet to the soul and healing to the bones" (Proverbs 16:24).

"The law of the Lord is perfect, refreshing the soul. The statues of the Lord are trustworthy, making wise the simple" (Psalm 19:7).

A mother cares for and nurtures her young child. Animals of the wild also care for their young in gentle ways and nurture them until they are able to survive on their own. As children grow, parents and care givers provide emotional support and encouragement as well as assist them in working through difficulties. It is your God given responsibility to initiate the nurturing of your own soul. You nurture your soul by taking very special care when you heed the Word of God and maintain your relationship with God. You cannot feed your heart and soul with the food you use to feed your body. The body is physical for it is from natural material the dust of the ground. The soul is immaterial (spirit) and cannot be fed with the same food. Jesus says, "***It is written: Man shall not live on bread alone but on every word that comes from the mouth of God***" (Matthew 4:4). To stay alive physically and be healthy, we must eat healthy food, we need fresh air, clean water, adequate sleep, regular rest and whatever else we should do to properly care for our physical bodies. If we neglect to take proper care of our bodies over time our health will decline.

In comparison, the human soul is the same. We must nurture our souls by intentionally feasting on the things of God that are found in the Word of God to stay healthy spiritually. "***Therefore, rid yourselves of all malice and all deceit, hypocrisy, envy, and slander of every kind. Like newborn babies, crave pure spiritual milk, so that by it you may grow up in your salvation***" (1 Peter 2:1-2).

> ***Then the Lord said to Moses, 'I will rain down bread from heaven for you. The people are to go out each day and gather enough for that day. In this way I will test them and see whether they will follow my instructions*** (Exodus 16:4).

The children of Israel needed a fresh supply of God's daily Manna and God did supply their daily food. In like manner God will give us His grace enough for each day. If we are to nurture and nourish our souls we must adhere to certain spiritual disciplines. The growth, health and good condition of the human soul requires that we read, meditate and study the Word of God daily. We also nurture our souls when we receive the Word through preaching and Bible study; the sacraments; worship; fellowship; and devotional times are all nutrients for the soul. Our hearts must be pure and we must reverence God and be in complete surrender to His will for our lives.

"*Blessed are those who hunger and thirst for righteousness, for they shall be filled*" (Matthew 5:6). To hunger and thirst means that one has a deep desire for more of God and the things of God. You are hungry and thirsty for righteousness by having a deep longing for more of God who will without fail satisfy your longing soul. "*As the deer pants for streams of water, so my soul pants for you, my God. My soul thirsts for God, for the living God. When can I go and meet with God*?" (Psalm 42:1-2).

The more we desire God and dwell in His presence is the more Christ like we will become and these Christ like qualities are The Fruit of The Spirit which are discussed in the next chapter.

CHAPTER 36

The Fruit Of The Spirit
Growing Into Wholeness

"But the fruit of the Spirit is love, joy, peace, patience, kind-ness, goodness, faithfulness, gentleness, self-control"
(Galatians 5:22-23).

"God is spirit: and they that worship him must worship him in spirit and in truth" (John 4:24).

A fruit bearing tree is known by the fruit it bears. So likewise a person's fruit will reveal the spirit you carry for the Scripture says that we are known by our love (John 13:35).

The Holy Spirit connects us to God for God is spirit and we cannot connect to Him in the physical. At this stage of your journey you intentionally cultivate the qualities of the Fruit of the Spirit and you have a deeper desire and thirst for more of God. It is here at this place that you are fully persuaded that the closer you get to God is the more you will grow to become more like the characteristics of the Fruit of the Spirit.

The Holy Spirit has only one fruit "***The Fruit of the Spirit***" and this fruit has nine godly attributes, characteristics or qualities which are actual manifestations of a true Christian's transformed life. In the natural (physical sense) we must eat food in order to nourish and sustain our physical life and well being. In the healing of your soul the Fruit of the Spirit is very essential. Our spiritual man, our souls must eat from the Word of God in order to live a healthy, victorious and prosperous spiritual life and grow daily in God's grace and knowledge of Christ. As we grow and become more like Christ it is the more pronounced the qualities of the Fruit of the Spirit will be in our lives.

Love: Love is the foundation that undergirds what the Holy Spirit is doing and love undergirds all the other qualities of the Fruit of the Spirit. Love is much more than a "word" it is action. Love is an attitude of good thoughts and actions towards others. God is love and Jesus says we should love God with all our heart, soul, mind and strength (Like 10:27). If we love God the way He requires of us it will not be hard to love one another. We cannot love God and walk in darkness by doing evil deeds.

> *Love is patient, love is kind. It does not envy, it does not boast, it is not proud. It does not dishonor others, it is not self-seeking, it is not easily angered, it keeps no record of wrong. Love does not delight in evil but rejoices with the truth. It always protects, always trusts,*

always hopes, always perseveres (1 Corinthians 13:4-7).

Joy: Joy is an inner gladness that you will have in the good times and also in the bad times. The indwelling Holy Spirit is the source of your joy and this joy makes you glad. "**Thou wilt show me the path of life; in thy presence there is fullness of joy; at his right hand pleasures for evermore**" (Psalm 16:11). If you linger in God's presence through His word, prayer, worship and songs of praise you will experience joy for to be in the presence of God gives joy. Someone can behave to be happy and still not have joy. "**In the presence of the Lord there is fullness of joy and at His right hand there are pleasures forevermore**" (Psalm 61:11). There is much strength in your joy. "**The joy of the Lord is my strength**" (Nehemiah 8:10). "The original Hebrew for "joy" in Nehemiah is "**chedvah**," meaning joy or gladness. The root word for joy in this context means to rejoice or to make glad. "Strength" in the same verse is a Hebrew word "**maw-oze**" which means "a fortified place, figuratively a defense force, rock, strength, fort or fortress, a place or means of safety, protection, refuge, or stronghold." The root word of strength means "to be strong, prevail, to make firm, and to strengthen." The joy of the Lord is a constant gladness and reason to rejoice. This joy comes from an inner strengthening from our relationship with God. Your joy rests in God through Christ Jesus. The joy of the Lord is strength of will, purpose, character, honesty and truth to do the right thing even if it is not the popular thing to do. (*Strong's Hebrew and Greek Dictionaries* explain joy).

Peace: The peace that God Himself gives is the assurance that God is in control of the universe. This peace is a place of power and reassurance from which you gain strength. Having this peace does not mean the absence of earthly problems and trials but it is the presence of a God who protects His people. "*Peace I leave with you, My peace I give to you; not as the world gives do I give to you. Let not your be troubled, neither let it be afraid*" (John 14:27). This is not an earthly peace that comes from earthly possessions, this peace comes from God Himself. "*Therefore, since we have been justified through faith, we have peace with God through our Lord Jesus Christ*" (Romans 5:1). We must first have peace with God in order to enjoy the peace of God.

Patience: (Longsuffering, perseverance, steadfastness): With this quality called patience you have the ability to endure mistreatment of life and from the hands of others. With this characteristic you are able to maintain your positive attitude without reacting and treating others unkindly. "*With all lowliness and meekness, with long-suffering, forbearing one another in love*" (Ephesians 4:2). Love undergirds everything and because of God's great love for us He is compassionate towards us. "*The Lord, the compassionate and gracious God, slow to anger, and rich in kindness and love (fidelity)*" (Exodus 34:6). With patience you wait just a little longer and you learn not to always be in a hurry.

Kindness: (Gentleness): Having a kind spirit will allow you to avoid thinking evil thoughts about others even if they did you wrong. With kindness in your heart you will find ways to be good to others and serve them in kindness and show favor to them. Our heavenly Father desires and expect us to live "*in purity, understanding, patience and kindness; in the Holy Spirit and in sincere love; in truthful speech and in the power of God; with weapons of righteousness in the right hand and in the left*" (2 Corinthians 6:6-7). We should seek to be kind to others in every way including our speech, behavior, and attitudes. "**And be ye kind one to another, tenderhearted, forgiving one another, even as God for Christ's sake hath forgiven you**" (Ephesians 4:32).

Goodness: With the character of goodness you desire to see goodness in others as well and not just in yourself. "**For the Fruit of the Spirit is in all goodness and righteousness and truth**" (Ephesians 5:9). Goodness is the quality of being morally good or virtuous. Goodness is good moral living by doing what is right and making good choices. With this character we do that which is good to others and we avoid doing that which is wrong.

Faithfulness: When a person is faithful that person has integrity and others can count on them. Faithfulness is evident in our actions when we cultivate and practice this quality. "**Let not steadfast love and faithfulness forsake you; bind them around your neck; write them on the tablet of your heart. So you will find favor and good success in the sight of God and man**" (Proverbs 3:3-4). When you are faithful others can count on you and your word will have meaning to them. In faithfulness you say what you mean and you mean what you say.

Gentleness: (Meekness): Gentleness is quiet strength it is sincere love and rooted in the Holy Spirit. "**Thou hast also given me the shield of thy salvation: and thy**

right hand hath holden me up, and thy gentleness hath made me great" (Psalm 18:35). Someone who is gentle is not abrasive in the treatment of others for this person considers the wellbeing of others. To be gentle means that you have the quality of being kind, tender, or mild mannered and there is a softness in your actions to others.

Self-Control (Temperance): Self control is a discipline and it requires patience. Someone who has self control does not act in an impulsive way but is subjected to the Holy Spirit's control. The person who exercises self control does not seek the desires of the flesh and the self but instead seeks the desires of the Holy Spirit. "*With all lowliness and meekness, with longsuffering, forbearing one another in love*" (Ephesians 4:2).

Cultivate these essential qualities of the Fruit of the Spirit and become a better you for yourself and others! You should manage and control your emotion, actions and feelings. With self control you wait and serve other before serving yourself. Self control helps us to resist temptation. The qualities of self control should include but are not limited to control of your thoughts, temper, fear, speech, and your actions.

CHAPTER 37

Integrity And Holiness
Growing Into Wholeness

"Because of my integrity you uphold me and set me in your presence forever" (Psalm 41:12).

"Make every effort to live in peace with everyone and to be holy; without holiness no one will see the Lord" (Hebrews 12:14).

"My integrity and uprightness protect me, because my hope, Lord, is in You" (Psalm 25:21).

To do what is right and just is more acceptable to the Lord than sacrifice (Proverbs 21:3) and this is integrity. With integrity you do the right thing whether or not it benefits you and whether or not it is the popular thing to do. Integrity is a fundamental value of Christian living. Holiness and integrity are intertwined and holy or godly living is what God requires from everyone. The goal of every Christian who is in a serious relationship with God is holiness and integrity without which no one will see God. "***Blessed are the pure in heart, for they will see God***" (Matthew 5:8). A person who lives a life of integrity cultivates the qualities of the Fruit of the Spirit which are love, joy, peace, patience, kindness, goodness, faithfulness, gentleness and self-control. "***For we are taking pains to do what is right, not only in the eyes of the Lord but also in the eyes of man***" (2 Corinthians 8:21). The person with integrity will always seek out the Lord's standards and live according to those standards. When you have integrity you are honest and truthful and all your other values are grounded in integrity which is godly living. God knows your heart and He can trust you to do the right thing even when it hurts if you have a heart of integrity.

> ***In everything set them an example by doing what is good. In your teaching show integrity, seriousness and soundness of speech that cannot be condemned, so that those who oppose you may be ashamed because they have nothing bad to say about us*** (Titus 2:7-8).

With a heart of integrity you seek to heal your heart from the hurt others inflicted on your soul so that your hurt does not become hate towards them. The standard of integrity that you seek in loving and serving God completely allows you to work on your inner healing so that your healing will flow in the spirit from your heart as living waters of righteousness. "***Whoever believes in*** *me, as Scripture has said, rivers of living water will flow from within them*" (John 7:38). This living water is the power of the Holy Spirit flowing freely from your heart because God finds integrity in your heart. God will always in His own time reveal to you the plot of the enemy so do not seek to take things in your own hands maintain your integrity. "*Because the Lord revealed their plot to me, I knew it, for at that time he showed me what they were doing*" (Jeremiah 11:18). There is no need for you to seek "payback" and turn the hurt of your broken heart into the pursuit of revenge on those who hurt you because the Good Lord has revealed their plots to you. Diligently work at maintaining your integrity and a clear conscience so that God can work with you without your interference. "*Keeping a clear conscience, so that those who speak maliciously against your good behavior in Christ may be ashamed of their slander*" (1 Peter 3:16). With integrity and holiness of heart you do not keep worrying about what people have done to you for this could drag your heart and soul into a place of hate and bitterness.

"*Whoever walks in integrity walks securely, but whoever takes crooked paths will be found out*" (Proverbs 10:9). Integrity of heart is the Christian and moral quality that you should always take a strong grip of and not let go so that the way you live your life and react towards those who mistreat you will reflect the bright light of God's love in you. The way you respond to those who mistreat you will reveal if you operate from a heart of integrity or not. Joseph is an excellent example of a life lived with integrity. In the book of Genesis we have the beautiful account of Joseph being sold by his brothers to Egyptians who took him to Egypt as a slave. While there in Egypt Joseph lived an impeccable life of integrity for which he experienced severe challenges of attacks and hardships including imprisonment but God favored him every step of the way because he lived a life of integrity. Eventually over time Joseph became the governor of Egypt and was able to rescue his family from the famine and also reunite with his brothers, his father and all of his family. Joseph was rewarded for his integrity for God was with him and prospered him, God showed him kindness, and God granted him favor. God will do the same for anyone with integrity and holiness of heart.

> **Finally, brothers and sisters, whatever is true, whatever is noble, whatever is right, whatever is pure, whatever is lovely, whatever is admirable- if anything is excellent or praiseworthy, think about such things** (Philippians 4:8). This is God's standard of integrity.

Soon after David became king he learnt of the death of his predecessor Saul and his son Jonathan. Although Saul was relentless in pursuing David to kill him due to jealousy, David was respectful to Saul. Jonathan knew David had done no wrong and they both forged a trusting and sincere relationship. Integrity of heart and love for his friend Jonathan guided David in not taking revenge on Saul's family members but instead he showed them favor for Jonathan's sake. Forgiving others will come easier when we have integrity of heart.

> **David said to him, 'Do not be afraid, for I will show you kindness for the sake of your father Jonathan; I will restore to you all the land of your grandfather Saul, and you yourself shall eat at my table always** (2 Samuel 9:7).

God please give me the grace to do what is right and honest for I want to be consistent in my love, uprightness and ethical principles according to the teachings of the Bible. My desire Lord is to be blessed with a heart full of integrity enough to be honest in maintaining a sincere and Christ like character.

REFLECTION

The Tunnel: Healing

Wow! Here you are at the end of your journey through the second and final **tunnel healing** and this is a great accomplishment which is worthy of celebrating. This was the goal from the beginning of your brokenness to wholeness journey to travel through the difficult tunnel of purging and then that of healing. Having gone through these two tunnels it is my prayer that you are now purged and healed enough to be able to pray sincerely for those who caused you such great heartbreak and pain. At this point you are very well positioned to continue your journey in pursuit of your wholeness and purpose.

You are at a place right now where many will try to pull you back and pull you down when they see what God is doing in your life and ministry. You should be comforted that having gone through these two tunnels you now have unmatched strength to press your way forward and your strength is much greater than the strength of those who wish to pull you back or pull you down.

Moving forward the goal is that you will fully embark on operating wholeheartedly in your divine purpose with great passion. I am convinced that your experiences gained from this journey have refined who you are in all or most areas of your life. Those to whom the Lord will have you minister are waiting on you. Be reminded that this is not the end of your purpose journey it is only the beginning of a new phase for you are **growing into wholeness and purpose**.

Part Five

Deliverance And Restoration

Biblical Examples
Of Deliverance From Brokenness

*"**You are my hiding place; you will protect me from trouble and surround me with songs of deliverance**"* (Psalm 32:7).

Deliverance: To be delivered is to be set free! In deliverance one is delivered and set free from physical bondage as in the case of the two biblical accounts of the two stories below. In deliverance one is set free in heart and soul from inner hurt and pain. This painful inner hurt is replaced with truth, forgiveness and repentance to bring about emotional and spiritual healing and liberation.

Restoration: In restoration God forgives us and cleanses our hearts and restores us to our original condition that He intended. Our hearts and souls are rescued from inner hurt and we are restored to peace with God and a heart full of joy.

The Bible gives numerous accounts of people who rose from brokenness to wholeness including Adam and Eve; The Prodigal Son; The Woman with the Issue of Blood; and Jesus Himself. "***The sacrifices of God are*** *a broken spirit; a broken and contrite heart, O God, you will not despise*" (Psalm 51:17). These individuals whom you will read about below were delivered and restored to wholeness. When we submit ourselves to God we give Him full control over our lives. He delivered the children of Israel with His mighty hand and He will do the same for you if you allow Him. In our present age God has delivered countless people including me and He will deliver you. "*Submit yourselves, then, to God. Resist the devil, and he will flee from you*" (James 4:7).

Peter's Miraculous Deliverance From Prison:

So Peter was kept in prison, but the church was earnestly praying to God for him. V6 The night before Herod was to bring him to trial, Peter was sleeping between two soldiers, bound with two chains, and sentries stood guard at the entrance. V7 Suddenly an angel of the Lord appeared and a light shone in the cell. He struck Peter on the side and woke him up. 'Quick, get up!' he said, and the chains fell off Peter's wrists. V8 Then the angel said to him, 'Put on your clothes and sandals.' And Peter did so. 'Wrap your cloak around you and follow me,' the angel told him. V9 Peter followed him out of the prison, but he had no idea that what the angel was doing was really happening; he thought he was seeing a vision. V10 They passed the first and second guards and came to the iron gate leading to the city. It opened for them by itself, and they went through it. When they had walked the length of one street, suddenly the angel left him.

V11 Then Peter came to himself and said, 'Now I know without a doubt that the Lord has sent his angel and rescued me from Herod's clutches and from everything the Jewish people were hoping would happen (Acts 12:5-11).

Deliverance of the Three Hebrew Boys:

And these three men, Shadrach, Meshach, and Abed-nego, fell down bound into the midst of the burning fiery furnace. V24 Then Nebuchadnezzar the king was astonished, and rose up in haste, and spake, and said unto his counselors, Did not we cast three men bound into the midst of the fire? They answered and said unto the king, True, O king. V25 He answered and said, Lo, I see four men loose, walking in the midst of the fire, and they have no hurt; and the form of the fourth is like the Son of God. v26 Then nebuchadnezzar came near to the mouth of the burning fiery furnace, and spake, and said, Shadrach, Meshach, and Abed-nego, ye servants of the Most High God, come forth, and come hither. Then Shadrach, Meshach, and Abed-nego, came forth of the midst of the fire. V27 And the princes, governors, and captains, and the king's counselors, being gathered together, saw these men, upon whose bodies the fire had no power, nor was an hair of their head singed, neither were their coats changed, nor the smell of fire had passed on them. V28 Then Nebuchadnezzar spake, and said, Blessed be the God of Shadrach, Meshach, and Abed-nego, who hath sent his angel, and delivered his servants that trusted in him, and have changed the king's word, and yielded their bodies, that they might

not serve nor worship any god, except their own God
(Daniel 3:23-28).

> "*You are my hiding place; you will pro-
> tect me from trouble and surround me
> with songs of deliverance*" (Psalm 32:7).

CHAPTER 38

Adam And Eve

And the Lord God commanded the man, 'You are free to eat from any tree in the garden; but you must not eat from the tree of the knowledge of good and evil, for when you eat from it you will certainly die (Genesis 2:16-17).

The first broken heart experience of humanity is recorded in the Bible and it is that of Adam and Eve the father and mother of humanity. The Bible tells us that everything God made was good. God spoke everything into existence but He made man, Adam and Eve. God placed them in the Garden of Eden and gave them specific and clear instructions concerning what they could and could not do.

Not only did God give them a choice but He also advised them how to choose. God clearly instructed them that there was one tree in the garden that they should not eat from. God also clearly pointed out what the consequences would be if they did not choose wisely.

The couple disobeyed God and did the very thing God told them not to do. Adam and Eve chose consequences over obedience and fellowship with God. The moment they ate of the fruit their eyes were opened and they realized that things were no more the same. **Adam and Eve were heartbroken**! The couple became ashamed and unworthy of continued fellowship with their God. They plunged into crisis and they no longer looked forward to having God come to the Garden to visit them. Shame and sorrow gripped hold of them and they realized that they failed God and themselves. The first couple could not face God and so they hid themselves. Prior to their disobedience by eating the fruit from the tree of the knowledge of good and evil, they were naked and yet not ashamed. "***And Adam and his wife were both naked, and they felt no shame***" (Genesis 2:25). Before eating the fruit Adam and his wife were walking in obedience to God's required instruction so there was no need to be ashamed.

Adam and his wife Eve made a conscious decision to disobey God and as a result sin crept into their hearts and shame consumed them. God is holy and He cannot and will not share His space with sin. "***This is the message we have heard from him and declare to you: God is light; and in him there is no darkness at all***" (1 John 1:5). In Scripture darkness represents sin and God cannot tolerate sin "***Now the serpent was more crafty than any of the wild animals the Lord God had made. He said to the woman, 'Did God really say, 'You must not eat from any tree in the garden***?" (Genesis 3:1). Child of God, notice carefully that the serpent twisted what God had said. Eve replied to the serpent saying, "*We may eat fruit from the trees in the garden, but God did say, 'You must not eat fruit from the tree that is in the middle of the garden, and you must not touch it, or you will die*" (Genesis 3:2-3).

The serpent deceived Eve and she was not alert to that fact for she was distracted and drawn away by her own lust. "*You will not certainly die. For God knows that when you eat from it your eyes will be opened, and you will be like God, knowing good and evil*" (Genesis 3:4). The serpent enticed Eve and she saw the fruit as pleasing to her eyes and she did not resist the temptation. "*Submit yourselves, then, to God. Resist the devil, and he will flee from you*" (James 4:7). If we resist the devil he will flee from us for this is God's promise. We resist the devil by using the Word of God as Jesus did after He fasted for forty days and forty nights and was tempted by the devil. There were many other occasions Jesus resisted those who attacked Him with the Word of God.

Eve took the fruit and she did eat then she gave some to her husband who also ate. After Adam and Eve eyes became opened they realized for the first time that they were naked. Then they sew fig leaves together and made covering to protect themselves (Genesis 3:6-7). This couple was truly broken. Things dramatically changed for them and they now found out that things will never be the same. Without the covering of the blood of Jesus we are all naked and exposed to the ravishing evil of sin.

As in former days, God was on His way to fellowship with His favorite couple Adam and Eve in the cool of the day as He always did. Unfortunately for the couple, Adam and Eve, when they heard the sound of the Lord God walking in the garden shame and fear gripped hold of their broken heart (Genesis 3:8). They knew not what to expect and they were very scared for things were certainly not the same. They could not face God in such a state of brokenness, guilt, and shame, so they quickly devised a plan. The man and his wife hid themselves from God. As a result, God did not find them at the usual place of meeting and fellowship. In our own lives we find that sometimes we allow our circumstances to pull us away from God instead of drawing us closer to Him in prayer and Bible study. This is a time when we should seek God's forgiveness, grace and mercy which we will find for God is quick to forgive and redeem us. "***The Lord is not slow in keeping His promise, as some understand slowness. Instead He is patient with you, not wanting anyone to perish, but everyone to come to repentance***" (2 Peter 3:9).

In His loving mercy and grace God reached out to Adam and his wife Eve. The all knowing all wise God knew that they were lost in sin, helpless, hopeless and probably wished to be rescued. "***But the Lord God called to the man, 'Where are you***?" (Genesis 3:9). God is truth and therefore He loves honesty and Adam was honest for when God called him, he answered and told God that he was afraid. "***I heard you in the garden, and I was afraid because I was naked; so I hid***" (Genesis 3:10). What was Adam afraid of? Adam was afraid to face God for he was afraid of the consequences of his disobedience. I suspect that at this point Adam clearly remembered God's instructions to him and he was disappointed in himself for not following God's request. God had a conversation with Adam and Adam told God the whole story although he made some excuses for his disobedience by casting blame on his wife Eve who gave him the fruit. This story shows that each person is accountable to God for his or her own actions. Child of God you are responsible for your healing. "*So then, each of us will give an account of ourselves to God*" (Romans 14:12).

God rebuked Adam and Eve and cursed the serpent. Not only did God rebuke Adam and Eve but He outlined to them the details of what their punishment would be moving forward (Genesis 3:14-20). God restored them and made proper covering for them from animal skin (Genesis 3:21). The fig leaves that they used to cover themselves were insufficient. So likewise, we cannot save ourselves from sin. We cannot cover our sinfulness. It is only the blood of Christ Jesus that can cleanse and cover us and protect us from the wrath of Almighty God.

There is no denying that this journey from brokenness to wholeness is difficult and can sometimes be very challenging. Even with your *survival kit* (see chapter one) this journey can from time to time force you to stop and take inventory and assess what is working and what changes you may need to make if any as you move forward. Above all take God at His word for He will certainly take you safely through and He will follow through on His consequences if you disobey His instructions.

"***Even though I walk through the darkest valley of the shadow of death, I will fear no evil, for you are with me; your rod and your staff, they comfort me***" (Psalm 23:4). Be assured that the Good Lord is always with you so count on Him. You could also have a trusted friend with whom you can talk if and when you feel the need to speak with someone concerning your challenges. You should not suffer alone.

CHAPTER 39

The Prodigal Son

What man among you, if he has a hundred sheep and has lost one of them, does not leave the ninety nine in the open pasture and go after the one which is lost until he finds it?
(Luke 15:4).

This is a beautiful story of repentance, forgiveness, deliverance and restoration. Individually, we have to take the initiative in order to bring about our own deliverance and restoration from broken heartedness. There are many accounts in the Bible of God telling individuals what they should first do in order for Him to act. For example God said, "***Call unto me, and I will answer thee, and shew thee great and mighty things, which thou knowest not***" (Jeremiah 33:3). We first must call on God, and when we do, He will act on our behalf by doing what is necessary for us.

In the story of the Prodigal Son, the younger of two sons decided one day that he wanted to leave home and go on his own. I guess he felt grown enough to explore the outer world on his own and capable enough of managing on his own and not needing his father's protection any longer. He felt confident and independent enough to leave home. As a result, he boldly went to his father and asked his father for his share of the inheritance. His father gave it to him and he left home and went into a very far country. Notice that he did not stay in a familiar place close to home. Instead, he went into a far unknown country. This is one of the things sin does to us it moves us far away from God's divine protection. I will submit to you that when our hearts are broken we sometimes are driven from who we really are to a faraway unfamiliar place emotionally where we try to protect our hearts from further hurt and pain. This faraway place is a secret place to which we escape and there we try to survive on our own.

After being there in this strange land for a while, things got severely difficult for this young man. Things did not work out the way he thought they would. This young man became desolate after he had spent all that he had. The people whom he met and became friends with were now all gone and he was now deserted and in an emotional state of emptiness. This young man was not only emotionally empty but he could no longer provide for his physical needs. The Bible says that he wasted his substance with riotous living for this young man lived carelessly. After a while there was famine in that place and he became very desperate that he accepted a job to feed swines. He actually had to eat after the swines since he had nothing else. This is brokenness at its lowest. His condition was grave to the extent that he was forced to do something he had never done before. Moreover, to mingle with swines was against his customs and personal beliefs.

Being broken is one thing but to acknowledge you are broken and try to do something about it is quite a different thing. Eventually the time came when this young man realized how far he had removed himself from home and the terrible mistake he had made to have left home. His place of safety and security is home where all his needs were met. He acknowledged and owned up to his wrong-doing and made a conscious and difficult life changing decision to return home. He realized that his life and survival depended on his taking drastic action to return home and admit to his father that he had done wrong.

> *And when he came to himself, he said, How many hired servants of my father's have bread enough and to spare, and I perish with hunger! I will arise and go to my father, and will say unto him, Father, I have sinned against heaven, and before thee, And am no more worthy to be called thy son: make me as one of thy hired servants. And he arose, and came to his father. But when he was yet a great way off, his father saw him, and had compassion, and ran, and fell on his neck, and kissed him* (Luke 15:17-18).

The father in the story is an example of God's forgiving love towards us. This father forgave his son because of his love and compassion for him. It seems clear to me that his father anticipated that his son would one day return home. One lovely day the father saw his son from a distance which suggests to me that he was always looking out for his son with expectation. The son was repentant and expressed to his father his regrets for having left home. He did not ask for much and he was not expecting to be returned to his original status in the family. The father forgave his son and welcomed him back home with a magnificent celebration. The young man's father expressed his joy of having his son back home and he restored him to his original place in the family. The Bible teaches that in heaven the angels rejoice when a sinner is saved. "*I tell you, there is rejoicing in the presence of the angels of God over one sinner who repents*" (Luke 15:10).

This son's journey from **brokenness to wholeness** is a very beautiful one. He made the choice to leave home and he made the conscious decision to return home. In our brokenness to wholeness journey we make choices daily. However, if by chance we make the wrong decision that affects our soul's health when we come to our senses and call for God's help, without doubt He will come to our rescue. Not only will He come to our rescue but He will restore our soul and fill your soul with pure joy to the overflowing. God will restore us to our rightful place in Him. "*Together, we are his house, built on the foundation of the apostles and the prophets. And the cornerstone is Christ Jesus himself*" (Ephesians 2:20).

CHAPTER 40

The Woman With The Issue Of Blood

*"**Seek the Lord while He may be found. Call upon Him while He is near**"* (Isaiah 55:6).

I n times of desperation we seem to find the strength and courage to do the things we could not do under most normal circumstances. In the story of the *Woman with the Issue of Blood* (Mark 5:24-34), this woman who suffered for twelve years to be healed did the extraordinary when she became very determined in pursuing her healing. During this period of twelve years she tried different means to get well and be whole. The Bible tells us that she was under the care of many doctors and none could help her but instead she got worse. This story makes clear that brokenness can put a strong hold on you and hold you captive for a mighty long time. To escape from this strong hold you must be determined to be delivered from your brokenness and be willing to do what it takes to be set free.

When the woman with the issue of blood heard about Jesus she was fully persuaded that she could be healed from her twelve years of bleeding. The Bible did not say exactly what she heard about Jesus but we can safely assume that what she heard convinced her enough that He could heal her. She exercised her faith and she encouraged herself and got to where Jesus was. You have to want healing badly enough to press your way through the barriers of the customs of the time. She was driven to do what it took to secure her healing. This woman had purpose and passion. She had a very strong conviction of faith. Her faith was so strong that she did not wait to have a conversation with Jesus she just wanted to touch the edge of his cloak. Without doubt this is unwavering faith. "**She said to herself, 'If I only touch the edge of his cloak, I will be healed**" (Matthew 9:21).

With all the strength that she could muster she got herself close enough to touch Jesus' garment. This woman had what I will call "limitless faith." The Word of God says, "**Now faith is the substance of things hoped for, the evidence of things not seen**" (Hebrews 11:1). Her faith convinced her to envision and claim her healing even before she touched Jesus. The moment she heard about Jesus her faith was activated. Her touch was a very special touch and one that got Jesus' full attention. When she touched Jesus she felt the change in her body immediately and Jesus also felt power left His body. After her touch Jesus called out, "*Who touched me?*" Certainly, Jesus knew who had touched Him but I believe He was giving the woman the chance to testify publicly about her deliverance. She was honest and acknowledged that she was the one who touched Jesus. "***Daughter, your faith has healed you. Go in peace and be freed from your suffering***" (Mark 5:34).

Her faith in Jesus was strong enough to propel her to take the risk and break the law by being in the public square. The law and custom declared her unclean and she should not be in the public square. She was desperate enough for her healing and she felt that the risk was worth taking by any means necessary. Are you desperate enough to be healed from that which has caused your heart to be so broken, torn and hurting very badly? The great faith of the Woman with the Issue of Blood secured for her a double portion of healing. Jesus said to her, "***Go in peace***" and with this Jesus addressed the healing of her heart. Then Jesus said to her, "***Be free from your suffering***" and this was the healing of her physical body.

Brokenness to wholeness and purpose is a journey that no one can escape from and no one can take this journey for someone else. Everyone at some time is broken in a different way and in different areas of life for this brokenness journey is a natural part of the human condition. Everyone goes through the process of healing at a different pace and in a different way. With the awareness that we are all at sometime broken we should pray one for the other and we should help to bear the burdens of others. "***Bear one another's burdens, and so fulfill the law of Christ***" (Galatians 6:2).

As you pursue your deliverance from broken heart you should not only focus on yourself but you should also find someone in need to help and God will in turn send someone to help you. "*Rejoice always, pray without ceasing, give thanks in all circumstances; for this is the will of God in Christ Jesus for you*" (1 Thessalonians 5:16-18). Like the *Woman with the Issue of Blood*, if you are desperate enough for your healing, and you are courageous enough to do what it takes, you will have to ignore your surroundings with everyone and everything in them and go after what you need and desire to have, which is your deliverance from heartbreak. Your restoration to wholeness depends on your determination to do what is required. Find encouragement in the Woman with the Issue of Blood and grow your faith in God for your healing is according to the measure of your faith. Jesus said that the woman had great faith and so must you and me.

Invite and allow God to heal your heart. "*He heals the broken hearted and binds up their wounds*" (Psalm 14:3). Everything we do originate in our hearts, and then they get to our minds as thoughts and ideas. Our thoughts and ideas become spoken words and actions and they influence our emotions. Notice that Jesus first took care of her heart issues. "*Above all else, above everything that you do, it is most important, that you guard your heart, for everything that you do flows from your heart*" (Proverbs 4:23).

CHAPTER 41

Jesus The Son Of God

He is despised and rejected of men; a man of sorrows, and acquainted with grief: and we hid as it were our faces from him; he was despised, and we esteemed him not. Surely he hath borne our grief, and carried our sorrows: yet we did esteem him stricken, smitten of God, and afflicted. But he was wounded for our transgressions, he was bruised for our iniquities: the chastisement of our peace was upon him; and with his stripes we are healed (Isaiah 53:3-5).

The ultimate brokenness to wholeness experience known to man is that of Jesus Christ our Lord and Savior. Jesus' brokenness is His rejection, suffering and eventually His cruel death on the cross of Calvary. I have concluded that Jesus' resurrection and ascension to heaven is His wholeness and fulfilled purpose.

Jesus knew His purpose for coming to this earth and that was to save mankind from the broken relationship with God caused by sin. "*For God so loved the world that he gave his one and only Son, that whoever*

believes in him shall not perish but have eternal life"
(John 3:16). Jesus gave up His royalty, wholeness, and
his perfection in heaven and came to earth in the form
of man. "*God made him who had no sin to be sin
for us, so that in him we might become the righteousness of God*" (2 Corinthians 5:21). Jesus took our
place by His death on the Cross of Calvary to redeem
us back to God.

The opposition Jesus experienced during His earthly
ministry as He went about doing good; teaching about
the kingdom of heaven; healing the sick; and raising
the dead; had to be heartbroken. It is heartbroken when
you do good to others and instead of being appreciated,
evil presents itself in ways that are discouraging. Do not
forget the verbal abuse that Jesus experienced by being
called all kinds of names one of which was Beelzebul
(prince of demons). "*But when the Pharisees heard
it, they said, 'It is only by Beelzebul, the prince of
demons, that this man casts out demons*" (Matthew
12:24). Jesus was mocked, beaten, humiliated and
arrested. People accused Him of eating with sinners and
not knowing that they were sinners. "*When the teachers
of the law who were Pharisees saw him eating with
the sinners and tax collectors, they asked his disciples: 'Why does he eat with tax collectors and sinners?* (Mark 2:16).

A vivid picture of Jesus' brokenness was evident
in His final days leading up to His crucifixion and this
was the climax of His brokenness as man. The Bible
tells us that as Jesus journeyed towards Jerusalem the
weight of the sin of the world was unbearably heavy on

Him. As man, this experience was too much for Him to bear on His own and this was when He called on His Father to ask for help. Throughout His ministry prayer was Jesus' bedrock for it was often that He would call on His Father in public prayer. So too should we call on God for help in private and in public. There are several examples of Jesus seeking His Father's help in prayer. One such example was when He fed the multitude of people. Jesus was intentional in the value He placed on prayer which was to model for His disciples and us the importance of prayer. Jesus also took time out to teach His disciples how they should pray. "**But when you pray, go into your room, close the door and pray to your Father, who is unseen. Then your Father, who sees what is done in secret, will reward you**" (Matthew 6:6).

As Jesus drew closer to Jerusalem where He would give up His life on Calvary, He was so overcome by the burden of the sin of the whole world that He stopped in the Garden of Gethsemane to pray to His heavenly Father for support and deliverance. Jesus' brokenness was so severe that He had second thoughts about going to the cross. He requested of His Father to remove the assignment from him yet He desired to be in His Father's will.

> **Father, if it is Your will, take this cup away from me; nevertheless not My will, but Yours, be done.' Then an angel appeared to Him from heaven, strengthening Him. And being in agony, He prayed more earnestly. Then His sweat became like**

great drops of blood falling down to the ground (Luke 22:42-44).

God answered His prayer right on time because He was constantly watching over and looking out for His Son Jesus. This is exactly what God will do for us. God sent an angel who ministered to Jesus and restored His strength. We too when our hearts are broken we must labor in prayer and pray without ceasing and God will restore our strength. Jesus was still in agony as He continued to pray but He was not alone for God sustained Him. Child of God, be encouraged as you labor through your brokenness. Jesus should be your model for He is the perfect example for us. You too can be successful on your soul's healing journey if you rely on The Most High God for help and call on Him whenever you need Him.

In our time of brokenness we will undoubtedly find help in the Word of God, fervent prayer, and the reliable support of the Holy Spirit will be extended to us. Some tests that God allows for us to experience can be grievous and extremely difficult but if we are willing to submit ourselves to go through these tests and follow His plan God will sustain us and bring us through victoriously. Your way may seem dark now but there is light at the end of the tunnel.

When Jesus got to Calvary He suffered shame and He endured the cross in our place. No one took Jesus' life from Him He gave it up. He was buried and just like He said He rose on the third day. Jesus gloriously and triumphantly rose from the dead and appeared to His disciples to reassure them that He was alive. Before

Jesus' ascension to heaven He promised his disciples that He would send the Comforter, in the person of the Holy Spirit and He did. Jesus is not here in the world in person anymore but we have the indwelling person of the Holy Spirit with us to comfort and guide us along this journey. Jesus kept His promise of the Comforter and because He dwells within us we are not alone and we will not be defeated.

If we take time to pause long enough and look around we will find enough people who are broken in ways that will cause us to forget our own condition and extent compassion and help to other travelers along this journey of life who may be in a worse situation. Sometimes we think that we are in the worst of situations when there are others who are worse than us. We are our brothers and sisters keeper, therefore, we should not be self centered, instead, we should see the needs of others and help to restore them. God will be pleased and we will be blessed.

CHAPTER 42

The Potter And The Clay

*"**Humble yourselves, therefore, under God's mighty hand, that he may lift you up in due time**"* (1 Peter 5:6).

A visit to the art gallery will expose you to various master pieces of pottery. The process that each pottery had to go through was quite meticulous which you did not see. You have no idea of how very painstakingly the potter worked with the clay in breaking, molding, firing, and painting of the pieces. When we visit the art gallery we are drawn to admire the beauty and uniqueness of each piece of pottery but we take no time to think of the rigorous process that the pieces went through. In like manner, no one knows what you went through on your journey of brokenness to reach this place in your healing process.

God is the potter and you are the clay. The potter has total control over the clay. I recommend that you yield yourself completely to God who is your maker, the Potter. When you yield you allow God to break you, mold you, fill you and use you for His purpose and glory. The breaking can and will be painful but through it all know that in order for God to make you over and anew He must first break you. You are especially chosen by God for a specific purpose so follow His lead and divine plan.

The prophet Jeremiah was instructed by God to go down to the potter's house and that He God would cause him to hear His words. In obedience Jeremiah went down to the potter's house and he noticed that the potter was working at the wheels. The potter made a vessel that was marred (defective) and so he made it again and this time it seemed good to the potter. "***Then the word of the Lord came to me. He said, 'Can I not do with you, Israel, as this potter does?' declares the Lord. Like clay in the hand of the potter, so are you in my hand, Israel***" (Jeremiah 18:5-6). God will break you and mold you into the person he wants you to be for His purpose if you allow Him.

The Lord gave Jeremiah a message to speak to the nation of Israel and to warn them to repent of their evil ways and turn back to God. God is faithful and ready to forgive us of our sins if we ask his forgiveness and turn to Him. "***If we confess our sins to him, he is faithful and just to forgive us our sins and purify (cleanse) us from all unrighteousness***" (1John 1:9). The Lord promised that if the children of Israel were to repent He would withhold the punishment that He had in store for them.

And if it does evil in my sight and does not obey me, then I will reconsider the

good I had intended to do for it. Now therefore say to the people of Judah and those living in Jerusalem, This is what the Lord says: Look! I am preparing a disaster for you and devising a plan against you. So turn from your evil ways, each one of you, and reform your ways and your actions (Jeremiah 18:10-11).

Child of God, the test that God gives us, because of His faithfulness He supports us in passing the test. If you trust him and obey him you will have His full support. You are God's master piece and there is no one like you for you are wonderfully made. "*I will praise thee; for I am fearfully and wonderfully made: marvelous are thy works; and that my soul knows right well*" (Psalm 139:14).

Submit yourself to God completely and allow Him to do His great work in and through you and you will be better for doing so. Like the "**potter and the clay**" God will do His work in you to perfection taking you from brokenness to wholeness, peace, joy and purpose. Praise God! You are one of a kind and God has a very special purpose for you to fulfill which no one else can do for it is your divine assignment.

CHAPTER 43

The Struggle Is Over

"It was good for me to be afflicted so that I might learn your decrees" (Psalm 119:71).

So I will restore to you the years that the swarming locust has eaten; The crawling locust; The consuming locust; And the chewing locust,; My great army which I sent among you. You will have plenty to eat, until you are full, and you will praise the name of the Lord your God, who has worked wonders for you; never again will my people be shamed (Joel 2:25-26).

When we struggle mentally or physically it means that we do not have enough fortitude, strength or will to deal with the challenges with which we are faced. Whenever we struggle it means that we have to make extra special efforts and challenge ourselves to keep going while we stay focus on our ultimate goal which is healing. *"It is for freedom that Christ has set us*

free. Stand firm, then, and do not let yourselves be burdened again by a yoke of slavery" (Galatians 5:1)

Praise God Almighty the struggle is over and this is now your period of recovery and victory! This is the victory of your soul from the enemies, the cares of life and all that caused your heart's pain. While the circumstances might not change your attitude and approach in dealing with those circumstances could and should change.

The brokenness experience is a struggle, a real struggle, an internal struggle. Broken heartedness is a struggle because we wrestle not against flesh and blood for it is not a physical fight. This is a fight in which you are fighting against the forces of evil. This is a fight against the principalities, powers and the rulers of the darkness of evil in this world. For this fight, God will give His **angels** charge over you. In this fight your responsibility will be to declare the glory of God and proclaim your deliverance in the process. Remember, there is power in the word of your testimony and your testimony could help others to some degree along their way so share your amazing story gladly.

When God delivered Daniel in the lion's den King Darius said to Daniel, "May your God, whom you serve continually, rescue/deliver you!" (Daniel 6). Since God cannot lie and cannot fail He delivered Daniel. God will deliver you in a way that will bring honor to His name and peace to your soul. God will deliver you in a way that you will not be able to deny or fully explain. God will deliver you in a way that will cause you and those around you to marvel. The night prior to Daniel's deliverance, King Darius was very restless and had no desire for food, drink or rest. Did you know that God will cause your enemies to be restless? God will confuse your enemies. "***But God chose the foolish things of the world to confuse the wise; God chose the weak things of the world to confuse the strong***" (1 Corinthians 1:27).

Early the next morning the king hurried to the lions' den and he called for Daniel in a very loud, anxious and troubling voice. "***Daniel, servant of the living God, has your God, whom you serve continually, been able to rescue/deliver you from the lions***?" (Daniel 6).

> ***Daniel answered, "O king, live forever! My God sent his angel and he shut the mouths of the lions. They have not hurt me, because I was found innocent in his sight. Nor have I ever done any wrong before you, O king***" (Daniel 6).

The king was overjoyed and relieved when he realized that Daniel was not hurt but was safe. He ordered that the men who falsely accused Daniel be thrown into the lions' den along with their wives and children. King Darius also ordered and decreed that every part of his kingdom people must fear and reverence the God of Daniel. So likewise your experience can cause others to recognize the mighty hand of God and be drawn to Him by giving their lives to Christ because you stood the test. In his brokenness and times of trials Daniel held on to his faith and in the end he was delivered and his God was glorified as the God of the Israelites. God will do the same for you if you stay true to Him and true to yourself. God has a perfect timeline so be patient and trust him completely.

In Peter's experience an angel of the Lord was sent to deliver him from prison. "***But during the night an angel of the Lord opened the doors of the jail and brought them out. "Go, stand in the temple courts, "he said, "and tell the people the full message of this new life***" (Acts 5:19-20). Child of God, allow God to fight your battles, the outcome will be sweet and joyous like honey from the honeycomb.

> ***The fear of the Lord is pure, enduring forever. The decrees of the Lord are firm, and all of them are righteous. They are more precious than gold, than much pure gold; they are sweeter than honey, than honey from the honeycomb*** (Psalm 19:9-10).

The lesson taught during your brokenness state is not for you only. All of your steps along the way should be used to help others in some way directly or indirectly. This victory is not for you only but for all those who are acquainted, if at all, with your brokenness to learn from it concerning what God can do for them also. Therefore it becomes your responsibility to do as God will have you do to ensure that you have learned the lesson. This can be accomplished in many ways one of which is through the power of our testimony. The Israelites struggled for a long time with the Philistines and God in his time delivered them.

David said to the Philistine, 'You come against me with sword and spear and javelin, but I come against you in the name of the Lord Almighty, the God of the armies of Israel, whom you have defied. V46 This day the Lord will deliver you into my hands, and I will strike you down and cut off your head. This very day I will give the carcasses of the Philistine army to the birds and the wild animals, and the whole world will know that there is a God in Israel. V47 All those gathered here will know that it is not by sword or spear that the Lord saves; for the battle is the Lord's, and he will give all of you into our hands (1 Samuel 17:45-47 & 50).

As the Good Lord did for the Israelites He will do for you and all of us. You cannot and should not live with the pain of broken heartedness for the rest of your life so give the struggle over to God. Allow God to fight for you, deliver you and free you to worship Him with all of your heart in spirit and in truth. The struggle is over so you are not bound any longer! Your mind is free and clear for you are not held captive by your broken heart any longer. Praise God! You are delivered and set free to praise God with all of your heart, soul, mind and strength! Your heart is now mended and your spirit is set free. By the power of God you are ***growing into wholeness*** your purpose to fulfill. The struggle, my struggle,

and your struggle are over! This means that you and I
have stopped fighting with man and with Almighty God
and are ready to operate in our purpose.

CHAPTER 44

Seed Time And Harvest

"Those who sow with tears will reap with songs of joy"
(Psalm 126:5).

"Truly I tell you, unless a grain of wheat falls to the ground and dies, it will never be more than one grain. But if it dies, it will produce lots of wheat" (John 12:24).

T he farmer at a certain time of the year prepares the ground for sowing with the hope that someday there will be a big harvest. At the appropriate time the seeds or seedlings are placed in the ground. Over a period of time they grow and mature into fruit bearing trees and produce a great harvest. There is a time for sowing and a time for reaping of the harvest. *"A time to be born and a time to die; a time to plant and a time to reap"* (Ecclesiastes 3:2). Seed time and harvest is a process and if you desire to reap the harvest you must first sow (plant) the right seed. Sowing and reaping is a divine and profound principle taught by God Himself. Harvest is God's provision and blessing for us His children.

Seed time is a time of dormancy for you cannot see anything above ground. In dormancy a seed is alive but the plant is not actively growing above ground. While in the ground the seed appears to be dead but it is not dead it is going through a natural process of growth in the ground. Harvest is a time of abundant life, growth and reaping from the tree which developed from the seed. Sometimes we just have to die a little on the inside in order to be reborn and be raised again to new life as a stronger, wiser, and more spiritually healthy and vibrant with clarity of our purpose. "*God made him who had no sin to be sin for us, so that in him we might become the righteousness of God*" (2 Corinthians 5:21). Christ died so that we may live a full and abundant life in Him. This is a perfect example of seed time and harvest.

There are those of us who desire to live but we refuse to first die. *To live is conditioned on our willingness to die*. We cannot have one without the other. We must die if we want or wish to live. In our lives we get rid of some things to make room for others and so likewise we die to sin in order to live a Christian life in Christ. Brokenness is death and death brings change which is newness of life and healing. Change can be challenging and at the same time rewarding. "What we sow is what we reap." Although this is a proverb it is true. "*For he who sows to his own flesh will from the flesh reap corruption. But he who sows to the Spirit, from the Spirit shall reap eternal life*" (Galatians 6:8). We must sow according to what we desire to reap. We must invest our time and efforts wisely keeping in mind our vision and purpose.

There are numerous stages in the order of the processes that are taking place during this time of seed dormancy. Take a moment to think of a buried seed in the ground. There is a period of different changes that the seed must go through underground for before the seed begins to grow it must first die. While the seed is in the ground going through the changes and process of death, germination and preparing for growth there is no sign of life above the ground. We cannot see what is taking place with the seed that is in the ground because it is underground in the soil but by faith we know that it is there and it will only be a matter of time before it begins to burst through the ground.

The Parable of the Sower and the Seed: Planting is the most significant time in the life of the seed. This is the first of many stages of growth that the seed will have to go through in the process of changing from seed to fruit bearing tree. When the seed is in the ground it is at this time that the seed will germinate and the root will be established to prepare for the anchoring of a great tree that will come forth and bear much fruit. This must be good ground with no obstruction such as rocks for the seed to be well established. In the parable of the **Sower and the Seed**, Jesus told the story of a sower who went out to sow some seeds. Some of his seeds fell by the **way side** and the birds of the air came and eat them up; Some seeds fell on **stony places** and because they had no deepness of earth they were scorched by the sun and they withered away for they had no root; Some seeds fell among **thorns** (weeds) and they grew up but the thorns choked them and they died; Other seeds fell into **good ground** and they brought forth fruit, some an hundred fold, some sixth-fold, and some thirty-fold (Matthew 13:1-23).

Four environments for the seed: Jesus' ultimate goal was to use this parable to teach the truth about the kingdom of God. He presented the four types of conditions or environments where the seeds had been sown (planted) by the sower. In the parable Jesus explained that these are the four types of attitudes of the human heart that people have towards the Word of God when they hear the Word. Jesus concluded the parable by saying, "***Whoever has ears, let them hear***" (Matthew 13:9). Jesus emphasized that people who hear and obey the Word of God by putting it in practice will grow in grace and in the knowledge of Christ the Lord. As I examined these four types of soils that represent the four types of heart attitudes toward the Word of God, I began to discern how these four types of soils also could represent four distinct characteristics of people in the church and their attitudes toward other Christians especially those with multiple and or outstanding gifts.

Caring for the buried seeds: It does take someone with special skills to properly care for the seeds that are buried in the ground. Seeds are buried at different times and seasons of the year and at different depths under the ground. Buried seeds absorb water differently and some require more water than others. Seeds take different lengths of time to germinate and grow. Some seeds can die underground if they are not nurtured appropriately according to their needs. If a seed is buried too deep it could run out of nutrients before the seedling can spring forth and open up above ground and get light energy. Once the seedling springs forth above ground it requires a different type of care and nurturing such as clearing away the weeds and providing adequate amount of water. The life cycle of the plant dictates how the process works.

Is my heart good ground for the seed of God's Word? This is a personal and self reflective question that each person must answer for himself or herself. It is God Himself who is the sower and He has planted the seed of His Word in each person's heart before birth. *"Before I formed you in the womb I knew you, before you were born I set you apart, I appointed you as a prophet to the nations"* (Jeremiah 1:5). You are the one who will determine the type of soil that you will make available in your heart for the seed of the Word of God to grow. In your time of heartbreak this is where your faith is required and you must rely on God's faithfulness towards you for He is always with you even during the darkest of times. The purpose seed in your heart will need your time and your attention to successfully go through the changes and stages of growth. To neglect your seed that is in your heart by not caring for it will prolong the length of time it will take to go through the various stages to get to maturity. Nurture your seed by taking heed to the Word of God. First and foremost you must get closer in your relationship with God. Sometimes we have to reach out and seek the help of other people. There are people who will invest in you by supporting you because they see the anointing upon you and they believe in you.

While you are waiting for your seed to take root in your heart and grow forth you must be careful of the people around you and in your circle. There are those who will stop at nothing to discourage you when they see the anointing upon you, and the potential in you, and they have a suspicion of what is to come. During this time in your journey you may feel alone because of all the work that is taking place on the inside of your heart and soul which you cannot share with anyone. You may even feel overwhelmed by the power of God's presence with you. This is a time when you must grow and exercise your faith in God and trust Him completely for your purpose must take root in your heart and be well established first so be very patient. This is a very significant time in the life of your purpose. During this time you keep a low profile while you are thinking, wondering, planning, reflecting, pondering, praying, hoping, preparing, and rejoicing too for you know what is on the inside of your heart is by God's divine order.

The seedling emerges from the ground with great anticipation to continue growing and to start another phase of its wonderful life but it could be vulnerable to all sorts of dangers and must be protected. For example, if there are weeds around the seedling the gardener could mistakenly cut it down as weeds. In your case you must be observant and very careful for there are people around you who will intentionally try to destroy your seed by speaking to you words that are unkind and words of discouragement. This behavior is to distract you from your divine purpose so be alert and be careful of these kinds of relationships. Be encouraged for no one can stop or fight against the seed that God has planted in your heart. You must get rid of distractions and focus fully on your purpose seed.

Remember that in the parable of the Sower and the Seed there were birds that came and ate some of the seeds; The sun scorched some of the seeds and they died; Other seeds were choked by the thorns (weeds) and they died. The Holy Spirit has revealed to me that there are people around including within the church with these same kinds of characteristics and attitudes who if they get the chance will destroy your God given purpose seed.

Some people protect themselves during this time of emotional upheaval by wearing a "mask" such as avoiding negative people while they are pursuing their healing and purpose. Over time these people will eventually emerge and claim their rightful place in this global community by changing lives. Be hopeful for sooner than later you also will emerge healed, and completely whole again. Like the seed that emerges from the ground as a vibrant plant ready to grow and bear much fruits in its season so too will be your big reveal in God's own time when you emerge from your brokenness into rapid growth leading to your divine harvest of purpose.

Seed time gives you the opportunity to reevaluate all of your circumstances and make God directed decisions at this stage of your healing and purpose journey. It should be at this point in your journey of seed time (dormancy) that you are more determined and ready to let go of "those things" and you are ready to move on in new dimensions of wholeness of life in Christ Jesus. Once you let go of those "dead things" and "dead situations" you should no longer sow in those "dead places" you must instead plant in fresh new and healthy soils. There is no denying that sometimes we have to physically change our environments for our seed to grow. In some environments there are people who will go to the extreme to do you wrong but be assured that God will turn it all around to benefit you and the purpose seed inside of your heart. *"But Joseph said to them, 'Do not be afraid. Am I in the place of God? You intend to harm me, but God intended it for good to accomplish what is now being done, the saving of many lives"* (Genesis 50:20).

Child of God, be careful not to curse your broken pieces and the difficulties you had to endure while your seed was being developed inside of you for out of those broken pieces and difficult times will emerged your purpose, new life, healing, strength, passion, courage, boldness, compassion, love, humility, gratitude, new attitude, freedom and liberation of spirit all of which you will need and should use to succeed in your services to humanity. Remember that you have been **Especially Chosen to be Broken for Purpose**. Every person is born with a seed or divine purpose planted in the heart by God. Whatever your calling is you must bear in mind that first and foremost you must serve and worship God and then serve humanity by ministering to them as God directs you.

Therefore go and make disciples of all nations, baptizing them in the name of the Father and of the Son and of the Holy Spirit, and teaching them to obey everything I have commanded you. And surely I am with you always, to the very end of the age (Matthew 28:19-20).

God expects all of us His children to be good stewards who will be fruitful and bear much fruit and when we do God will maintain and sustain us in the bearing of much more fruits. "***I am the vine; you are the branches. If you remain in me and I in you, you will bear much fruit; apart from me you can do nothing***" (John 15:5). If we fail to be fruitful and multiply by operating in our gifts and purpose we must be prepared to answer to God for we will have a price to pay. Jesus and His disciples were leaving Bethany in Jerusalem and Jesus was hungry. Jesus saw a fig tree in the distance and hoped that there were figs on it for Him to eat but when He got to the tree there were no figs only leaves. Although it was not the season for figs Jesus was angry and He cursed the tree saying, "***May no one ever eat fruit from you again***" (Mark 11:12-25). God expects us to produce and there will be consequences if we do not.

He told them another parable: The Kingdom of heaven is like a mustard seed, which a man took and planted in his field. Though it is the smallest of all seeds, yet when it grows, it is the largest

of garden plants and becomes a tree, so that the birds come and perch in its branches (Matthew 13:31).

Identify and claim where you are in the process and push forward. You should be at one of these stages such as the seed underground, germination, root establishment, seedling, young plant, tree, grown tree, or fruit bearing tree. God expects you to produce in season and out of season regardless of the stage where you are. You must study the Word of God always and know it with understanding and confidence showing yourself approved by God. "*Preach the Word; be prepared in season and out of season; correct, rebuke and encourage with great patience and careful instruction*" (2 Timothy 4:2). It is from our hearts that we speak for everything we do is from our hearts. "*Above all else, guard your heart for everything that you do flows from your heart*" (Proverbs 4:23).

Hide the Word in your heart for God knows the thoughts and intentions of your heart. "*A good man brings good things out of the good stored up in his heart, and an evil man brings evil things out of the evil stored up in his heart. For the mouth speaks what the heart is full of*" (Luke 6:45). From the abundance of the heart the mouth speaks and this means that the Word is in our hearts first and when we speak the Word comes from our hearts. The seed is the Word of God and we must speak it for when we do it is sown in the hearts of those who hear leading to exponential growth of the kingdom of God. The seed of God's Word is in our hearts where we store it away. The Word of God is in our minds for we are told to meditate on the Word day and night. The Word of God is in our mouths when we speak. "*But his delight is in the law of the Lord, and in His law he meditates day and night*" (Psalm 1:2)

> *Finally, brothers and sisters, whatever is true, whatever is noble, whatever is right, whatever is pure, whatever is lovely, whatever is admirable, if any-thing is excellent or praiseworthy think about such things* (Philippians 4:8).

I earnestly encourage you to apply the principles of God's kingdom in your life and ministry for these princi-ples have been tried and stood the test of time. These principles are God ordained and they will not fail. Do not fail to nurture your seed for your seed is your God given purpose, passion, dream and future. You must guard your seed and nurture it diligently. I have a note of caution for you and it is that you should not com-pare your seed and purpose with those of someone else for everyone is different. "*We have different gifts, according to the grace given to each of us. If your gift is prophesying, then prophesy in accordance with your faith*" (Romans 12:6). Your purpose will flourish like the mustard seed when grown. Jesus said that the mustard seed is the smallest of all seeds, yet when it grows, it is the largest of garden plants and becomes a tree that all the birds come and lodge in the branches

(Matthew 13:31-32). Regardless of the size of your seed and purpose the impact will be great as long as you operate in God's divine will for you and the ministry to which He has called and ordained you.

I am very excited because God's purpose seed in my heart is quite *potent* for it has great power; great influence; great effect; and it is ordained by God to produce greatly much fruit. No person can successfully stand in the way and no person can stop what God has put in motion. The power of the Holy Spirit is in supreme control. Enjoy God's perfect plan for you!

> *On the mountain heights of Israel I will plant it; it will produce branches and bear fruit and become a splendid cedar. Birds of every kind will nest in it; they will find shelter in the shade of its branches. All the trees of the forest will know that I the Lord bring down the tall tree and make the low tree grow tall. I dry up the green tree and make the dry tree flourish. 'I the Lord have spoken, and I will do it* (Ezekiel 17:23-24).

Part Six
Gratitude And Praise

Journey Reflections

"Give thanks in all circumstances; for this is God's will for you in Christ Jesus" (1 Thessalonians 5:18).

"I will give thanks to you, Lord, with all my heart; I will tell of all your wonderful deeds" (Psalm 9:1).

My transparent thoughts concerning my own experiences in overcoming severe heart pain; the process in healing and growing into wholeness and purpose will shed much insight on my journey. Had it not been for God on my side the outcome would have been different. I thank God for His grace and mercy that sustained me through it all. *"All this is for your benefit, so that the grace that is reaching more and more people may cause thanksgiving to overflow to the glory of God"* (2 Corinthians 4:15).

Reflection is an intentional effort by someone to look back and re-examine where they have been in contrast to where they are right now and a look ahead to answer how to get there. Hindsight is 20/20 which means that "it is easy to know the right thing to do after something has already happened, but it is hard to predict the future." Insight is looking within with an understanding that you are able to see or understand clearly. Foresight is the ability to predict what will happen in the future. "*I always thank my God for you because of his grace given you in Christ Jesus. For in him you have been enriched in every way, with all kinds of speech and with all knowledge*" (1 Corinthians 1:4-5).

My journey through the tunnel of purging where I purged myself of the impurities in my heart and soul gave me the opportunity to reflect on my journey and make an informed self assessment on what I could have or should not have done and how to move forward. My emotions were real and it was well worth my determination and effort going through all the journey experiences to the very end of each tunnel. I am very sure that I could not have made this journey without my **Survival kit**. My word of caution is that you must continue to use the tools in your survival kit, personal choice, prayer, the Word of God, faith, trust, humility, time, the whole armor of God, songs of praise and endurance. You still need these tools at every point of your daily journey for they are your spiritual nutrients (See chapter one). Do not be fooled for you will need your survival kit even more now because the fight not only continues but it intensifies. Be watchful and do not let your guard down so stay covered under God's mighty wings of protection.

Once one battle is over another begins for the fight is real. It is my hope that having gone through your brokenness to wholeness journey you have gained much spiritual insights, strength, knowledge and understanding, to truly purge yourself and that you have grown in grace and in the knowledge of your Lord and Savior Jesus Christ. From my personal experiences although my heart hurt and pain were unwelcomed at first I grew exponentially from them and can now truly thank God for those experiences. Each victory along the way did help me and should have helped or will help you to win other fights or challenges. Now I am better prepared for the unknown challenges that lie ahead and I hope that you are as well.

> *I have fought the good fight, I have finished the race, I have kept the faith. Finally, there is laid up for me the crown of righteousness, which the Lord, the righteous Judge, will give to me on that Day, and not to me only but also to all who have loved His appearing"* (2 Timothy 4:7-8).

Child of God, you too have fought a good fight because you are not defeated instead you are victorious, you won! That particular fight is over but your race is not yet completed for there will always be another fight so you must fight on. In your past fight you kept the faith and so too you must keep the faith moving forward. Revisit chapter one where I talked about faith and why it is extremely essential to our very survival spiritually. Without faith it is not only hard but impossible to please God (Hebrews 11:6). As we fight for ourselves let us also fight on the behalf of others.

God did a great work in my heart and He opened my eyes so that I could see in the Spirit that which I could not see in the natural. God delivered me with His Mighty hand to my purpose and to where I was needed and needed to be. At the onset of my broken heart I considered it very strange but now I do understand enough for God has exposed what He wanted me to know.

CHAPTER 45

From Death To Newness Of Life

"A new commandment I give unto you, That you love one another; as I have loved you, that you also love one another" (John 13:34).

"And he hath put a new song in my mouth, even praise unto our God: many shall see it, and fear, and shall trust in the Lord" (Psalm 40:3).

The journey, your journey now takes on a new meaning and new dimension. The focus now is to continue growing into wholeness and excel in your purpose. During the dark and difficult places of this journey that you had to travel God was indeed preparing and fashioning you for your exceptionally unique purpose. God has all the human and material resources that you will need in carrying out your task and assignments secured for you. *"Behold, the days come, saith the Lord, that I will make a new covenant with the house of Israel, and with the house of Judah"* (Jeremiah

31:31). God is in a divine covenant with you and your purpose in ministry is exponential growth going forward. You will now reap in joy!

The life cycle dictates that something has to first die in order to keep living. Let's face it, brokenness kills. To be broken hearted can draw your very life out of you and kill your spirit, desire, dream and hope. A broken heart can leave you just existing and moving around in circles like a shadow instead of living your full life and operating in your God given purpose. At the same time there is no life without death for when one dies in the physical they continue to live on in the spirit. Moreover, one has to die to sin in order to live in Christ. "*So you also must consider yourselves dead to sin and alive to God in Christ Jesus*" (Romans 6:11). Wholeness is life, fulfilled life. Wholeness brings about new birth which is new life and new beginning. GLORY TO GOD, HALLELUJAH!

Sometimes along this journey we spend too much of our time holding on to grief for we mourn over that which is broken to the extent that we miss out on the beauty and growth of the new life that is vibrantly springing forth in our hearts and lives. "*Therefore, if anyone is in Christ, the new creation has come: The old has gone, the new is here*" (2 Corinthians 5:17). God has a perfect plan for you and you need to trust Him in that plan. You should know that when something is dead, it is dead and if you are not sure ask God for discernment and spiritual wisdom so that you can see and know the spiritual truth of that deadness. Sometimes we try to breathe life into that which is already dead and not meant to live any-more. I am encouraging you to let go of that dead "thing" and celebrate your new life that is ordered by God. Do not continue to mourn the death of that which God has removed you should try to focus on your purpose and advance in that path and newness of life.

Spirit: "*Create in me a pure heart, O God, and renew a steadfast spirit within me*" (Psalm 51:10). As you continue to navigate your way through this journey of wholeness and purpose you have to be strong in the Lord and maintain a strong spirit. "*Finally, be strong in the Lord and in the power of his might*" (Ephesians 6:10). If you are not very careful and observant you will be tempted to look back at your brokenness and this will kill your spirit and take all of your drive away from you. You cannot allow that to happen for you must focus on your wholeness and purpose. "*A happy heart makes the face cheerful, but heartache crushes the spirit*" (Proverbs 15:13). Your spirit is who you are. Man is spirit possessing a soul and lives in a body. "*Do you not know that your body is a temple of the Holy Spirit within you, whom you have from God? You are not your own, for you were bought with a price, So glory God in your body*" (1 Corinthians 6:19-20). Child of God, "*Be renewed in the spirit of your minds*" (Ephesians 4:23). You must put on and have the mind of Christ in order to think differently of new and healthy thoughts and think differently of your purpose.

You should not consider yourself a victim of broken heart any longer you are now a trailblazer. Personally speaking, after God brought me through my purging and healing tunnels He anointed me as a trailblazer in many ways. Trailblazers are leaders who point the way and they are risk takers who are not afraid of change. On this journey God has led me in and through experiences that have grown my faith and turn my dreams into reality and He will do the same for you. People of God you cannot be concerned any longer about how people feel, think or what they have to say about your purpose. You are accountable to God and God you must obey so do not allow barriers and obstacles by man to distract you any longer.

> **Finally, brethren, whatever things are true, whatever things are noble, whatever things are just, whatever things are pure, whatever things are lovely, whatever things are of good report, if there is any virtue and if there is anything praiseworthy think (meditate) on these things** (Philippians 4:8).

Train your mind to entertain the thoughts that are heavenly and pure. You must rebuke any negative thoughts that may creep in your mind and not entertain them for the focus must be your purpose. It was revealed to me in July 2019 while I was in London England that the spirit that we carry will attract or repel people. Certainly I knew that fact before but on this particular day it was very direct and profoundly demonstrated to me causing me to think more deeply about this reality.

Motivation: You are determined to stay motivated on this new segment of your journey with new purpose. To be frank you cannot wait around for others to motivate you for that motivation may never come. It is important to know that self encouragement is also essential so learn how to encourage yourself. Sometimes there will be no one to encourage you and give you a helping hand along the way. King David encouraged himself in the Lord and so must you. "*Why, my soul, are you downcast? Why so disturbed within me? Put your hope in God, for I will yet praise him, my Savior and my God*" (Psalm 42:5). If you are not careful the unknown could reduce or kill your motivation and leave you uninspired, hopeless, helpless, and without joy or peace and you cannot allow this to happen.

Keep moving forward for God has blessed your path. You must look to God who is your ultimate helper for He will surely motivate you. "*May the God of hope fill you with all joy and peace as you trust in him, so that you may overflow with hope by the power of the Holy Spirit*" (Romans 15:13). God is the great source for your spiritual, physical, emotional and psychological needs and this is motivation. Focus on your desired outcome to help you stay motivated while you stay focus on your journey and on God. "*I will lift up mine eyes unto the hills, from whence cometh my help. My help cometh from the Lord, which made heaven and earth*" (Psalm 121:1-2). God is your strongest supporter and motivator and you will have to trust Him. Each victory along the way should serve to motivate you to keep going.

Attitude: Attitude is a natural human expression of emotion. Your healing and wholeness will result in new attitudes. Our attitudes could be positive or negative and they are expressed in many ways to include verbal or non-verbal behaviors. Our expressed attitudes positive or negative are byproducts of our thoughts and our will or choices. When a person's heart is broken it could kill that person's positive attitudes but when the heart is healed the attitude is positive. Child of God our attitudes are expressions of how we are feeling and so it is hard to mask our true feelings when we are hurting on the inside but with healing our joy will be radiant. Know that for our spiritual journey to be successful it will require that we desire and maintain a positive, cheerful and warm attitude. "*Have this attitude in yourselves which was also in Christ Jesus*" (Philippians 2:5-8). Jesus in all His experiences good or bad maintained a positive attitude so let us emulate His example.

Do not be forgetful concerning what the Good Lord has done for you along the way on your journey from brokenness to wholeness. Be thankful and praise God's holy name for He brought you through and to this place of wholeness and purpose. "*Then your heart will become proud and you will forget the Lord your God who brought you out from the land of Egypt, out of the house of slavery*" (Deuteronomy 8:14). In humility you should remember what God has already done for you since it will always serve to support and sustain you along the way. "*Humble yourselves before the Lord, and he will exalt you*" (James 4:10). God loves a humble spirit and He has a way to lift up and promote the humble in spirit so remain humble in attitude and in God's presence. "*Pursue peace with all men, and the sanctification without which no one will see the Lord*" (Hebrews 12:14). Be sure to pursue peace for it is a Christian quality that is essential for you to have. Peace is one of the qualities of the Fruit of the Spirit. This peace does not mean the absence of problems but it does mean the presence of God that gives you the assurance that all is well. This assurance of peace makes a happy heart. "***Though He slay me, I will hope in Him. I will surely defend my ways before Him***" (Job 13:15). Job had a positive attitude and a gentle spirit with which God could work and God desires from all of us a gentle and obedient heart with which He can work.

Do not depend on your own understanding for that attitude will be a losing game to play so seek help from "special people" and most importantly from God. "***But this people has a stubborn and rebellious heart; They have turned aside and departed***" (Jeremiah 5:23). Try not to turn away from help by trying to fix things on your own for no one can successfully stand alone in all circumstances. The conclusion then is that we must rely on God for His grace and mercy! A "can do it all" attitude does not help anyone.

Giving: Be very watchful so that the experiences of your broken heart do not kill your spirit of giving. At a time when you are broken it can be a challenge to give of yourself fully in any meaningful way. In all areas of our lives we are called upon to give every day in so many ways. God gave to mankind His best gift in the person of His Son Jesus and we should give of our best to God by serving Him completely without reservation. A clean and pure heart is our best gift to God and that is what He requires. "***The one who has clean hands and pure***

heart, who does not trust in an idol or swear by a false god" (Psalm 24:4).

Giving is a requirement in serving God and to give in any way to others is an opportunity to bless someone and God Himself will reward us in return. "**Give, and it will be given unto you. A good measure, pressed down, shaken together and running over, will be poured into your lap; For with the measure you use, it will be measured to you**" (Luke 6:38). We should not limit ourselves to the giving of money for there are many other ways in which we can give to others. Some people may not need money but instead they may need help in preparing a meal for a sick and shut-in, someone may need a ride to the store or some words of encourage-ment. "**Every man shall give as he is able, according to the blessing of the Lord your God which He has given you**" (Deuteronomy 16:17).

Giving is God's expectation of everyone according to the blessings He gives. "**He who is generous will be blessed, for he gives some of his food to the poor**" (Proverbs 22:9). God promises that those who are generous in giving will be specially blessed. "**Then the people rejoiced because they had offered so will-ingly, for they made their offering to the Lord with a whole heart, and King David also rejoiced greatly**" (Chronicles 29:9). Notice how the people rejoice when they give for there is great joy in giving. "**Do not with-hold good from those to whom it is due, when it is in your power to do it**" (Proverbs 3:27). "**The righteous gives and does not hold back**" (Proverbs 21:26). In whatever way we serve others this too is giving.

Desire: I believe that our greatest desire is to be whole and happy. With newness of life come new desires. When we are broken in heart there is one desire that we all do have and that is for the experience to immediately go away. We all have a desire to be "whole" in spirit, soul and body for we all want to be healthy. "*I delight to do your will, O my God; your law is within my heart*" (Psalm 40:8). If the desire in your heart is to do God's divine will He will provide for you the resources that are needed to get it done. "*With my whole heart I seek you; let me not wander from your commandments*" (Psalm 119:10). God is the one who directs your steps therefore He will protect you from wondering away from your purpose. "*Delight yourself in the Lord, and he will give you the desires of your heart*" (Psalm 37:4). As long as your desires are lined up with the precepts of God's Holy Word He will in His perfect timing grant the desires of your heart. "*Blessed are those who hunger and thirst for righteousness, for they shall be satisfied*" (Matthew 5:6). Anyone who desires to have more of God He will make Himself available to them and bless them with the anointing of the Holy Spirit thus giving them more power to operate in their purpose. "*But one thing is necessary, Mary has chosen the good portion, which will not be taken away from her*" (Luke 10:42). We all should desire and seek that one important thing which is life in Christ Jesus.

Remember that "*personal choice*" is one of the tools in your **survival kit** for this journey (see chapter one). Whatever we desire is a conscious and personal choice that we make when we choose to desire that thing. God

307

does not force us in what we should choose instead He gives us the power to choose wisely. However, at the same time He advises us on the choice that we should make and what the consequences will be if we deviate from His instructions and make wrong and foolish choices.

God is always watching over us and He is aware of the choices that we make. "*But he knows the way that I take, when he has tested me, I will come forth as gold*" (Job 23:10). Whenever God puts us through a test He gives us the grace to preserve us in that test and he brings us out as pure gold. "*He fulfills the desire of those who fear him; he also hears their cry and saves them*" (Psalm 145:19). "*For I desire steadfast love and not sacrifice, the knowledge of God rather than burn offerings*" (Hosea 6:6). "*In the path of your judgments, O Lord, we wait for you; your name and remembrance are the desire of our soul*" (Isaiah 26:8). "*My soul yearns for you in the night; in the morning my spirit longs for you. When your judgments come upon the earth, the people of the world learn righteousness*" (Isaiah 26:9).

Child of God, I encourage you to cultivate a desire for more of God and the desire to operate fully in your purpose. You must make the concerted effort to have your desire met. "*One thing have I desired of the LORD, that will I seek after; that I may dwell in the house of the LORD all the days of my life, to behold the beauty of the LORD, and to enquire in his temple*" (Psalm 27:4). No wonder David desired to dwell (abide, stay) in God's presence all the days of his life for it is a safe, peaceful, comforting and wonderful place to be.

"***You make known to me the way (path) of life; You will fill me with joy in Your presence, at Your right hand there are pleasures forevermore***" (Psalm 16:11). God delights in your desire to dwell in His presence for this was His original plan from the beginning when He made Adam and Eve (Genesis chapter 3).

CHAPTER 46

Brokenness Produces And Leaves Scars

*"**Jesus said to Thomas, 'Put your finger here; see my hands. Reach out your hand and put it into my side. Stop doubting and believe**" (John 20:27).*

I have a few scars on my body that I received as a child from playing and falling. Whenever I look at these scars they remind me of my happy and playful childhood. Today there are adults who still have scars on their bodies such as their hands or feet from bruises they received from falling as children. Some of these scars wear away over the years while others remain for a lifetime.

Now that my broken heart is healed I can praise God for my scars for when I look at them they serve as reminders of how I overcame the pain and sufferings of my broken heart and so can you. Convert your scars into blessings of hope, wholeness, miracles, purpose, vision, growth, forgiveness, passion and ministry. Jesus himself got scars from His wounds and His scars served a purpose. "***Then he said to Thomas, 'Put your finger here; see my hands. Reach out your hand and put it into my side. Stop doubting and believe. Thomas said to him, 'My Lord and my God!***" (John 20:27). Your scars serve as evidence of your wounded and broken heart experiences and they help you to tell your amazing story. Pull strength from your scars. Although my heartbreak has been healed there are scars that remain. I will always praise God for those scars for they serve to remind me of my purpose.

There is no brokenness to wholeness and purpose journey without scars. This is about your scars that are left on your heart and soul and they cannot be seen with the natural eyes. Some people will be amazed when you tell them your story for they cannot see your scars because they are not physically visible. If you were ever wounded and broken in heart those wounds undoubtedly left scars. When I look at my scars they remind me of my struggles, defeats, heartbreak, fears, wounds, tears and praise God my victories too. No one saw the tears I shed at nights groaning before God without sleep, or my time spent in devotion seeking God. No one knew of the longing in my heart to share with someone my unbearable heart pain. No one knew of my many moments of self examination and my intense prayer and fasting asking God for an extra supply of His sustaining grace. No one knew of how much alone time I spent with God in praise and worship or the many times I minister with compassion to those in pain from my own pain.

When you look at your own scars they will and should remind you of where the Good Lord has brought you from and the many blessings you have experienced along the way. Please do not despise your scars. Your scars will also remind you of the assistance that you received from others directly or indirectly (if any) and also the assistance you provided to other travelers along this journey of life. Joy should flood your soul realizing where you are right now as opposed to where you have been. It is God's grace and mercy that brought you this far. GLORY TO GOD! God's strength is made perfect in your weaknesses. "*But he said to me, 'My grace is sufficient for you, for my power is made perfect in weakness.' Therefore I will boast all the more gladly about my weaknesses, so that Christ's power may rest on me*" (2 Corinthians 12:9).

Our scars serve as great reminders that will help us to never forget what we have been through and these scars will help to fuel the fire of our testimonies and our determination in moving forward in our wholeness and purpose. The Bible states that we overcome by the blood of the Lamb of God and the word of our testimony. It is very important to share with others our experiences of God's provision and deliverance. When we share our journey experiences others will be benefited by being empowered and encouraged on their journey as well. "*And they overcame him by the blood of the Lamb, and by the word of their testimony; and they loved not their lives unto the death*" (Revelation 12:11). Because we have gone through the tunnels of our journeys from brokenness to wholeness, our testimonies become authentic and believable to those with whom we share them for we are sharing our personal experiences with passion and sincerity.

In our testimonies, we speak of our own personal scars and how we got them. To be transparent we also share how we dealt with those situations and how we overcame them. You will determine how much you want to share and with whom you choose to share. It will be empowering to also share the lessons you learnt along the way and how those lessons have changed you in becoming a better person and a better Christian and one who wants to make a difference. Whenever I share my personal testimonies I speak from a place of deep self confidence, honesty, passion, purpose and humility. I trust that you will do the same.

I discovered that my scars serve me very well for they remind me not only of my pain but most importantly of how God sustained me, prepared me and delivered me. To be honest, some of my scars I found hard to accept and look at, but I soon realized that I must own them all and use them as added strength. It is very important that you know that some scars are from self inflicted wounds. Take comfort in knowing that some of your scars are per-mitted or allowed by God Himself and for a purpose that He knows quite well and that these purposes will serve for your own good as you advance in your wholeness and purpose to fulfill.

Wholeness: Whenever I look at this scar it reminds me of the mighty hand with which God delivered me from the heartbreak and painful experiences that leave this scar and it inspires me to rejoice in my wholeness in Christ. "***I urge you, therefore, to reaffirm your love***

for him" (2 Corinthians 2:8). This wholeness I speak of is wholeness of heart, soul and body. This is a state of wholeness especially of your heart and soul. Your soul is the eternal part of you that is non-material. Your soul is spirit. The body is flesh and is therefore material and cannot inherit the kingdom of God. Also, your body is the temple of the Holy Spirit. This means that your soul which is spirit lives in your body the temple. "*I declare to you, brothers and sisters, that flesh and blood cannot inherit the kingdom of God, nor does the perishable inherit the imperishable*" (1 Corinthians 15:50).

This spiritual state of wholeness is not a destination instead it is a daily journey that is growing forth from your broken pieces. "*Then He (Jesus) said to them all; Whoever wants to be my disciple must deny themselves and take up their cross daily and follow me*" (Luke 9:23). By the revelation of the Holy Spirit I found that this wholeness is only the beginning of new adventures in your fullness of life in Christ and your God ordained ministry. This wholeness of heart means knowing God in a deeper way, and having a closer, personal relationship with Him. This wholeness means that your heart, soul and body work in a harmonious balance with nothing broken and nothing damaged.

When God takes you from brokenness to wholeness it means that you are in a new dimension of your relationship with God. Can you hear God calling you to come up higher? During the time of your test God was preparing you for the task He has in mind for you to undertake which is your purpose and ministry. From my experience I can tell you that this tedious journey which you overcame will serve as a background and foundation on which God will build your unique purpose and ministry that will impact many lives near and far.

Do not look at your broken pieces and scars with regret but instead look at the possibilities of those broken pieces. Look at the gains in your spiritual growth as a result of your broken pieces. Look through the lenses of faith and see in the future what is hoped for and call it into existence as your evidence of what is to come in God's perfect will and purpose for you and in his perfect time for you. YOU ARE TRIUMPHANT! Sing songs of praise to God. "*Enter his gates with thanksgiving, go into his courts with praise; give thanks to him and praise his name*" (Psalm 100:4).

Final and complete wholeness will be perfect wholeness with Christ after this life when Jesus will say to all His faithful ones "well done." "***His master replied, 'Well done, good and faithful servant! You have been faithful with a few things; I will put you in charge of many things. Come and share your master's happiness***!" (Matthew 25:23).

Miracles: Whenever I look at this scar it reminds me of the many miracles God performed on my behalf along my journey of brokenness, healing, wholeness and purpose. Rejoice for all the miracles you experienced along the way. God came through for you when you thought there was no hope of continuing your journey to the end in pursuit of wholeness. These miracles served to support you with needed encouragement and strength to keep going. It is from your miracles that you gained physical, moral and inner spiritual strength that kept you going just a little longer and just a little further by the grace of God. God promises that He will never leave you or forsake you and He was true to His Word to you. King David expressed his personal experience of God's faithfulness in the following way. "***Even though I walk through the darkest valley, I will fear no evil, for you are with me; your rod and your staff, they comfort me***" (Psalm 23:4). If you examine the brokenness to wholeness journey of the children of Israel from Egypt to Canaan you will be amazed by the numerous and mighty miracles that God performed on their behalf along their journey.

Your broken pieces provide tools for God in His infinite mercy to work with and perform miracles on your behalf. It is from our "nothing" that God can call forth into existence something wonderful and "plentiful" to renew our hope and confidence in Him and be able to see clearly His divine purpose. God sure knows how to restore our souls. "***He refreshes my soul. He guides me along the right paths for His name's sake***" (Psalm 23:3). Be very careful that all of your glory, honor and praise must go to God! All the miracles that God performed on your behalf moving forward He will use you to do even greater. "***Very truly I tell you, whoever believes in me will do the works I have been doing, and they will do even greater things than these, because I am going to the Father***" (John 14:12).

Purpose: Whenever I look at this scar it reminds me of my divine purpose in Christ. God Himself planted a purpose seed inside of my heart and that purpose is very clear to me now more than ever before. God has a divine purpose for you as well, so walk in it consistently and diligently. In my personal brokenness to wholeness journey God used several strategies, methods and approaches in making clear to me my purpose. God did this for me, for in my case I wanted to be very sure of my purpose and so I sought God earnestly in prayer and sometimes in prayer and fasting asking for clear revelation.

> ***Therefore I do not run like someone running aimlessly; I do not fight like a boxer beating the air. No, I strike a blow to my body and make it my slave so that after I have preached to others, I myself will not be disqualified for the prize***" (1 Corinthians 9:26-27).

"***For it is God who works in you to will and to act in order to fulfill his good purpose***" (Philippians 2:13). God in His divine plan has a special purpose for your brokenness to wholeness journey and He watches over you always to protect and perfect that plan. "***For the eyes of the Lord range throughout the earth to strengthen those whose hearts are fully committed to him***" (2 Chronicles 16:9). As you commit to God you must seek to know and always abide in His divine purpose for you. I find it refreshing and rewarding to operate in my purpose

God had a divine purpose for Abram (Abraham) and God told him, "***I will make you into a great nation, and I will bless you; I will make your name great, and you will be a blessing***" (Genesis 12:2). The experiences of your brokenness to wholeness journey were not for you only but to also serve as a blessing to others. With God nothing happens by chance to His people for God does not make mistakes or take chances for He is intentional in all that He does. *"The lot is cast into the lap, But its every decision is from the Lord"* (Proverbs 16:33). Be assured that our every step is ordered by the Lord. *"The mind of man plans his way but the Lord directs his steps"* (Proverbs 16:9). *"And we know that in all things God works for the good of those who love him, who have been called according to his purpose"* (Romans 8:28).

With purpose you can move forward in the establishment of what you are called to do. You must travel on forward with great purpose, passion and determination. Having taken this journey and carefully learning the lessons along the way, by this time you should have some degree of clarity concerning your divine purpose in God. It is this journey that leads you to the end result which is your purpose. The person you are now will not be the same person at the end of both tunnels for you will have grown and change. If you are not sure about your purpose ask God who will make it clear for you.

It is God's desire that you operate in your purpose and bring glory and honor to his name while you live a victorious life in Christ. Therefore, God will without doubt make your purpose clear to you each day. I can attest to you that once you are clear about your purpose you will be liberated and will want to operate in that purpose with passion. You will find that there are numerous opportunities to do ministry if you look beyond the four walls of the church. My mission and passion is to lead people through their inner healing to wholeness and purpose in Christ. When you are operating in your purpose which is what God has called you to do *no weapon that is formed against you will prosper for you will have the divine protection of God* (Isaiah 54:17).

Passion: Whenever I look at this scar it reminds me of the passion that I must have for my purpose. Loving God and doing service for Him requires passion. With passion you are consumed with your purpose. Passion ignites and fuels your purpose. In my case I have clarity concerning my God given gifts and what God will have me to do in His vineyard. I take great delight in what God has called me to do and this gives me great passion which is a strong feeling of inner enthusiasm in fulfilling my assignment. Someone can have purpose and yet has no passion in carrying out that specific purpose. I believe that in order to maximize one's potential and purpose one should seek to blend that purpose with passion.

The passion that I have for my purpose pushes me to want to learn more about my purpose so that I can be excellent at what I do. If someone has a passion for playing golf that person will seek to learn more about the sport of gulf and will practice to be proficient at playing that sport. One may have a passion for dancing, music, fishing, evangelism, reading or mountain climbing. I have a deep passion for preaching and teaching among other things. Loving and enjoying your purpose increases your passion in your engagement of that purpose. If you are not sure what your purpose is seek God and He will use various creative means to reveal and make it clear to you.

Jesus is our perfect example as one having great passion for His purpose. Jesus' passion was wrapped up in His purpose and His purpose was wrapped up in His passion. Passion and purpose are intertwined and they are inseparable. "*Then he said, 'Here I am, I have come to do your will.' He sets aside the first to establish the second*" (Hebrews 10:9). "*I delight to do Your will, O my God; Your law is within my heart*" (Psalm 40:81).

Vision: Whenever I look at this scar it reminds me of the clear vision that God has placed before me and how I should remain steadfast and focused. Hopefully you can see clearly now what is God's purpose for you. It will require faith for you to see those things as though they were and also to trust God fully. "*Now faith is the substance of things hoped for, the evidence of things not seen*" (Hebrews 11:1). Having a clear vision or picture of what the end of your journey will be will have to be seen through the lenses of your faith eyes and broken pieces. This vision cannot be seen only through your natural eyes for your eyes of faith are needed in order for you to see beyond the natural and see clearly in the Spirit. Neither can these things be understood in the natural but rather in the realm of the Spirit. The Word of God says "*But the natural man receives (understand) not the things of the Spirit of God: for they are foolishness unto him: neither can he know them, because they are spiritually discerned*" (1 Corinthians 2:14).

Instead of gazing endlessly at your broken pieces, you should now see through your eyes of faith your wholeness which God has prepared and is awaiting your arrival at the "finish line" at the end of each task. God has tried and proved you to be faithful enough to embark on the task He has for you which is your **purpose**. When you understand your calling and operate in that calling you will have a significant impact on the lives of people. It is true that people do not know the process in the journey you had to go through to get to where you are right now, and where you are going, but you can share your story and make a big difference in the life of someone. Child of God, you must complete this test in victory and with God's help you have it in you to do so! Find your strength in the Lord and get it done by His grace!

Growth: Whenever I look at this scar it reminds me of my growth experiences along this journey from brokenness to wholeness. This scar also reminds me of my growth in the knowledge and things of Christ and my divine purpose. This has been timely and exponential spiritual growth in grace and the knowledge of Christ. *"But grow in grace, and in the knowledge of our Lord and Savior Jesus Christ. To him be glory both now and forever"* (2 Peter 3:18). This brokenness to wholeness journey produces abundant growth in all areas of your life especially your spiritual growth in Christ. During this period of growth as you spend more time with God in solitude, His Holy Word, and in prayer, you should experience abundant growth from your broken pieces. You will find too that your power and faith will be strengthened in the Lord due to your journey experiences.

In multiple areas of your life, especially your spiritual life, growth should have taken place on this journey. It is during this time of your broken heartedness that you call on the name of the Lord more than ever before. In our times of desperation we seem to call out to God and seek after Him even more and with greater intensity. Jesus on many occasions did the same thing by calling out to His Father God for help. God knows that your faith is tested and during these times you must rely on Him completely for help and He will without doubt provide you with the grace you need.

Relying on the Lord your God is the recipe for your victory and growth. "*It shall come to pass that before they call, I will answer; and while they are still speaking, I will hear*" (Isaiah 65:24). "*In my distress I called to the Lord; I cried to my God for help. From his temple he heard my voice; my cry came before him, into his ears*" (Psalm 18:6). You should learn from the Children of Israel who never fail to call on God when in deep trouble and He delivered them over and over again. The more time we spend with God is the greater our anointing, spiritual power, and spiritual growth in Christ. Like a seed that is planted in fertile soil that grows rapidly so likewise we grow in the things of God when we spend more time with Him.

Forgiveness: Whenever I look at this scar it reminds me of God's forgiveness extended to me and how I should forgive those who have wronged me. From my own experiences I find that peace of heart and soul cannot be fully realized until you have forgiven those who caused you pain in your heart and soul. To forgive others will bring deliverance in your spirit. Child of the Most High God, take it from me, you free yourself from bondage and *liberate* your own soul when you forgive others. With your heart full of forgiveness you will grow rapidly into becoming whole in heart, soul, and mind. Therefore, free yourself from the slavery and bondage of the unforgiveness, if any, that seeks to entrap your soul. Unforgiveness is certainly not an environment in which your precious and priceless heart and soul can live and thrive. There is nothing in the environment of unforgiveness that is healthy to feed your soul. If you dwell there for too long your precious soul will suffer and die from spiritual malnourishment.

Complete forgiveness is born from a heart of love. This love is your deep love for God and your love for others. Wholeness of heart cannot be experienced without the willingness to forgive other people. I had to learn to love others and forgive as if I had never been hurt. It must be clear that to forgive requires love. Be quick to forgive even if one did not ask for your forgiveness. God requires that you forgive and you must. "*But if you do not forgive others their sins, your Father will not forgive your sins*" (Matthew 6:15). According to the Word of God to not forgive others is sin. You must pray to God for a tender and loving heart of forgiveness. The spirit of unforgiveness will hinder your growth into wholeness and purpose. Moreover, an unforgiving heart could develop into a heart of bitterness which you do not want to have.

The nature of humanity is to take revenge on the person who hurts them but God has warned against taking revenge. "***Do not take revenge, my dear friends, but leave room for God's wrath, for it is written: 'It is mine to avenge; I will repay,' says the Lord***" (Romans 12:19). I recommend that you revisit chapter 15 on bitterness and chapter 26 on forgiveness. These are two heart conditions that you must be clear about.

Ministry: Whenever I look at this scar it reminds me of, and it keeps in focus my ministry "***Soul Care Healing***" that was born from this particular brokenness experience. From my experience of pain a ministry is born. This brokenness experience is also the "seed" from which this amazing book of ministry is born. I now fully understand that my broken heart was *God's divine launching pad* for the expansion of my ministry. "***It was good for me to be afflicted so that I might learn your decrees***" (Psalm 119:71). Throughout my life since my teen years onward, I have always been engaged in Christian ministry in various capacities. Like most people, I have had numerous heartbreak experiences throughout my life some of them I wish that I never had. In every sense this particular brokenhearted experience that led to the growth and expansion of my ministry was the most severe of them all because it happened in the church, the body of Christ and I suffered severely beyond words can explain.

This particular brokenhearted experience was extremely difficult for me. However, although my journey was tedious and very long I never thought for a moment that it was time to quit for I understood that this Christian walk has many valleys too and not just mountain top experiences. I thank and praise God that I have a solid Christian foundation and a deep unfailing love for God on which to rely. Thank God I believe in and practice prayer and fasting as one of my spiritual disciplines which was my bedrock that gave me strength.

I was able to survive my heartbreak because the Word of God was stored away in my heart and I clung on to it daily and in my devotion and meditation I called on the name of the Lord. Glory to God, my Christian foundation is built on the Solid Rock of God's Word! During this particular journey I had to exercise my faith in God daily and pray for grace and mercy like never before. It was often that I had to seek God in prayer and fasting. "*But this kind does not go out except by prayer and fasting*" (Matthew 17:21). With the help of the Blessed Holy Spirit, I had to draw on all the strength deep within my heart and soul in order to keep on believing and keep standing on God's promises.

***ESPECIALLY CHOSEN To Be BROKEN for PURPOSE*: Overcoming Brokenness Growing Into Wholeness And Purpose** is my reality! During my own journey from brokenness to wholeness there were times when the pain in my heart was so severe and difficult to endure I often fell on my face and wept to God in prayer and praise Him for the strength He provides. One of my requests in constant prayer to God was for a forgiving heart to be ready and willing to forgive those who hurt me so deeply. Forgiveness does not mean that your heart heals from its wounds overnight. Although you have forgiven your offender your healing will take some time. Severe heart hurt does take time to heat and may take a long time for some people depending on the degree of hurt. However, you do not forgive in increments your forgiveness must be complete.

It is very hard emotionally for me to open up and talk about my church hurt but it is part of the healing process and must be done. Seeing the light at the end of the tunnel was still a painful situation. I found that every segment of my journey comes with different emotions and challenges. When I emerged from my tunnel "***Purging***" and looked at my "scars" left by the wounds I received along the way my emotions were uncontrollable and I wept like I had never done before. Yet, I could praise the Good Lord for how far I had come. Yes, I am healed but these scars are for a lifetime.

In order for your soul to remain healed you must take care of it daily by taking heed to the Word of God. "***Watch out that you do not lose what we have worked for, but that you may be rewarded fully***" (2 John 1:8). "***Watch your life and doctrine closely. Persevere in them, because if you do, you will save both yourself and your hearers***" (1 Timothy 4:16). "***Be careful, or you will be enticed to turn away and worship other gods and bow down to them***" (Deut. 11:16). You must be watchful and be very careful in this walk for there are snares of the enemy awaiting to entrap you so follow Christ closely.

From your broken heart experiences your ministry, passion and purpose could be discovered and it should. Your story just might be your ministry or part of it that could be ignited from your broken pieces. "***They triumphed over him by the blood of the Lamb and by***

the word of their testimony; they did not love their lives so much as to shrink from death" (Revelation 12:11). Your purpose will burst forth like a spring welling up within your heart and soul and it will be so strong that you will have no doubt. "**But whoever drinks the water I give them will never thirst. Indeed, the water I give them will become in them a spring of water welling up to eternal life**" (John 4:14). God has planted a purpose seed inside of your heart which no one can take away from you or destroy. You are the only person who can destroy this seed which is your God given purpose. Your purpose will be manifested in the natural in God's own perfect time when God Himself launches your ministry whatever that ministry might be. God will make your ministry to be very clear to you and it will be one that you will be passionate about.

> "***It was good for me to be afflicted so that I might learn your decrees***" (Psalm 119:71).

> "***I know, Lord, that your laws are righteous, and that in faithfulness you have afflicted me. May your unfailing love be my comfort, according to your promise to your servant***" (Psalm 119:76).

> "***May I wholeheartedly follow your decrees, that I may not be put to shame***" (Psalm 119:80).

CHAPTER 47

The Fight Continues

"If your law had not been my delight, I would have perished in my affliction. I will never forget your precepts, for by them you have preserved my life" (Psalm 119:92-93).

"Those who sow in tears shall reap in joy. He who continually goes forth weeping, Bearing seed for sowing, Shall doubtless come again with rejoicing, Bringing his sheaves with him" (Psalm 126:5-6).

Celebrate your healing and deliverance and keep going and keep on fighting. You cannot and should not put your weapons down for the "*real fight*" has only just begun. This is not a time to lay down your armor and be off guard you have to stay alert. This is the time to expect and prepare for greater battles. You must be prepared to expect the unexpected. Satan is furious! Satan hates that you won, for his desire has always been to take you out completely. Satan is angry that he lost this fight with you and he will not give up so be very watchful.

Be aware that Satan is now strategizing to return with new arsenal of assaults on you. Satan's weapons of military style equipment will include persons and groups you least expect and even some of those things you have purged yourself from in **tunnel purging**.

Child of God, you must take courage and stand firmly on the Word of God. "***Stand fast therefore in the liberty wherewith Christ hath made us free, and be not entangled again with the yoke of bondage***" (Galatians 5:1). The Lord Himself will give His angels charge over you and God will build a wall of defense around you so do not allow the enemy to intimidate you. Continue to use the essential tools in your **survival kit**. You still need those tools now more than ever before and you will always do moving forward (see chapter one). Although you are now fearless and strong because of the victories you have won on this journey in the name of Christ Jesus your Lord you still need to be watchful.

> ***So shall they fear the name of the LORD from the west, and his glory from the rising of the sun. When the enemy shall come in like a flood, the Spirit of the LORD shall lift up a standard against him***" (Isaiah 59:19).

On this journey there were times when it seemed as if we were singled out for severe attacks from the enemy on every side. The pressures of such attacks were like floods and we were overwhelmed. Many times the forces against us were more powerful than we were and it was very hard for us to resist and defend by ourselves. Glory to God the spirit of the Lord lifted up a standard against the enemy. Although the forces against us are strong the power of God is stronger and greater. Use the Mighty Word of God and the enemy will have no choice but to flee from you. "***But you belong to God, my dear children. You have already won a victory over those people, because the Spirit who lives in you is greater than the spirit who lives in the world***" (1 John 4:4). The standard the Lord lifts up in our defense is the Word of God and anointing power of the Holy Spirit. Jesus defeated the enemy Satan and also His human enemies with the Word of God and so can we. "***Submit yourselves, then, to God. Resist the devil, and he will flee from you***" (James 4:7).

The end of the tunnel unfortunately is not the end of our journey it is just the end of a segment of our journey. The journey continues and this is a new beginning with new experiences, dimensions and challenges. I believe that you are now better prepared for the next leg of your journey. Remember, wholeness is not a destination it is a journey. Those lessons learned and those victories you won along the way should help you in the continuation of your journeys and you should be better prepared as you move forward. I hope that you take time to enjoy your journey even in the difficult times and that you are able to count each experience as joy that will propel you further as you travel onward. Praise God as you go along for it will make your journey just a little easier as you move onward!

Brothers and sisters, I count not myself to have apprehended (taken hold of it): But this one thing I do, forgetting those things which are behind, and reaching forth toward those things which are before, I press on toward the mark (goal) to win the prize of the high calling of God in Christ Jesus (Philippians 3:13-16).

Your spiritual and emotional growth that you gained as a result of what you went through should serve to make you stronger and unmovable always abounding in God's grace. Now is the time for you to stand and face the giants that confronted you just like David did when he faced Goliath and defeated him in the name of the Lord (1 Samuel 17). So also you and I must face our giants in the name of the Lord our deliverer.

Therefore, my dear brothers and sisters, stand firm. Let nothing move you. Always give yourselves fully to the work of the Lord, because you know that your labor in the Lord is not in vain (1 Corinthians 15:58).

CHAPTER 48

Are You Saved?

"For everyone who calls on the name of the Lord will be saved" (Romans 10:13).

"Just so, I tell you, there will be more joy in heaven over one sinner who repents than over ninety nine righteous persons who need no repentance" (Luke 15:7).

"For the wages of sin is death, but the free gift of God is eternal life in Christ Jesus our Lord" (Romans 6:23).

Y ou are a child of the Most High God and if you are not saved you need Christ Jesus the only Savior of mankind! Christ Jesus is Life and He is the source of your life, physical and spiritual present and eternal. Your very existence depends on Him. There is a life after this physical life. Your life does not end at death. There is a life after death and it is eternal life. This eternal life is only found in Christ Jesus who is the Way, Truth and Life. *"Salvation is found in no one else, for there is no other name under heaven given to mankind by which we must be saved*" (Acts 4:12). "*For God so loved the world that he gave his one and only Son, that whoever believes in him shall not perish but have eternal life*" (John 3:16). Ask God to forgive you and cleanse you from your sin. "*Purge me with hyssop, and I shall be clean, wash me, and I shall be whiter than snow*" (Psalm 51:7).

Everyone will have to make the personal choice to accept Christ Jesus as Savior or to reject Him and perish by the wrath of God. "*So then, each of us will give an account of ourselves to God*" (Romans 14:12). In this present life, when we leave God out of our lives we become that "*lost sheep*" and we expose ourselves to the dangers and challenges of this world. "*We all, like sheep, have gone astray, each of us has turned to our own way; and the Lord has laid on him the iniquity of us all*" (Isaiah 53:6). Christ your Savior is the only one who will protect and shield you from all harm. "*Even though I walk through the valley of the shadow of death, I will fear no evil, for You are with me; Your rod and Your staff, they comfort me*" (Psalm 23:4).

If you are not saved, I encourage you to choose Christ today as your Savior for you belong to Him anyway, you are not your own, you belong to God for He made you and it is in Him that you live, move and have your being. "*For every animal of the forest is mine, and the cattle upon a thousand hills. I know every bird in the mountains: and the insects in the fields are mine*" (Psalm 50:10-11). "*In his hand are the depths of the earth, and the mountain peaks belong to him.*

The sea is his, for he made it, and his hands formed the dry land (Psalm 95:5).

The world belongs to God including you and Jesus Christ bought you with the price of His own life on the Cross of Calvary (1 Corinthians 6:20). To accept Christ as your Savior you must give yourself to Him willingly by giving Him your heart for He will not force you. For you to do otherwise is to loose in this life and the one to come. "***For what shall it profit a man, if he shall gain the whole world, and lose his own soul?*** (Mark 8:36 KJV). You will spend your eternity in heaven or in hell and the choice is yours to make. "***Jesus replied, 'I tell you the truth, unless you are born again, you cannot see the Kingdom of God***" (John 3:3). "***If I take the wings of the morning, and dwell in the uttermost parts of the sea; Even there shall thy hand lead me, and thy right hand shall hold me***" (Psalm 139:9). There is no place for you to go and hide from the wrath of God. If you reject Christ as your Savior, He too will reject you before His Father. "***But whoever disowns me before others, I will disown before my Father in heaven***" (Matthew 10:33). If you are not saved, today is your day of salvation, so if you hear God's voice speaking to your heart, do not harden your heart because you need Christ Jesus.

> ***Come, let us bow down in worship, let us kneel before the Lord our Maker, for he is our God and we are the people of his pasture, the flock under his care. Today, if only you would hear his voice;***

> ***Do not harden your hearts as you did at Meribah, as you did that day at Massah in the wilderness, where your ancestors tested me; they tried me, though they had seen what I did*** (Psalm 95:6-9).

Turning away from God is to go the wrong way which leads to destruction which is actually a death sentence. "***There is a way that appears to be right to man but, in the end it leads to death (destruction)***" (Proverbs 14:12).

Accepting Christ as your Savior is not hard to do. You just need to make a conscious decision to invite Christ in your heart and follow Him. Admit to God that you are a sinner and repent of your sins by asking God's forgiveness. If you believe in your heart and confess with your mouth it will be done. "***Because, if you confess with your mouth that Jesus is Lord and believe in your heart that God raised him from the dead, you will be saved***" (Romans 10:9). God will forgive you and cleanse you from all of your sins.

I OFFER CHRIST TO YOU!

Pray this prayer: Father God I am a sinner and I desire to be saved. Lord Jesus, please forgive me of my sins and cleanse my heart. Jesus, I believe in my heart and confess with my mouth that You are the Christ. Lord, I receive Your forgiveness and I receive Jesus as my Savior. Thank you for your sustaining grace. Amen.

Create in me a clean heart, Oh God, and renew a right spirit within me. Cast me not away from thy presence; and take not thy Holy Spirit from me. Restore unto me the joy of thy salvation; and uphold me with thy free spirit (Psalm 51:10).

"***And be not conformed to this world: but be ye transformed by the renewing of your mind, that you may prove what is that good, and acceptable, and perfect, will of God***" (Romans 12:2).

If you prayed the above prayer sincerely God has forgiven you and He will sustain you by giving you the grace to live above sin. Jesus says, "***All those the Father gives me will come to me, and whoever comes to me I will never drive away***" (John 6:37). Be confident that no one will be able to pluck you out of the Mighty Hand of God. "***I give them eternal life, and they shall never perish; no one will snatch them out of my hand***" (John 10:28).

Be warned for if you did not pray the prayer of forgiveness one of these days God's patience is going to run out so do not let it run out on you. "***Then the Lord said, 'My Spirit will not contend with humans forever, for they are mortal; their days will be a hundred and twenty years***" (Genesis 6:3). "***Blessed is the one who fears the Lord always, but whoever hardness his heart will fall into calamity (evil)***" (Proverbs 28:14). "***Rid yourselves of all the offenses you have***

committed, and get a new heart and a new spirit. Why will you die, people of Israel?" (Ezekiel 18:31). "**I will praise you because I am fearfully and wonderfully made, your works are wonderful made; your works are wonderful, I know that full well**" (Psalm 139:14).

I trust that you did pray the prayer of forgiveness and accept Christ as your Savior. If you are already saved then I encourage you to recommit your life to Him and continue to serve Him with all of your heart, soul, mind and strength.

CHAPTER 49

Concluding Thoughts

The Spirit of the LORD is upon Me, Because He has anointed Me To preach the gospel to the poor; He has sent Me to heal the broken hearted, To proclaim liberty to the captives, And recovery of sight to the blind, To set at liberty those who are oppressed; To proclaim the acceptable year of the LORD (Luke 4:18-18 & Isaiah 61:1).

As I objectively reflect on my journey of healing, wholeness and purpose, I am truly grateful for the process and valuable lessons I gleaned from those situations which were emotionally oppressive at times especially in the earlier stages which I will call *my joy in unrelenting pain*. My experience of heartbreak has taught me a great deal about myself and others. The healing that I experienced during and after the process has served me well. With these lessons I have become the purpose driven person that I am today. "*At least I can take comfort in this: my joy in unrelenting pain, that I had not denied the words of the Holy One*" (Job

6:10). It was the Word of God and the comforting presence of the Holy Spirit that kept me through it all. While I do not wish for anyone to endure such experiences of heart pain I am grateful that I can use my experiences to encourage and support you as you navigate your way through to your healing from heart pain.

The reliable formula is that if you allow God free access to work with you, in your heart, and through you, He will heal your broken heart and make you completely whole again. God will put your broken pieces back together perfectly and your latter will be greater than your former according to God's promises. Your scars that remain due to those broken places in your heart will serve you well as reminders of God's goodness to you and the strength inside of you due to His grace.

"*The glory of this present house will be greater than the glory of the former house,' says the LORD Almighty. 'And in this place I will grant peace*" (Haggai 2:9). "*Though your beginning was small, yet thy latter end would greatly increase*" (Job 8:7). To God you are worth more than you could ever imagine for to God you value more than the whole world. In God's eyes you are priceless, beautiful, kind, wise, funny, unique, and more precious than gold. "*They are more precious than gold, than much pure gold; they are sweeter than honey, than honey from the honeycomb*" (Psalm 19:10).

Remember, God is the Potter and you are the clay, the work of His hands. "*Yet you, Lord, are our Father. We are the clay, you are the potter; we are all the work of your hand*" (Isaiah 64:8). Your journey was not in vain for God has and will continue to reward you greatly. God has a wonderful purpose for you and He had to prepare you for that purpose by taking you through the journey. What you went through will serve to help shape your ministry and fuel your passion as you serve in your divine purpose. I learned these truths on my journey and I am sharing these truths with you.

> *To all who mourn in Israel, he will give a crown of beauty for ashes, a joyous blessing instead of mourning, festive praise instead of despair. In their righteousness, they will be like great oaks that the LORD has planted for his own glory* (Isaiah 61:3).

HALLELUJAH! Glory to Almighty God! It does not matter what forces are aligned against you, you will always be like the great oaks. Your brokenness was a time for you to listen to God's still and quiet voice and prepare for your assignment. God's word is true, He says that when He has tried us we will come out as pure gold, "*But he knows the way that I take; when he has tested me, I will come forth as gold*" (Job 23:10). Child of God, you endured your *brokenness to wholeness and purpose* journey and came fourth victoriously and now you are a better person because of those challenges. You are now like "pure gold" you are the victor, for you overcame your trials and now you are refined. Your life now takes on new meaning, purpose and passion.

This was how I felt when I got to the end of my ***tunnel purging and tunnel healing***. For me it was a victorious experience and one of renewed hope. I can see clearly now through my eyes of faith and in the realm of the spirit God's purpose for my ***brokenness*** journey and I truly rejoice and praise Him for those experiences. With confidence and from a heart full of compassion I can sincerely encourage you to be steadfast and trust God's divine plan for your purpose.

From my own experiences I believe that you are now probably praising God as you take a look back on your own journey and see what you have been through and how God kept you through it all and now you are delivered, restored and free. Rejoice and praise God for your experiences and praise Him for His sustaining grace. Then, tell your amazing story with great joy, fullness of joy in the Lord and help someone else who is going through their journey of brokenness.

Self Assessment: Objective self assessment is very important for you to do. At the place where you are right now on your journey from ***brokenness to purpose*** you should examine carefully all the details. Hopefully you are not still at the entrance of the ***Tunnel Purging*** gazing on the inside at whatever you can see and imagining what you cannot see while you are contemplating if or not you should embark on the journey ahead of you. If you are actually on your journey through the "***Tunnel Purging***" you should hold on to your Shepherd's (Jesus') hand and patiently travel onward. It could be that you are on your way through the "***Tunnel Healing***" to heal your wounded heart and that would be wonderful. Please make sure that you are not standing at the crossroads until you become stagnant you should keep moving. Listen, each step you take going forward you are further removed from your brokenness and those same steps will bring you closer and closer to your complete healing and wholeness state of heart and mind in Christ Jesus your Lord.

As you know, there are various stations along your personal healing journey which you have discovered by reading this book. Each station is extremely important and has implications for all the other stations. These stations could be compared to the various members of the human body in which each member is very important and depends on the other members for the full function of the whole body. In the Word of God we are told of the importance of the human body which has many members and they are all interdependent (1 Corinthians 12:12-27). Likewise, in the Body of Christ each person within the church and the larger Christian community is an important member and we are all interdependent on each other. Please understand each stage of your "*purpose*" journey experience in this light, for each stage of the journey lays the foundation for the success, difficulty or failure thereof moving forward.

My heart is full of gratitude to God and I am thanking God for an overflow of His divine anointing of the Holy Spirit upon me. The Holy Spirit has been my companion and helper working with and through me on this book which is a divinely directed and anointed ministry project. **To God be the glory for the things He has done**! I am fully persuaded that the ministry that is embodied

in this very special book has been a source of tremen-
dous blessing to you. Now it is for you to introduce this
"**healing manual**" to others and be a blessing to them
in their pursuit of healing and wholeness of heart and
soul. Make this book known to as many people as you
can, concerning the blessing it has been to you and the
possibilities of the blessing it could be to them in their
pursuit of healing and wholeness.

*In that day you will say: 'Give praise to the
Lord, proclaim His name; make known among the
nations what He has done, and proclaim that his
name is exalted. Sing to the Lord, for He has done
glorious things; let this be known to all the world*
(Isaiah 12:4-5).

With a heart full of gratitude and praise I thank God for
the journey He took me on and for leading me faithfully
to the fullest manifestation of my purpose. There was a
time when I thought that I was in a birthing and nurturing
place but it later turned out that I was not. Instead, I was
in a place that sought to suffocate my purpose. I was
not in a birthing place and I would not be able to give
birth to my purpose in that place but it was part of God's
divine plan in preparing me. In the end, God delivered
me from that "*barren and sterile*" place that would not
nurture me. In His own time, God changed my season
and environment so that I could give birth to His divine
purpose. There was a time when I could not help but
wonder if my heartbreak was a form of punishment but it
turned out to be an enormous blessing in disguise. Now
I truly praise God for that season.

I want to encourage you not to hold on to what you are going through any longer if you know God wants you to let go. Just let it go and move forward in the path God is taking you. Looking back, I cannot thank God enough for when He led me through "the valley of the shadow of death" during which time I fed on prayer, praise, and the Word of God. As painful as my **Broken for Purpose** journey was I did not blame God instead I sought strength from prayer and fasting and I got closer to God. Through it all, God now has me right where He wants me to be and He can trust me with His specific assignment for me. There was nothing that the enemy could have done to abort the purpose God placed inside of me. The enemy tried extremely hard to abort my purpose but I held on to God's faithful promises and I used the weapon of God's Word and the enemy failed. Glory hallelujah!

Child of the Most High God your experiences have prepared you or should prepare you for your God ordained assignment which is your purpose. Your experiences are not curses instead, they are blessings and your testimonies for your lifetime. My deepest desire is that this book has blessed you.

ENDNOTES

Empower Yourself
For Your Healing Journey:

For a successful healing journey you must take control of who you are and operate in your true self. It is of great importance that you know and understand your strengths and your weaknesses in order to embrace them fully while you work to improve those areas that may need improvement. You have the ability inside of you and with the help of the Holy Spirit you will know what is best for you. With vigor and conviction you should pursue your goals without apologies.

These spiritual and necessary tools which I am giving you will significantly impact your holistic approach to your healing. This is a continuous journey which requires that you be well equipped for a more successful journey. *"Then he said to them all; Whoever wants to be my disciple must deny themselves and take up their cross daily and follow me"* (Luke 9:23).

- Do not allow the burden of the past to stand in your way preventing you from fulfilling your purpose
- Be pleased with yourself and how far you have come
- Spend daily quality time in the presence of God through prayer, fasting, praise, worship and Bible study
- Do not be afraid of the evil one who has no authority over you
- God will prepare a table before you in the presence of your enemy (Psalm 23:5). They will watch God's blessings upon you and will not be able to do anything to stop the flow of anointing and blessings on you and your purpose.
- God will hide you in a place where the enemy will not be able to find you or lay hands on you. You will be in front of them but what they will see is the glory of God and not you. The inner peace, joy and strength of the Holy Spirit within you will burst forth in radiance.
- Respond to God with obedience always for it is better to obey God.
- Obstacles are what you see if and when you take your eyes off Jesus. When you take your eyes off Jesus you will see the great gulf which to your natural eyes is impossible to go over. This will frighten and scare you away from your purpose.
- In your situation always give God thanks in spite of what you have to go through for His grace will always sustain you. Yes, the situation is breaking you now but God has a great blessing awaiting

you at the end of it all when you overcome. God has fixed the outcome to benefit you.

- The world will know God's children by their character. Be kind and compassionate to others. Having a positive attitude, patience and respect are winning qualities.
- Be of good courage while you wait on God. Be careful not to become impatient. While you wait you must remember that God has a perfect set time. God does not operate on our time.
- God may take you to a place where only the anointing of the Holy Spirit and His divine grace and mercy can keep you there to test you so be steadfast, be faithful, and be patient. Honor that place as very sacred for there, God will test your faith, patience, endurance and love for Him and your purpose.
- Do not forget God's promises to you for that could be self defeating. "***Be strong and courageous. Do not be afraid or terrified because of them, for the Lord your God goes with you, he will never leave you or forsake you***" (Deuteronomy 31:6; Psalm 23).
- One way to protect your purpose is to keep it secret in your heart until it is God's time for its manifestation. Seek heavenly wisdom from God who will grant it to you generously. "***Do not give dogs what is sacred; do not throw your pearls to pigs. If you do, they may trample them under their feet, and turn and tear you to pieces***" (Matthew 7:6). Do not be wise in your own eyes.

- Maintain a strong internal (in your heart) and open (publicly declare) relationship with God always
- In your midnight hour, which is your most difficult circumstances you should call on the name of the Lord for His divine help.
- Believe and trust God above everyone else.
- Be healed so that you can be an inspiration in the healing of others. You cannot be a blind leading the blind for you both will be in serious trouble. "*If the blind lead the blind, both will fall into a pit*" (Matthew 15:14-16). "*You hypocrite, first take the plank out of your own eye, and then you will see clearly to remove the speck from your brother's eye*" (Matthew 7:5).
- Trust the process for it will make you more valuable and stronger
- Use the negative that you are given to your advantage as part of the solution. Parts of this journey can be dangerous. It was quite dangerous for Jesus. Do not be overcome by the negative for that is the enemy's desire. The negative should motivate you to envision, think, reflect, strategize, and reassess what is going on and be more determined to overcome.
- Know when to lead and who to lead. Ask God for discernment.
- Know when to follow and who to follow. Follow those who have positive influence upon you and those who will add value to your journey and purpose. Paul says, "*Follow my example, as I follow the example of Christ*" (1 Corinthians 11:1).

- Know when to serve and whom to serve. Know what they need in order to serve.
- Taking a stand to operate in your purpose does not mean that you are defiant it means that you are aware of your accountable to God. It is always better to obey God.
- Work on those internal "issues or concerns" so that you can be your best self. Purge yourself! David asked God to purge him and make him clean. "***Purge me with hyssop, and I shall be clean: wash me, and I shall be whiter than snow***" (Psalm 51:7)
- God has to break you first before releasing you to your purpose. Remember, Jesus broke the bread first before giving it to the people and in the process the bread multiplied to be more than enough for the need of the people (Luke 9:16). God is breaking you now and in your brokenness you are growing exponentially in faith, your purpose, perfecting your gift, growing in your passion.
- How clearly do you see what God is showing you? Do you see clearly through your eyes of ***compassion*** what God wants you to see? Do you see clearly through your eyes of ***faith*** what God wants you to see? Do you see clearly through your eyes of ***love*** what God wants you to see? Do you see clearly through your eyes of ***mercy*** what God wants you to see? Do you see clearly through your eyes of the spirit? God Himself will bless you with clear vision.

- Avoid fear! Fear is the friend of evil and fear makes you irrational.
- Trust God completely to the extent that you have faith in His plan and you are not discouraged when your plan does not materialize the way you envision.

Tips For Maintaining Your Mental Health: Your mental health is your emotional, psychological and social wellbeing.

- Be humble in heart and attitude, for God cannot deal with the proud.
- Pray with authority to release God's divine power of anointing upon your life. Pray in the Spirit.
- Remind God of His Word and promises. God says that we should remind Him. "***Put me in remembrance, let us plead together, declare you, that you may be justified***" (Isaiah 43:26).
- Dwell in God's presence and avoid evil and wrongdoing (Psalm 91).
- Receive and share God's Word. You cannot give what you do not have so, hide the Word of God in your heart. "***Thy Word have I hid in my heart, that I might not sin against thee***" (Psalm 119:11).
- Thanksgiving and praise go hand in hand with healing. "***Enter into his gates with thanksgiving, and into his courts with praise, be thankful to him, and bless his name***" (Psalm 100:4).
- Learn how to deal with stress by thinking positive thoughts.

- Store away good treasures which is the Word of God in your heart. From the abundance of the heart the mouth speaks (Luke 6:45).
- Nurture and care for yourself emotionally, spiritually and physically
- Have unwavering faith in God for without faith it is impossible to please God (Hebrews 11:6).
- Sing songs of praise to the Lord. Sing unto the Lord a new song. "***Sing to the Lord, praise his name; proclaim his salvation day after day***" (Psalm 96:2).
- Do some form of physical exercise regularly.
- Maintain a healthy diet and be consistent.
- Drink adequate amount of water daily.
- Memorize Scripture verses and use them.
- Reach out and help someone who is in need.
- Practice forgiving those who hurt you.
- Count your blessings and give God thanks.
- Practice praying for others and not just for yourself.
- Speak encouraging words to someone and to yourself.
- Testify, share and tell what God has done for you.
- Read good Christian literature books.
- Eyes, be careful of what you see and watch.
- Ears, be careful of what you hear and what you are listening.
- Mouth, be careful of the words that you speak.
- Hands, be careful of the things that you do.
- Feet, be careful of the places where you go.

But mark this: There will be terrible times in the last days. People will be lovers of themselves, lovers of money, boastful, proud, abusive, disobedient to their parents, ungrateful, unholy, without love, unforgiving, slanderous, without self-control, brutal, not lovers of the good, treacherous, rash, conceited, lovers of pleasure rather than lovers of God having a form of godliness but denying its power. Have nothing to do with such people (2 Timothy 3:1-3).

Love the Lord your God with all your heart and with all your soul and with all your strength. These commandments that I give you today are to be on your hearts (Deuteronomy 6:5).

++++++++++++++++++++++++
#DivinelyDirectedPurpose
#DivinelyInspired
#Prophetic
#PurposePassionMissionService
#ReachTeachReleaseSupport

- DivinelyDirectedNewYear [12/24/2018]
- Love in many languages globally [3/28/2019]
- SAMC [3/29/2019] Best
- GRJ [5/19/2019] The Great Chain Reaction
- RDAI [9/14/2019] Signed
- LIHP [1/22/2020] Good to go
- PSA [6/22/2020] Soon
- VM [7/18/2020] Specially picked by God

About The Author

R ev. Dr. Jasmine Rosetta Gordon was born in Fort William Westmoreland Jamaica, and attended Williams Field All Age School. She comes from a very humble beginning that is quite interesting and one in which she takes great pride. Rev. Dr. Gordon is one of ten children, six girls and four boys, and she honors her parents for raising them well and in the fear of the Lord. She experienced a childhood full of fun and great memories. She is proud of her heritage, cultural background, and upbringing as a Jamaican. Her strong sense of self, determination, purpose, and perseverance in pursuing excellence in education and ministry and whatever she does fuels her. Dr. Gordon has devoted her time and life's work to the service of humanity mainly in education and Christian ministry. She obtained her basic and professional education in Jamaica which provided her with a solid background and foundation in the ethics of hard work, professionalism, professional ethics, and a strong sense of self awareness. It has been a very long and beautiful journey from walking over one mile to and from elementary school to this point of an amazing accomplishment in education and service to God and mankind.

Rev. Dr. Gordon distinguishes herself as a servant leader who cares about and ministers to humanity. She is an accomplished educator who has earned multiple degrees in education and Christian ministry. Rev. Dr. Gordon's credentials include: Doctor of Education Degree from the University of Sarasota, Florida (1999) and Doctor of Divinity (Hon) from Canadian International Chaplaincy Association & University (2019). She holds Master's Degree in Counseling Psychology and Human Development from Clark Atlanta University, Georgia (1994); Master's Degree in Educational Leadership from Georgia State University, Georgia (2007); and Master's of Divinity Degree from Luther Rice University & Seminary, Georgia (2015); Bachelor of Science in Education & Counseling from Western Carolina University, Cullowhee, North Carolina (1985); She is a graduate of Mico Teachers' College & University, Kingston Jamaica (1979); Certificate in Theology from Venture Bible College, Jamaica (1978). She is a Licensed and Ordained Minister, Certified Christian Chaplain, and state certified notary public.

Dr. Gordon is a certified educator for more than 30 years holding multiple certificates in Elementary; Middle Grades and High School Education in various content areas and levels and also in School Counseling. She has taught elementary, middle grades, high school, college, and university graduate education. She has worked as college and university professor and College and University Supervisor of practicing teachers doing internship. As a professional development specialist Dr. Gordon has served educators from different multicultural backgrounds in various school districts. Dr. Gordon held full time employment with the Atlanta Board of Education 1995-2015, while concurrently she taught as an adjunct college professor. Rev. Dr. Gordon continues to teach as a university adjunct professor in Metropolitan Atlanta. Dr. Gordon is a conference presenter at educational conferences nationally and locally. She is a state certified and approved level 3 (the highest level) trainer for the Georgia Department of Education Early Childhood Education. Prior to migrating to the United States Dr. Gordon's first teaching job was for two years prior to college as a pre-service teacher at Chatsworth All Age School in Saint James. After college Dr. Gordon taught at Mount Alvernia High School in Montego Bay, 1979-1987; Anchovy High School, Montego Bay 1987-1988; and then Bethlehem Moravian Teachers' College, Malvern Saint Elizabeth 1988-1991.

Rev. Dr. Gordon is an articulate, engaging, inspirational and motivational public speaker at religious and educational and community events. She has been recognized and honored for her accomplishments and contribution to education. Her honors and awards include: Recognition from the Atlanta City Council in 2002 and 2015; The Atlanta Journal-Constitution Honor Teacher Award 2002; Teacher Of The Year repeatedly; Master Teacher of teachers by Public Broadcasting Atlanta; Academic Honors from Clark Atlanta University 1994; Who's Who Among Students In American Universities

And Colleges 1995 and many Certificates from the educational and Christian Communities among others.

As a doctoral candidate due to her outstanding course work, dissertation, and dissertation defense Dr. Gordon was asked to be the commencement speaker at her own graduation in 1999. This acknowledgement was an outstanding achievement and humbling experience which Dr. Gordon fulfilled with great delight, humility, honor and gratitude.

As a minister of the gospel of Jesus Christ, Rev. Dr. Gordon shares the Christian message of Jesus with passion and holy boldness. She is a sought after speaker at religious events including conferences. She is an anointed Bible teacher, counselor, preacher, chaplain and mentor. She is the founder of "*DRJasmine RGordon Ministry Soul Care Healing.*" She has also founded *Jasmine Gordon Ministry Institute* which is the center of learning and training for Christian ministry and education professional development; *Soul Care Healing Prayer Ministry*; and *Gordon Chaplaincy Ministry*. Rev. Dr. Gordon has been engaged in Christian ministry from her early years in church at Fort William Westmoreland Jamaica and she still preaches at her childhood church whenever she goes home to Jamaica.

Author: Rev. Dr. Jasmine Rosetta Gordon has authored and published her first book in 2020 entitled "ESPECIALLY CHOSEN To Be BROKEN For PURPOSE: Overcoming Brokenness Growing Into Wholeness And Purpose".

Rev. Dr. Gordon serves humanity with compassion, sincerity and humility of heart. Her community services are numerous including visiting the sick at home and in the hospital. Rev. Dr. Gordon is a member of numerous professional organizations including National Certified Chaplains Association; American Chaplains Association; Concerned Black Clergy of Metropolitan Atlanta; National Association for the Education of Young Children; Georgia Association on the Education of Young Children; Georgia Association for Teacher Educators GAATE.

She is mother of two adult children, son Nigel (Andy) and daughter Marcia (Annie). She loves her children, six grand children and two great grand children. Her hobbies include writing, singing, sewing, gardening, needle craft, and reading.

Invite Rev. Dr. Jasmine R. Gordon for preaching, teaching, workshops, speaking, facilitating, conference keynote and book signing.

SOUL CARE HEALING

For more information contact:
Phone: 678-834-9618
DRJASMINE RGORDON MINISTRY
P. O. BOX 361421
Decatur, Georgia 30036
United States
drgordonministries@yahoo.com
https://drgordonministries.org

Follow me for spiritual growth and development support.
https://drgordonministries.org
https://www.youtube.com/drjasminergordon
https://www.facebook.com/drjasminergordonministry
https://twitter.com/DrJasmineGordon

Rev. Dr. Jasmine R. Gordon
Certified Christian Chaplain

God Almighty Himself has planted a purpose seed in my heart which no one could or can take away from me. This seed is freely blooming where it has been planted.

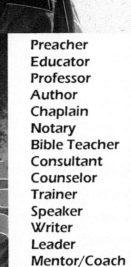

Doctor of Education 1999

Doctor of Divinity 2019

Preacher
Educator
Professor
Author
Chaplain
Notary
Bible Teacher
Consultant
Counselor
Trainer
Speaker
Writer
Leader
Mentor/Coach

drgordonministries.org

Product of Fort William Westmoreland Jamaica

CPSIA information can be obtained
at www.ICGtesting.com
Printed in the USA
BVHW040222280621
610626BV00015B/654

9 781630 509132